The Management of Conflict

The Management of
Conflict

Interpretations and Interests in

Comparative Perspective

Marc Howard Ross

Yale University Press

New Haven and London

Designed by James J. Johnson.
Set in Melior Roman and Optima types
by Marathon Typography Service,
Inc., Durham, North Carolina.

Printed in the United States of America
by Edwards Brothers, Inc., Ann
Arbor, Michigan.

The paper in this book meets the guidelines for permanence and dura-
bility of the Committee on Production Guidelines for Book
Longevity of the Council on
Library Resources.

Library of Congress Cataloging-in-
Publication Data

Ross, Marc Howard.
The management of conflict : interpretations and interests in comparative perspective / Marc
Howard Ross.
p. cm.
Includes bibliographical references
and index.
ISBN 0-300-05398-3

1. Political anthropology. 2. Conflict
management—Cross-cultural
studies. 3. Conflict (Psychology) —Cross-cultural studies.
4. Ethnopsychology. I. Title.
GN494.5.R66   1993   92-47397
303.6'9—dc20   CIP

A catalogue record for this book is
available from the British
Library.

10 9 8 7 6 5 4 3 2 1

To

Kimberly, Aaron, Kristin, and Ethan

May your generation manage conflicts
more constructively than mine

Contents

Preface

This inquiry into conflict management evolved from a prior interest in cross-cultural differences in conflict and violence. In 1989, as I approached the completion of a book on that topic, I realized that different ways of understanding conflict had important implications for how conflicts should be managed—so I added a half dozen chapters. After sharing the draft manuscript with several colleagues, I realized that my concern with linkage between theories of conflict and strategies of conflict management did not necessarily require addressing both in a single volume. Dividing the original manuscript into two permitted me not only to make each part of my argument more accessible to readers but also to emphasize differences in style and content between the components of my argument.

The first book, *The Culture of Conflict* (Yale University Press, 1993), examines cross-cultural differences in conflict using data from ethnographic reports on ninety small-scale preindustrial societies typically studied by anthropologists. I argue that a society's psychocultural features are critical in shaping its overall level of conflict and violence, whereas its social structure is the main factor in determining who the opponents will be. The book points to the important and independent role that interests and interpretations play as a cause in conflict.

This second book uses the theoretical framework developed in my cross-cultural investigation to explore conflict management. Whereas the cross-cultural study of conflict offers a formal test of a number of hypotheses derived from social structural and psychocultural conflict theories, this volume is an effort to discuss and develop hypotheses about conflict management, to build a comparative framework for its study, and to explore the concept of constructive conflict management.

Conflict management for many people focuses on the outcome—a solution that all the parties in a dispute can adopt. In contrast, my emphasis here is on the *process* of conflict management, as a conflict unfolds and as the parties, their interests, and their interpretations of what is happening change. I am concerned with how the parties understand their own actions and those of others, and how those perceptions affect the course of a conflict. The steps a party takes as a conflict develops and how it interprets the motives of others are directly related to its willingness to accept whatever outcome is reached. In other words, the viability of any conflict outcome is directly related to how it is achieved. Success and failure, from this perspective, are related to the process of conflict management as much as to any specific formulas the parties devise to work out their differences.

Unlike the weather, there is a great deal disputants and third parties can do to affect the course of many conflicts. By emphasizing alternatives and the efficacy of action, I raise the matter of two kinds of errors we make in conflict management—type I, in which we inappropriately act when doing something else or even nothing would have been better, and type II, in which we do nothing when action was needed. I believe the ratio of type II to type I errors is too high today because of ignorance and inertia. More attention to conflict management and more energetic efforts in this area will certainly increase type I errors, a price that may be worth paying if the number of successful cases also rises. Diminishing both types of errors requires the cultural expectation that parties can, and will, manage their differences in constructive ways and the development of specific institutions and practices to promote such behavior. My argument that constructive conflict management is often possible does not mean that it always is. In acute crises, such as shooting wars, the best we can often hope for is a cease-fire and a lessening of tensions. Development of more constructive solutions can only come later.

In our own society, constructive conflict management is not a topic that evokes widespread interest. In the face of bitter conflict, few people avoid taking sides or even rejecting the claims (and legitimacy) of all the disputants. Few ask whether there is a possible outcome that offers a solution attractive to all sides, transforming the conflict into a cooperative situation. A more common response is likely to be "Lock 'em all up and throw away the key."

Conflict management is surprisingly difficult to examine comparatively. One important source of resistance is the disputants themselves (and some scholars as well), who have a tendency to view the conflicts they are involved in as unique. Given the analysis I offer below, which recognizes the feelings and perceptions of disputants as legitimate rather than challenging them, I do not dismiss this point entirely. At the same time, I argue that while disputants may sincerely believe that the conflict they know from the inside is unlike any other, from an analytic point of view I can still search for the features it shares with other disputes.

Another barrier is conceptual. Our ideas about what effective conflict management entails are poorly developed. Evaluating the success of particular strategies is not always simple; making judgments across contexts is even more uncertain. Differences in cultural goals make judgments difficult even when the criteria for evaluation are clearly defined. One culture may emphasize an outcome in terms of the fairness of the substantive outcome, but another may consider the future of the parties' ongoing interpersonal relations. Evaluating outcomes comparatively must, then, deal with the issue of context-based multiple criteria.

In spite of the problems of comparison, attention to cross-cultural differences in conflict management encourages thinking about how cultures can learn constructive conflict management practices from one another. Cross-cultural borrowing to improve the quality of conflict management is based on the fact that interactions with outside groups have always shaped human communities in important ways. We most commonly think about contact and cultural diffusion in terms of technology and other aspects of material culture, but borrowing also involves norms, institutions, and a wide range of cultural practices. The pristine society, unconnected to and unaffected by any other, is a product of western thought, not human experience. Contact and selective modification and adaptation have been important in many domains—conflict management being only one.

A social scientist studying as charged a topic as conflict and its management must expect that his or her personal experiences and culture will influence the way the subject is studied and the emphasis on certain conclusions. It seems reasonable then, in a study that dissects the cultural dispositions of others, to try to describe my own as a way of helping readers to better understand my perspective.

My inspiration for this undertaking is twofold. One is George

Devereux's too little-known book *From Anxiety to Method in the Behavioral Sciences* (1967), in which he argues that the relationship between a social scientist and a community he or she studies can be viewed as similar to the transference and countertransference relationships between a psychoanalytic patient and a therapist. Deviations from objectivity are no cause for distress, Devereux says, in that they provide valuable data about the subject under study. That scholars react to certain subjects in specific ways is not surprising; the important thing is to use those reactions to enhance understanding.

A second source of my motivation is Marcus and Fischer's *Anthropology as Cultural Critique* (1986), which is built around the insights derived from recent ethnographer-centered ethnography. When ethnographers bring their own concerns and points of view to the fore, Marcus and Fischer argue, new understandings develop. In addition, Marcus and Fischer stress the importance of using the "sophisticated reflection by the anthropologist about herself and her own society that describing an alien culture engenders. This reflection can be harnessed . . . and redirected for full-scale projects of cultural critique at home" (1986:4). Marcus and Fischer's argument about ethnography can be applied to other kinds of cross-cultural investigation as well.

I have tried to be reflective about how my personal attitudes and feelings about conflict and violence influenced my emphasis on psychocultural factors, for example, and my decision to link the study of conflict with the study of conflict management. In providing some personal background, I hope to further clarify my approach; I hope also that readers will reflect on how their own predispositions about conflict and violence may affect their reactions to this study.

I think of myself as nonconfrontational and conflictual (sometimes both at the same time). I sometimes hesitate to challenge authority directly, but I sympathize with those who do (even when the authority is my own). Nonetheless, I have a hard time letting things pass, and I find myself involved in many personal and professional exchanges that sometimes evolve into active conflicts. There were always a good many open disagreements and disputes in my family when I was growing up; we all quickly said what we felt. An important lesson was that when this took place between people who cared about each other, the long-term consequences were productive rather than costly. I now realize how firmly I held on to this view, even when there was sometimes evidence that it was not always valid. The ways in which parties air grievances, I now understand, can be as important as the substance of what their disagreements are about. With my own children, I have tried to legitimate the idea of disputing, which I believe increases the likelihood that conflict will take constructive forms, and pay attention to what those forms might be in different contexts.

I have also always enjoyed political debate and confrontation. In high school I organized several friends refusing to stand up when the New York State-mandated prayer was recited over the loudspeaker. My father, though supportive of the idea that the state prayer should not be imposed on students, seemed horrified at the potential problems when I suggested to him that we ought to take the school district and the state to court. When the college newspaper I worked on was closed down, he once again was sympathetic on substantive grounds but warned me to stay away from the protests, fearing that I would be booted out of school. Some of his concern diminished over time when I later participated in civil rights and anti-Vietnam actions (including the takeover of university buildings to protest the war).

My personal style is rooted in readily tapped indignation at social injustice and a sense of efficacy not always warranted by results. My values are unabashedly utopian, as is the case with many in my generation: I believe not only that things can get better, but also that people can make this happen. While I recognize the intellectual naïveté of this position, I still find these old feelings cropping up in new political and personal situations. It is hard for me to believe that no constructive actions are possible, that any particular situation is hopeless, or that, in the long run at least, the good guys won't win. But at least I now know that lots of bad things can happen in the short run, and that a lot of good people get hurt in the process.

While I know that the challenge for those in oppressive and unjust situations is to creatively define alternatives that will bring about change, the paucity of real options in many intense conflict situations is not reassuring. In addition, the fact that a group seeks to replace a bad regime doesn't guarantee that much will change beyond the name of the exploiters.

In other situations, however, conflict can serve as a critical mechanism for the articulation of goals, for the definition of creative solutions to problems, and for the development of collective identity. Conflict and threats of conflict are important weapons of the weak. If disadvantaged groups and individuals refuse to consider open conflict, they deny themselves what sometimes is their most effective means for bringing about needed change. Yet violence or the threat of it, the most visible and emotionally primordial conflict option, is one that I am less ready to endorse than I once was. I used to believe that the end may sometimes justify the means, yet I now see that particular means have more serious consequences than I had understood: a regime that comes to power through violence rarely eschews it later.

We now live in the nuclear era, yet at least as important are the many other weapons of mass violence and repression available to governments and others who can afford them on a totally new scale. In addition, the majority of weapons (and power) are in the hands of those whose values are very different from my own. Challenging these regimes or groups directly is frequently futile, or even suicidal. Yet playing by the rules and focusing on law and order solutions often strikes me as no better, as the rules give all the advantages to those who already hold power.

What is needed is a new (and better) approach to conflict, not a refinement of the ways in which it was handled in the past. Violence, I am convinced, is most likely to produce more violence—for which many innocent people pay the price. A different approach to conflict needs to better recognize the central role of psychocultural sources of conflict and the peacemaking possibilities this opens up. In emphasizing the dispute management consequences of psychocultural interpretations of conflict here, I am aware that these forces can propel conflict in either constructive or destructive directions. Some readers will draw more pessimistic conclusions from my analysis than I have. If conflict is rooted in deep-seated cultural patterns, they will say, how can change in conflict behavior come about? Addressing the psychocultural interpretations of a conflict becomes possible when we take seriously the mutual fears adversaries have, reorganize the ways in which all parties view themselves and others in the dispute, and use these changes to develop integrative solutions.

This tall order will not be accomplished easily in all settings. One reality is that few groups are rarely so unified that all voices sing together; in any group there will be those who (for self-serving or other reasons) seek to counter movement toward accommodation by warning of its dangers. If the peacemakers invoke new metaphors and images in speaking about old enemies or animosities, those fearful of reaching agreements with former enemies will continue to emphasize deeply rooted opposing worldviews. It is not clear who will prevail. A second reality is the basic human disposition to form groups for social and political differentiation. Perhaps Volkan's (1988) "need for enemies and allies" is the right term for this phenomenon, for it refers to both a social and psychological dynamic very basic to human (and even nonhuman) communities. Peacemaking efforts cannot abolish all differences among groups but must recognize that these differences will continue to be important; conflict management institutions need to be particularly sensitive to ways in which group-based fears can grow into full-blown, intransigent battles. In short, cultural constructions are important in managing conflicts, and their influence on how interest-based solutions are built and experienced should not be underestimated.

Constructive conflict management should not be confused with selling accommodation to people who need far more radical solutions. I do not seek to present a position analogous to one who counsels battered wives to adjust to a "difficult" situation, or who teaches "stress management" to the underclass. There is no easy general answer to this dilemma, but developing more widespread institutions for constructive conflict management and meaningful indicators of their success and failure may be a good starting point. While there is no guarantee that conflict management will lead to justice, there are certainly dangers in failing to define alternatives to violent confrontation.

Finally, in making judgments about conflict and conflict management, I use my own cultural experiences as a point of reference, but I am hardly suggesting that they are the standard the world should emulate. I am only too aware that the United States is one of the most violent and most heavily armed societies in history. Cultural relativism evaluates each culture on its own terms, but from a broader universal human rights perspective even more important today is being aware of and questioning the standards with which one evaluates any culture. This I have sought to do here.

I have received generous support for my work from several sources. Bryn Mawr College has granted me several sabbatical leaves and has provided important institutional support over the years. The National Science Foundation's Anthropology Program provided support for the cross-cultural data collection (BNS82–03381). The Harry Frank Guggenheim Foundation provided generous support which was critical in completing the data analysis and writing. The Fund for Research on Dispute Resolution supported work on theories of conflict and peacemaking in ethnic disputes. Portions of chapter 5 appeared in "Ethnic Conflict and Dispute Management: Addressing Interests and Identities," published in *Studies in Law, Politics and Society*, edited by Susan S. Silbey and Austin Sarat.

Various individuals have also provided support and encouragement. Don Campbell vigorously encouraged me to pursue the peacemaking consequences of different theories of intergroup conflict as central to our common interest in ethnocentrism. Jay Rothman read several drafts the manuscript and suggested revisions and improvements for which I am very grateful. Bob Mulvihill has talked to me about Northern Ireland over the years and has encouraged me to think about how my general approach to conflict could offer insights into this long-standing conflict. Lou Kriesberg, as a reader for Yale University Press, made specific suggestions which were crucial in strengthening my argument. Ted Gurr gave me insightful comments which clarified my presentation. Carol Ember, Tom Weisner, John Darby, Jack Nagel, Marshall Segal, Frank Munger, Pat Gray, and Jim Silverberg all offered useful comments at different times on parts of the argument presented here. I want especially to thank Noreen O'Connor of Yale University Press for editing the manuscript meticulously, clarifying ambiguous meanings and tightening my overall argument. Not very many authors are blessed with such a thoughtful and capable editor.

Kimberly, Aaron, Kristin, and Ethan have patiently watched me work on this project for a number of years, occasionally asking me what it was about. What they did not realize was how much I have thought about them while writing this book, hoping that their generation will indeed learn to manage conflict more constructively than mine. For that reason I dedicate this book to them.

Katherine Conner, my wife, has been a tremendous source of support and ideas throughout this project. She encouraged me to pursue the dispute management implications of my earlier work on conflict. She listened to me talk about this project from start to finish and read every draft of every chapter. She never hesitated to tell me what needed changing, elaboration, cutting, or clarification and made suggestions when I felt stuck. Many of the ideas are hers as much as mine. For her tremendous commitment to this project and her continual assistance even while she pursued her own full-time interests I shall always be grateful.

The Management of Conflict

1

The Two Faces of Conflict

It is not difficult to find people who believe that there is too much conflict in the world. One can easily cite figures on family violence, overburdened courts, soaring homicide rates, terrorism, and war casualties to support this view. But instead of emphasizing these grim realities of contemporary life as evidence of excessively high conflict levels, I view them as testimony to our inability to manage conflicts in constructive ways. The problem is not conflict per se, but how we handle it.

In fact, it is easy to make the case—as Felsteiner, Abel, and Sarat (1980–81) have done—that only a small proportion of legitimate grievances actually turn into disputes, and that only a small proportion of these are effectively processed. Even more important, these researchers and others suggest, is a systematic tendency to value the concerns of some groups or individuals more than those of others. In such situations, conflict management becomes a tool of the privileged used to maintain their privileged positions, leaving the less-favored the unsettling choice between acquiescence and costly, often destructive, action.

Conflicts and disputes are found in all human, and many nonhuman, communities. At the same time, there is widespread variation in how different groups respond to conflicts (de Waal 1989; Ross 1993). People's choices in reacting to conflict situations are neither fully conscious nor fully rational in the sense that decision theorists use the term. A disagreement about control or use of a valued object like land, for example, may result in quiescent acceptance or it may unleash the unilateral use of force, intense negotiations, a meeting involving many members of the disputants' community, or action by administrative, political, or judicial authorities. Why do certain responses occur in particular situations? What are the consequences for the disputants and their communities when different reactions occur?

Students of political conflict and students of conflict management have explored these questions, but have all too often worked independently of one another in recent years. Those who examine conflict have told us a great deal about the roots and evolution of conflicts, but they have often paid far less attention to how disputes end, how alternative actions by the disputants might have led to other outcomes, or what consequences the settlements of disputes have for subsequent intergroup relations. Researchers in the emerging field of conflict resolution, in contrast, pay great attention to approaches to and techniques for managing conflicts in a range of settings but too rarely in a way that explicitly links conflict management to theories about conflict. To some people, conflict management consists of specific, discrete skills, such as mediation, negotiation, and adjudication, in the same way that cooking is a matter of mastering component skills like baking, broiling, and sautéing. By following simple directions, it is sometimes suggested, organizations and communities can manage conflicts easily and efficiently. The danger of this skill-based approach is that practitioners fail to grasp the enormous complexity of intransigent social and political conflicts where, ironically, new approaches are most needed.[1] Consequently, people become committed to particular strategies rather than appreciating the strengths and weaknesses of any method and evaluating not only what works but also why.

The lack of rapprochement between the study of conflict and of conflict management means that theories of conflict tell us too little about how to manage conflicts, while conflict management theories fail to consider many underlying sources of conflict that conflict theories have identified, thereby often yielding partial and inadequate solutions to complex, deeply rooted disputes. This, in turn, means that our institutions and practices for addressing severe and not-so-severe conflicts are often deficient.

Managing conflicts effectively is difficult because complex social and political conflicts invariably have multiple sources rather than a single clearly defined cause. Conflicts are about the concrete interests that adversaries pursue, as well as their interpretations of the motives of

---

1. For now I will set aside the question of the costs to disputants resulting from alternative dispute resolution methods.

opponents. Often a substantive issue becomes the focal point for more profound differences of which the antagonists may be only dimly aware. Managing a conflict effectively then means addressing both the issue about which the parties are contending and the deeper concerns which, if ignored, are likely to resurface in a short time. Conflicts are intense and hard to manage not only because of the intrinsic value of what is being fought over, but also because of the emotional importance of the object of contention. The argument from my cross-cultural study of conflict that I apply here to the question of conflict management is that conflict management is most effective when it addresses both disputants' differences in interests and their divergent and mutually hostile interpretations; an exclusive focus on either is biased (Ross 1993).

A central goal of the present volume is to suggest how our understanding of conflict leads to the adoption of particular methods of conflict management, expanding our awareness of the conflict management process in order to increase the proportion of disputes that are constructively managed. To do this, I shall raise a series of questions about how we understand conflict management choices and how we evaluate conflict management successes and failures. Insights drawn from a cross-cultural perspective contribute to the concept of constructive conflict management and are applied first to individual societies and then to particular disputes. Finally, by examining cases of conflict management success rather than just failure, I focus on how we can better manage intense, long-standing disputes, as between ethnic communities. To better understand the dynamics of success and to develop more nuanced criteria by which to judge it, we must explore the institutions and practices associated with successful conflict management.

I begin with a dispute that occurred in France in 1989, where I was living at the time, partially because I remember being astounded by the amount of news coverage and the intensity of feelings this seemingly insignificant matter provoked. Second, this not very successfully managed dispute introduces many themes explored in later chapters: the role of interests and interpretations in social conflicts, the power of psycho-cultural forces, and the criteria for evaluating success and failure in conflict management.

Islamic Scarves in French Schools

In recent years, people of North African origin have become the largest and most visible minority in France and have been the focus of sometimes intense political and social conflict (Grillo 1985). Throughout the 1980s there have been confrontations and local violent incidents, often associated with youth gangs and the National Front, a neofascist political organization.[2] On many occasions the role of North Africans in France has been questioned from a variety of points of view. The North Africans—often called Maghrebians in reference to their region of origin—are almost exclusively Muslim, and many are French citizens, yet they experience discrimination in a number of domains. In the view of many French people, the North Africans show little interest in integration.[3] Although the Socialist regime of François Mitterrand at first cautiously moved to extend social benefits and citizenship rights to immigrants, it has recently grown far more tentative and there have been calls from the center-right opposition to restrict immigration, social programs, and the availability of citizenship (Balinkska 1988). For some time hostility between Muslims and non-Muslims has been high and relations strained in many French cities. Incidents like the one in the summer of 1989 where the mayor of one small city ordered the bulldozing of the local mosque and later claimed it was an accident, have been all too common.

In the fall of 1989, Ernest Chenière, principal of a small junior high school in the town of Creuil, forty miles north of Paris, prohibited three Muslim girls from wearing in school the *chador* (a scarf with which traditional Muslim women cover their hair in public from adolescence onward). Within a month, one girl claimed that the principal had struck her, and her family called in representatives of two Islamic fundamentalist organizations to talk to the principal. The incident touched off a controversy that quickly involved the nation's top polit-

2. Race-related attacks against minorities (80 percent aimed at North Africans and most of the others against Jews) were a regular feature of the 1980s, and the number of racial threats has steadily climbed during this period (*Le Monde*, March 28, 1990:8).

3. France has historically been willing to accept immigrants. Between the wars, for example, it had the largest immigrant population in western Europe. Most came from Spain, Italy, and Poland—all Catholic nations—and had little difficulty with acculturation; consequently they were not viewed as a problem by the French majority.

ical figures and raised a series of issues at the core of French political life.

Chenière justified his action as a defense of the school as a secular institution, although for Chenière, a thirty-five-year-old native of the Antilles in his first administrative assignment, establishing the authority of the school in a downtrodden community with a large immigrant population was also important (Schemla 1989a). Creuil was not the only school in France where the issue arose; in fact, for years various modi vivendi had been worked out on a number of cultural and religious issues with Muslim students as well as with Jewish students (who in some cases wore yarmulkes and did not attend school on Saturday mornings).

Chenière's vigorous defense of the separation of church and state struck a responsive chord for many French, however, and soon the minister of education, Lionel Jospin, a high-ranking figure in the governing Socialist Party, was drawn into the affair. He declared that responsibility in this matter rested with school authorities, who were to talk to the families involved to make them understand the importance of secular public education and abandon the open expression of religion in school. He added, however, that wearing a scarf was not sufficient grounds for exclusion and if the family refused to change its mind, the child's education must come first (Beriss 1990). The Muslims must be accepted in the public schools, the minister declared, because "French schools exist to educate, to integrate, not to reject" (Schemla 1989b:78).

Jospin's hope for diffusing the dispute through dialogue, persuasion, and flexibility was unrealized, and the controversy continued to rage. On the political far right, members of the National Front talked about the evils of immigration and the problems created by foreigners. For many on the left, the incident evoked a threat to the central role of secular public schools played in the past century in the inculcation of democratic values. "The future will tell if the year of the bicentennial [of the French Revolution] will be seen as the Munich of the public school," declared five leading intellectual figures (Badinter et al. 1989:58). For many feminists, the dispute was about neither religious freedom nor the secularism of the public school, but rather the oppression of women in fundamentalist Islam. They felt that tolerating the chador in school amounted to a seal of approval for oppression. The center-right opposition, which, like the Socialists, was divided on the issue, was happy enough to see the government of President Mitterrand and Prime Minister Michel Rocard stumble.

For many, the critical image associated with the dispute was not cherubic faces peering out from under the scarves but Iran's Ayatollah Khomeini and the specter of Islamic fundamentalism. Several years earlier there had been a dramatic wave of terrorist bombing in and around Paris, and French hostages were still being held in Lebanon. The girls, some charged, were being manipulated by their fathers in the service of larger political or religious goals.[4] Teachers throughout France, feeling that their authority and secular principles in general were under attack, spoke out against allowing the chador to be worn, and brought up cases where Moslem students refused to attend gym classes or objected to biology, music, or even art classes on religious grounds. Teachers said that wearing the chador was not only a rejection of secular education but also represented a safety hazard in some situations, and they threatened to go on strike if the scarves were not banned.

Soon Jospin realized that there was little he could do to contain the conflict, which had now expanded to North African work habits, housing, social services, illegal immigration, and integration. The specific issue of the scarves and the more general issue of North African immigrants in France divided the ruling Socialists and generated such intense emotions that there was no obvious way to focus on the narrow issue of the scarves and put together a coalition around an acceptable solution.

So the minister of education kicked the matter upstairs, not to the president or prime minister (who certainly wanted to deal with it even less than he did) but to the Conseil d'Etat, the nation's top administrative tribunal (Escoube 1971). Within a month the Conseil d'Etat ruled that wearing religious symbols was not necessarily incompatible with the idea of a secular public school, as long as the symbols were not provocative, did not pressure other students, were not proselytizing, and were not tools of propaganda—a decision that satisfied neither those who saw the issue as one of religious freedom nor those who wanted to ban the chador from public schools (*Le Monde*, November 29, 1989:13). Accord-

---

4. Beriss (1990) suggests that for some French people the incident evoked images of the Algerian war in which some Muslim women carried bombs to be used against the French.

ing to the ruling, students could not refuse to attend certain classes or threaten the liberty or security and safety of others. The Conseil d'Etat said that the principal of each school was to decide on a case-by-case basis if a student's actions involved more than just a religious sign and ordered the minister of education to prepare a set of guidelines.

Most teachers' organizations and administrators, unhappy with the decision, suggested that what was most critical was its implementation. Some Muslim students and their families, citing the fact that Catholic students often wore crosses, saw the decision as favorable and returned to school wearing the chador, but some Muslim girls were sent home again, especially in the south. Parents in one high school in Marseille gathered 1500 signatures supporting a principal who refused to meet with the lawyer for an expelled student but said she would meet with the student and her parents in the school. A Dijon hospital refused to accept a young Muslim doctor when she told the authorities that she planned to wear a chador at work. In the next few months, local authorities were left to handle the issue as they saw fit. Some students were excluded when they refused to attend gym classes, but strikingly, almost none of these decisions received much publicity as the nation turned its attention to other matters.

The dispute over allowing the chador to be worn in French schools was settled through the imposition of an administrative rule, but the larger conflict was in no sense resolved. It was diffused and transformed as the arenas, actors, and issues shifted; as media coverage decreased, it seemed to go away. Many of the disputants (the families, school authorities, and even the public) would have preferred a different outcome to the one that resulted. Conflict over the questions of integration and immigration displaced the specific dispute over the scarves in a very short time. French suspicions about and anger toward North Africans seemed to increase, whereas North Africans felt more vulnerable and uncertain than ever about which, if any, of their basic rights the government would protect. Although it was possible to use administrative and judicial procedures to deal with the dispute over the scarves, the deeper issues were far more divisive and challenged the Socialist policy of supporting limited ethnonational expression from minorities within France (Safran 1985).

Accounting for Conflict Management Failure

Management of this conflict was ineffective for several reasons. At the simplest level the parties to the dispute kept shifting and had few direct interactions with each other. At first the dispute involved only the school administrators and the students in Creuil. Then the families brought in outsiders as a way of dealing with an unequal power situation. The issue escalated again when successive levels of educational administrators, including the minister of education, were drawn in, and the teachers' union, the media, political parties, and leading intellectuals joined the fray. Extensive television and newspaper coverage kept the public informed and fired up. The original disputants soon took a back seat to more prominent actors. The parties never engaged in joint problem solving and instead relied on "self-help" actions aimed at promoting their own position and not in reaching a solution. In asking the Conseil d'Etat for a ruling, Jospin turned to a third party to impose a decision on a situation that had gotten out of hand. None of these strategies were particularly effective, except insofar as they helped the Socialists remove a politically charged issue from the front pages. These conflict management methods failed, however, to bridge the apparently competing interests of the parties and, equally important here, to address the underlying concerns and deep fears of both the French majority and the North African minority—it only made them worse.

The way participants and conflict managers understand a dispute has a good deal to do with the steps they take to settle it. In the controversy over allowing the chador to be worn in school, Jospin saw the central issue as integration and ordered school officials to explain French values to the North African families. What he failed to recognize and therefore did not address was the intensity of the parties' fears, which got in the way of reaching a constructive solution that many (if not all) of the parties would find satisfactory. In addition, his integrationist perspective made it hard for him to conceive of a different, more pluralistic view of French society, for that would derail his strategy of using persuasion based on France's liberal democratic values.

As with this dispute, many conflicts are managed but not necessarily resolved. In this case, given the inequality in power between the government and the families, Muslim parents had the choice of acquiescing or removing their child from the public schools. Furthermore, the government's insistence that the matter concerned only the families and school authorities both reinforced the structural inequality of the situation and eliminated the possibility of the education officials working out a more general compromise solution.[5]

Probably the greatest barrier to managing the dispute over the scarves constructively, however, concerned its rapid transformation into a larger, more intense debate about immigration and integration in France where the government felt a real gap between its integrationist, mildly pluralist principles and political reality. Lack of agreement did not result in coalition building across existing political and social cleavages. Instead, those upset about the scarves issue responded with polemics, few people explicitly defended the students, and many said little and hoped the issue would go away. Even before the end of the dispute, Prime Minister Rocard created a high-level committee to address the integration of minorities, clearly hoping that the group would operate out of the limelight. The next spring the government sought to form a coalition with the opposition against the right-wing National Front on the question of integration, modifying its position on several key issues. A huge demonstration in Paris brought together political leaders of all groups (except the National Front) and all religious communities in the wake of the desecration of the Jewish cemetery in Carpentras in the south in May 1990, and other related anti-minority and anti-immigrant incidents during the spring. Yet it remained unclear whether the French had the ability or desire to address the divergent interests and fears which kept the issue of ethnic minorities on the political agenda.[6]

5. SOS–Racisme, a group concerned with discrimination, was one of the few organized non-Muslim groups to support the students actively. SOS-Racisme in no way represented the students or their families, however, and expressed more of an integrationist, rather than pluralist, position on the issue, which was at odds with the position of the students and their families. The fundamentalist organizations, which represented the families in early meetings with the school, played no public role in the controversy once it reached the national level. It should be noted that not all Muslims in France supported the students' positions.

6. The issue of immigration and migrant workers affects all prosperous EEC nations, not France alone. Each nation is struggling to deal with the issue and the EEC is seeking a common policy. With the political changes in central and eastern Europe since 1989, these issues have become even more charged in most EEC nations, especially Germany.

Conflict Management: Key Questions

The case of the chadors highlights central questions in the study of conflict and conflict management. Disputes are played out around what appear to be concrete interests, but participants' emotional interpretations are equally important in explaining why and how a dispute develops and whether it can be managed constructively. This conflict illustrates the transformation of disputes as they unfold, with one party's actions setting off responses from others (Schattschneider 1960; Mather and Yngvesson 1981). Issues shift as parties offer competing images of what is at stake, as different deeply held fears are evoked, and as new concerns are articulated (Cobb and Elder 1983). The transformation of this dispute from a conflict over the role of religious symbols in a secular school to a full-blown debate about racism, integration, and immigration in France is dramatic, but not necessarily exceptional. Finally, parties with interests that differ from those of the original disputants come to play prominent roles, often increasing polarization (Coleman 1957). The case shows how easily conflicts expand along existing social and economic divisions in a community and how some disputes evoke strong reactions and become harder to manage (Pruitt and Rubin 1986).

The main conclusion from my cross-cultural analysis of conflict provides a more general framework for examining this and other disputes: both social structural interests and psychocultural interpretations shape a society's culture of conflict, but in quite different ways. The core of my argument is that whereas psychocultural dispositions account for a society's overall level of conflict and violence, social structural conditions that underlie competing interests determine the selection of targets. Each source of conflict suggests contrasting strategies for managing conflict successfully. Structural theory gives a primary role to conflict-limiting approaches involving altering incentives, payoffs, or—most fundamentally—the organization of society. Divergent interests, in this view, are hard to bridge and lead to an emphasis on either unilateral action or third-party intervention. In contrast, psychocultural theory points to the need to alter either disputants' dominant images and metaphors concerning what is at stake or the relationships between key parties. In chapter 2 I shall discuss the implications of this cross-cultural theory of conflict for the study of conflict management. Here I want to spell out the more general aspects of the idea of the culture of conflict and how it can provide the basis for understanding conflict management.

It is easy to emphasize structural and psychocultural theories of conflict behavior as competing alternatives, yet these potential explanations for conflict have complementary strengths and weaknesses. Fears and threats identified in a psychocultural explanation can account for the intensity of feelings involved, but only the structural explanation speaks to why they are focused in particular directions. Interests arising from social structure and interpretations rooted in psychocultural forces are relevant to understanding conflict management as well. Patterns of escalation, redefinition, extension to new parties, and termination of disputes have both structural and psychocultural components. Because interests and interpretations interact, conflict management strategies will be successful only to the extent that they pay attention to both. Finally, success in addressing one enhances the prospects for dealing effectively with the other.

Societal and Dispute Levels of Analysis

What constitutes an adequate explanation of conflict behavior? Some explanations of conflict or conflict management examine the structure of conflict in a society or community, whereas others focus on the details of one or more disputes. In the controversy over the chadors in French schools, a dispute-level explanation would focus on the question "Why the scarves?" whereas a societal level consideration would ask "Why in France?" Societal level theories of conflict suggest why some communities are more prone to conflict or certain forms of it than others. Societal level comparisons, such as my cross-cultural study of conflict, stress cultural differences between groups and downplay differences within groups. This strategy is valuable because it highlights broad patterns of relationships that can be obscured when one views a question only from a perspective of intensive involvement in specific settings. Dispute-level approaches, in contrast, account for the forms conflicts take, the dynamics of individual incidents, the strategies used by different parties, and the stages in the evolution of the conflict (Swartz 1968; Kriesberg 1982, 1992; Pruitt and Rubin 1986). A dispute-level analysis suggests how particular shared and divergent understandings of what is at stake shape disputants' actions. Here actors' strategic choices are linked to specific cultural settings to show how individual and group interests are established and maintained and how the actors themselves understand events. In the case of the chador controversy, the actions of the school administrators, the responses of the students' families, the statements of public figures (Danielle Mitterrand, the president's wife, remarked that she saw nothing wrong with wearing the scarves in school), and the actions of the minister of education shaped the course of the dispute.

The societal approach identifies forces which make a community disposed toward characteristic forms and levels of conflict and styles of conflict management; the dispute-level approach tells us how particular disputes come about, develop, and end. Which explanation is best depends on the question one wants answered, but one need not choose between the two. In chapter 2 I construct an account of the chador controversy in France that includes both dispute and societal level elements in order to show how one enhances the other. Societal level forces provide the context in which a dispute occurs and shape the actions of the parties. Here the centralized character of the French educational system and its role in previous political battles shaped the dispute in certain ways. Likewise, racial tension, the rise of the National Front, and prior calls from the opposition to limit immigration and the granting of citizenship—calls which had received widespread public support—limited and directed the government response. Finally, the economic slowdown of the mid-1980s and the integration of the French economy into the EEC were also important. At the dispute level, the actions or inaction of particular figures mattered. The loudest voices in the dispute spoke out against allowing the scarves to be worn in school. While the government officials talked about integration and the media made some effort to show the diversity in the French Muslim community, their voices were far quieter in comparison. Few politicians and organized groups were prepared, it turned out, to take the unpopular position in defense of the students' religious rights—to challenge the idea that permitting them to wear the scarves was the first step toward an Islamic revolution in France or to ease the fears of the Maghrebian community in France.

Conflict As a Cultural Process

Culture—a shared, collective product—is particularly important for understanding conflict and conflict management and provides both a repertoire of behaviors and standards of reference to evaluate the actions of others (Cohen 1991; Ross 1993). Culture involves, as Avruch and Black put it, the social structuring of both the world outside the self and the internal world. The concept refers to widely shared practices and to commonly held "assumptions and presuppositions that individuals and groups hold about the world" (Avruch and Black 1991:28).

Culture shapes what people consider valuable and worth fighting over, investing particular goods, social roles, official positions, or actions with meaning. Unlike economists, who translate diverse values into a common standard of reference, cultural analysts are more likely to ask why certain objects or positions take on the value they do in particular settings (Wildavsky 1987, 1989, 1991). Cultural differences can explain why, in response to what appears to be a similar event, people in one setting feel their interests are threatened while those in another do not.

Conflict behavior is often highly structured because culture sanctions certain actions taken to pursue individual or group interests and disapproves of others. Anthropologists have learned, for example, about the highly stylized form tribal warfare takes in many settings (Meggitt 1977; Turney-High 1949). The same is true of other forms of conflict. Most cultures have clear expectations about what a party should do on its own when it feels aggrieved, to whom it can turn for help, and if and when it is appropriate to involve the wider community. The same event, such as a physical attack on a relative, warrants physical retaliation in one culture, a community meeting to discuss the situation in another, and an appeal to the authorities in a third.

Conflicts can be seen as a process of social communication (Gulliver 1979) whose messages are interpretable because disputants share a common frame of reference. Some messages seem quite cryptic to outsiders, but their cultural meanings in context are clear. Conflict occurs not only within a shared cultural framework, however, but also between groups and individuals who come from different cultures and whose common frame of reference may be small. Here, conflicts can escalate as each side relies on its own understanding of what is going on, reading unintended meanings into a situation (Cohen 1990, 1991).

The dispute over the scarves in French schools illustrates the importance of culture in the conflict process. First, cultural assumptions about the meaning of the scarves were at the core of the actions and reactions of the participants. For Islamic fundamentalists, wearing the chador in public stems from a central religious tenet, the indivisibility of the world into the private and the public or the secular and the sacred (Etienne 1989), whereas for many on the French left the necessity of separating these domains is just as basic a belief.

The dispute also revealed that the French can accept foreigners into their society, only on the condition that newcomers adopt core French values. Integration into French society, it has often been argued, is a cultural rather than a racial matter; the French historically have had trouble with the idea of a pluralist society and the idea of mutual accommodation in which all sides make adjustments to live together (Beriss 1990). Granting even modest sanction to the expression of regional cultural differences, for example, occurred only in the 1980s and has challenged French views of their cultural homogeneity (Safran 1985).

Culture is the vehicle through which many conflicts are played out. Cultural interpretations of particular acts (the wearing of the chador), or settings (the public school) become highly emotional. Symbols involved in the dispute quickly become associated with control, autonomy, power, and most important, identity, hopes, and fears. To understand the power of culture in this and other disputes, it is critical—as Avruch and Black (1991) argue—to consider the assumptions about the world held by the different participants in a conflict.

This became clear to me when, as an American living in France during the dispute, I tried to understand what was happening by using my own culture (American society) as a point of reference and as a result made several cultural miscalculations. I overestimated the importance of the value of cultural pluralism in France and was often surprised when even those who were most supportive of the students (and North Africans generally) continued to emphasize the necessity of their integration into French society meaning the need of North Africans to change and saying little about mutual accommodation. I underestimated the importance of the public schools as a symbol of the Republican left in its long-standing battles with the right and its Catholic clerical allies. Finally, I was struck by the fact that because the conflict cut across the country's profound left-right division (and united other potentially relevant groups), the matter was finally managed through administrative directives (see Crozier 1964), since the political process held no possibility of solving the dispute through direct involvement of the interested parties.

Plan of the Book

In this book the topics addressed in each chapter extend my earlier analysis of the culture of conflict to questions of conflict management. In chapter 2 I summarize the main findings from my cross-cultural research on conflict, emphasizing structural interests and psychocultural interpretations as central mechanisms and highlighting their implications for conflict management. I shall also explain how interests and interpretations emphasize different elements in the conflict over the scarves in France. In chapter 3 I further develop the cross-cultural perspective through the idea of the constructive conflict society, identifying the common features in five small-scale, low-conflict societies.

The following two chapters concern general connections between conflict and conflict management. In chapter 4 I propose that both are processes during which interests and interpretations of disputants change. I suggest that shifts in each indicate whether the parties are moving closer to or farther away from an acceptable settlement, illustrating my argument with the case of a public housing dispute in New York. In chapter 5 I discuss how three strategies of conflict management—self-help, joint problem solving, and third-party decision making—differently address social structural interests and psychocultural interpretations as causes of conflict.

In chapters 6 and 7 I evaluate the management of particular disputes, discussing them within the framework used to describe cross-cultural differences. When dealing with the complicated issue of success and failure in conflict management, it is easy to be ethnocentric in determining the effectiveness of particular outcomes. Another pitfall is making a single judgment where, in fact, multiple criteria may indicate more accurate yet complex views. Even when what seem like clear conceptual criteria can be used to evaluate particular cases, applying them to actual situations, especially in varied settings, is not always straightforward. Success and failure in conflict management is a nuanced, multidimensional phenomenon, not an either/or dichotomy. We have to resist asking only if a situation is "as good as it can be" following conflict management, for it rarely is. Rather, we should ask if and how things are better (or worse) than if there had been no conflict management efforts at all. To examine this question, I offer a series of case studies of successful and unsuccessful conflict management, including the conflict between

MOVE and the city of Philadelphia, the return to warfare in highland New Guinea, and the Camp David accords. Instead of considering only the final outcome in each situation, I focus on the small steps along the way and the relevance of disputants' interests and interpretations.

The case studies suggest that addressing disputants' mutually hostile psychocultural interpretations is necessary in order to deal effectively with conflicts over divergent interests, particularly in bitter disputes. In chapter 8 I discuss how various proposals for conflict management, such as problem-solving workshops, Track Two diplomacy and personal and cultural exchanges address psychocultural interpretations as a prior step to bridging divergent interests.

In the final chapter, I speculate about three issues needing further attention: the development of models of successful conflict management, the need to further spell out the connections involved in psychocultural models of conflict, and the concept of the constructive conflict society, concluding with a discussion of the importance of and possibilities for improving conflict management, especially in the case of intransigent disputes.

2

Interests, Interpretations, and the Culture of Conflict

Conflicts are rooted in differences both in interests and in participants' interpretations of events and other actors. To be effective, peacemaking must both bridge the parties' differences in interests and consider disputants' deep hurts and the strong distrust of adversaries.

Because my analysis of conflict management builds on my cross-cultural investigation of conflict, first I shall present its argument, emphasizing the role of interests and interpretations (Ross 1993). As in the cross-cultural study, I begin with an emphasis on societal differences. I shall argue in subsequent chapters, however, that the same concepts that are useful in examining the culture of conflict comparatively are also helpful in understanding conflict in particular societies and the unfolding of single disputes.

The complementarity of the mechanisms of interests and psychocultural interpretations ultimately makes an explanation for conflict linking the two at both the societal and dispute levels richer than a theory based on either one alone. Where structural conflict theory focuses attention on the apparently concrete interests actors easily cite, psychocultural conflict theory focuses on interpretations that point to deeper, less conscious, more ambiguous dispositions and motives of which parties often are only dimly aware, as people impose the structure of their inner worlds on external events. These motives, while intensely individual, are of interest here because they are shared by members of the same culture. Common interpretations of the world grow out of social support-seeking and the search for consensus and are especially important where group anxiety is high and where there is no assurance of a favorable future outcome (Noelle-Neumann 1984). In this process the social and psychological connection between individual and group identity is central to the link between the inner psychological world and external social concerns (Northrup 1989).

In this chapter I first discuss the results of my cross-cultural study with emphasis on its significance for conflict management. In the second section the concepts of interests and interpretations and their relevance for conflict and conflict management receive considerable attention. Finally I return to the case of the wearing of chadors in French schools to illustrate how a focus on interests or on interpretations yields different understandings of the dispute. In the next chapter I use these concepts to develop the idea of the constructive conflict society and its special structural and psychocultural features through the detailed analysis of five low-conflict societies.

Cross-Cultural Lessons About Conflict

Fifteen years ago I began investigating why some societies are more conflictual than others through a comparison of small-scale, preindustrial societies typically studied by anthropologists. While conflicts occur in all human societies, there is great variation in the forms they take. In some societies, like the Yanomamo of Venezuela and Brazil, conflict and violence seem to be a regular feature of daily existence (Chagnon 1967, 1983), whereas among other groups such as the Mbuti of Zaire's tropical rain forest (Turnbull 1961, 1978), differences among people living in the same community or among neighbors are rarely bitter and violent.

Why, I wondered, were communities so different in their conflict behavior? I started with two distinct plausible theories: social structural conflict theory identifies the primary source of conflict in the social, economic, and political organization of society and in the nature and strength of ties within and between communities; and psychocultural conflict theory emphasizes the role of culturally shared, profound "we-they" oppositions, the conceptualization of enemies and allies, and deep-seated dispositions about human action stemming from earliest development.

In more concrete terms, a structural analysis of conflict posits that the stronger the ties of kinship, economy, and politics in a society, the lower the chance of severe conflict among the individuals and groups

(Coleman 1957; LeVine and Campbell 1972). A psychocultural analysis, in contrast, is based on the understanding that much social action is ambiguous; this approach stresses the importance of the interpretation of words and deeds in explaining why some disputes unleash intense and violent sequences and why others do not.

Hypotheses derived from these two theoretical perspectives were tested systematically using data from a worldwide sample of ninety preindustrial societies (Ross 1986a, 1993). In the analyses, each preindustrial society was scored in terms of internal conflict and violence, external conflict and warfare, and total conflict.[1] Differences were then explained in terms of social structure (measured by socioeconomic and political complexity, patterns of marriage, the strength of social linkages across communities in a society, intercommunity trade, and the existence of fraternal interest groups—localized related males with common material and political interests) and the psychocultural features of a society (measured in terms of early socialization: the extent to which it is affectionate and warm, the degree to which it is harsh and punishing, and the strength of male gender-identity conflict).

Although I initially somewhat naïvely sought to find clear-cut evidence in favor of one theory or the other, the results were more complicated—and more interesting. Although psychocultural dispositions shape a society's overall conflict level, structural features are critical in determining the targets of hostile action. To understand this pattern better I then examined individual societies, such as the warlike Mae Enga of highland New Guinea (Meggitt 1977; Ross 1986b, 1993:104–112), which are consistent with the model, and cases where the model and results were more at odds (Ross 1993:129–145). I also applied the model developed from preindustrial settings to explain conflict and violence (or their absence) in Northern Ireland and Norway, two small-scale modern polities (Ross 1993:146–167).

These detailed analyses provided a sense of how the culture of conflict—a society's relevant norms, practices, and institutions—allows the society to manage conflicts in characteristic ways. The case studies balanced the statistical results with knowledge of particular contexts as I puzzled over how socioeconomic structure and psychocultural disposi-

1. Detailed descriptions of the specific variables used in the statistical study are described in Ross (1983, 1993).

tions affect conflict levels and targets. It became clear to me that the *mechanisms* linking social structure and psychocultural dispositions to conflict are distinct. Specific individual and group interests connect social structure and conflict, and shared interpretations of the world link psychocultural dispositions and conflict.

The mechanisms of structural interests and psychocultural interpretations are very different, and integrating them into a single explanation initially seems problematic. However, the distinct theoretical assumptions and languages of social structural and psychocultural theories may be united in an integrated explanation, for weaknesses in one theory may be precisely those points receiving the greatest attention in the other. It follows that some central questions in one approach may be all but ignored in the other. Furthermore, the two theories do not necessarily explain the same features of conflict. Psychocultural theory is more relevant to the intensity of conflicts, whereas structural theory best explains the specific ways societies organize conflict and cooperation.

The identification of interests and interpretations as the mechanisms linking social structure and psychocultural dispositions to social and political action, I shall argue later, points to specific strategies for constructive conflict management. A critical consequence of this argument is that addressing interests and interpretations may provide effective steps peacemakers can take in the short run rather than having to wait for a long-term shift in social structure and psychocultural dispositions, forces they cannot control.

Consider societies that are highly polarized along ethnic lines such as Northern Ireland, Israel, Sri Lanka, or South Africa. Cross-cutting ties linking the members within each different community are weak. In addition, there are distinctive psychocultural dispositions that perpetuate positive in-group and negative out-group images. Strong within-group ties are associated with specific interests in land, jobs, housing, and political rights. Similarly, psychoculturally shared interpretations are critical to the hostile intergroup images and fears of group survival associated with the continuation of conflict at high intensity (Horowitz 1985). Because the social structure and psychocultural dispositions are difficult to address directly let alone modify, in these conflicts it is often far more useful initially to focus on the specific interests and the interpretations that grow out of them. Policies can be developed to promote a more equitable distribution of jobs or housing, for example, or to rectify the more blatant aspects of ethnic discrimination, as occurred in Northern Ireland in the early 1970s. Steps can also be taken to address disputants' deep-seated fears concerning their existence, as seen in dramatic cases such as Egyptian President Anwar Sadat's trip to Israel in 1977, or the South African government's release of Nelson Mandela and subsequent recognition of the African National Congress in 1990. Many less dramatic steps address particular interests and modify the organization and salience of group interpretations, which can alter intergroup images, diminish perceived threats, and create conditions where substantive agreements become possible.

Before elaborating on this argument, which is the substance of chapters 4 through 8, I shall spell out here the idea of the culture of conflict and consider how social structure gives rise to concrete interests and how psychocultural dispositions produce interpretations that become the focus of social and political conflicts.

The Culture of Conflict

The culture of conflict refers to culturally specific norms, practices, and institutions associated with conflict in a society. Culture defines what people value and what they are likely to enter into disputes about, suggests appropriate ways to behave in particular kinds of disputes, and shapes institutions in which disputes are processed. In sum, culture affects what people fight about and how they go about it. It is an emergent concept, something which appears on the aggregate, not individual, level; culture is not an individual characteristic, but consists of understandings and practices shared by many people in a society.

Culture affects conflict behavior, and conflict can also be understood as cultural behavior. All conflict occurs in a cultural context which shapes its course in important ways. Culture frames people's understanding of their social worlds, how they classify people, how they evaluate possible actions, and it sanctions certain responses. Conflict reflects cultural priorities, but it also can be used to alter them. Culture is political because control over the definition of actors and actions favors certain people and groups over others. The culture of conflict both summarizes a society's core values and reflects prior conflicts which favored some individuals and groups over others.

Central to the culture of conflict are social structural interests and psychocultural interpretations. In societies where interests are sharply divergent and outsiders are seen as threats, as among the Jivaro of western Ecuador (Harner 1972), the culture of conflict is violent. In contrast, where cross-cutting interests exist and images of in-groups and out-groups are not highly polarized, as among the Mbuti of Zaire, the culture of conflict is more likely to facilitate the constructive management of disputes.

Social Structure and Interests

The structure of society is a ready source of hypotheses about political conflict and conflict management, which are linked through the common interests shared by individuals and groups occupying similar positions in the social structure, and pursued through collective action. Socially rooted interests can be defined in several ways. Some interests (often competing) are defined through the inequalities of power and resources inherent in particular levels of social complexity. Other interests are formed through interaction and exchange among people in a society or between groups in different societies and can be described in terms of the strength of cross-cutting versus reinforcing ties (LeVine and Campbell 1972).

The cross-cultural study supports the proposition that cross-cutting ties inhibit the severity of internal and, at the same time, increase the likelihood of external conflict. In societies with strong cross-cutting ties, individuals cannot count on a large core of fixed supporters who share the same interests, since people mobilized on the basis of one loyalty, such as kinship, may be opposed on the basis of another one, such as residence or ritual affiliation. In contrast, in societies in which several bases of social differentiation reinforce one another, the mobilization of one's core group is relatively easy so that conflict is often expansive and difficult to contain. Cross-cutting ties communities limit escalation in ways not found in reinforcing ties societies, since divided loyalties make it difficult to organize diverse and often dispersed groups and individuals who will be at odds with each other for extended periods of time.[2]

2. Gluckman's concept of multiplex (as opposed to simplex) ties, not quite the same as cross-cutting ties, refers to the number of links among groups or individuals. He hypothesizes that the greater the number of links the higher the commitment to the relationship and the more likely the disputants are to resolve differences through compromise (Nader and Todd 1978).

Finally, although communities with strong cross-cutting ties may be relatively successful in limiting internal conflict, the same conditions which promote internal unity can, at times, make such groups more ethnocentric and bold when facing outsiders (LeVine and Campbell 1972).

In preindustrial societies, cross-cutting ties that limit the intensity of conflict can be achieved in a variety of ways. One common mechanism is through ritual groups, such as cults or age organizations, whose membership regularly brings together individuals in different communities. Another frequently used mechanism is a system of kinship and marriage that disperses closely related males who might provide the core of fighting groups. In this way, internal conflict is contained in societies such as the matrilocal Mundurucu (Murphy 1957) and the Tikopia (Firth 1963) who have strong multiple group memberships that extend beyond local communities.

In contrast, a prototypical case of a weak cross-cutting ties society with a high level of conflict is one where localized groups of related males defend common interests in land, livestock, and women and their offspring (Otterbein 1970; Paige and Paige 1981; Thoden van Velzen and van Wetering 1960). In politically uncentralized societies these fraternal interest groups exercise effective political control within many communities. Fraternal interest groups, in the pursuit of common goals, can develop high levels of intragroup coordination, while their relationships with outside groups are often unstable and punctuated by outbreaks of conflict and violence (Meggitt 1977).

This pattern is relevant in general terms, even though fraternal interest group theory concerns the power of localized male kin groups in uncentralized societies. In fact, at each level of societal complexity the specific interests male groups defend differs, but the existence of groups of males having common interests that they defend is widespread. For example, the men's house in highland New Guinea, male social clubs in London, and American college fraternities are crucial institutions for pursuing the interests of their members, although the basis of membership and the ways in which the interests are pursued are not the same.

Social structural conflict theory is better at predicting likely opponents in a community conflict than in determining if a conflict is likely in the first place. Not all potential lines of division become open disputes, and in many situations the hypotheses of social scientists (and other observers) about which lines of social cleavage will achieve political significance have been proven wrong, and divisions that at first seem to be firm can later turn out to be ephemeral.[3] In great part this is because we have too broad a notion of what interests are and too readily attribute them to actors without first making sure that the disputants view events as observers suppose they do. If one assumes that actors necessarily pursue their own interest in a rational manner—as both microeconomic and rational-choice theory do—one must either decide what action actors should take or declare that whatever they did was necessarily rational.

Many structural analyses make problematic action seem self-evident largely because these theories are asked to explain more than they can. Few ask why individuals equate their self-interest with that of the group so easily in certain situations.[4] Although the identification of social structural and ecological interests in a conflict is rarely wrong, explanations for conflict based on these considerations alone are often incomplete and therefore misleading. Interests are rarely as self-evident to either participants or observers as structural conflict theory makes them seem; similarly the intensity of affect associated with many interests is so much higher than a "rational" observer would expect that something else is clearly involved. Here psychocultural theory can fill in important gaps in our understanding of conflict.

Psychocultural Dispositions and Interpretations

Psychocultural dispositions are deep-seated, socially constructed internal representations of the self, others, and one's social world that are widely shared in a society. I use the term psychocultural because it emphasizes both the psychological processes by which these dispositions are acquired and their socially constructed and shared character (LeVine 1973; Whiting and Whiting 1975). Examples of relevant psychocultural dispositions include the degree of trust of people within and outside one's kin group; beliefs about the supernatural; and feelings about personal and social identity. Such dispositions become critical

3. A dramatic but not uncommon example is the shift in voters from class- to ethnic-based parties as a political campaign heats up. Melson and Wolpe (1970) document this in a Nigerian election.

4. See Campbell (1983) for an excellent discussion of the linkage between individual and group interests and their role in biosocial theories of conflict and cooperation (also see Ross 1991a).

building blocks (but not the only elements) in the interpretations that explain the origin and development of conflicts.

Psychocultural dispositions are acquired in different ways. Some, Whiting (1980) suggests, arise from situational forces, contain relatively low affect, and involve such learning mechanisms as trial and error, direct instruction, and modeling. Understanding how culture places certain individuals in various social situations, she suggests, can teach us a great deal about their subsequent orientation to the world. Other dispositions, which Whiting calls "expressive" and "projective," are acquired through processes best described by modern psychoanalytic theory. Religious beliefs and interpretations of illness fit into this category, but, as I suggest, so too do views of conflict and its management. In these later cases high ambiguity and a strong affect combine with a lack of direct evidence that could alter beliefs or action.

Contemporary psychoanalytic ideas are particularly helpful in thinking about the psychocultural construction of social worlds (Greenberg and Mitchell 1983; Stern 1985; Volkan 1988). This work emphasizes social communication and interaction from the first days of life, placing psychological development squarely in the social realm. The approach draws our attention to how early relationships create a model, or template, for later ones and provide a set of standards by which groups and individuals evaluate their social worlds.[5] Without making assumptions about cultural homogeneity or the distribution of personality types in a society, psychoanalytic ideas help us to build a plausible explanation of the intensity of conflict-related beliefs and behaviors and identify social processes associated with the acquisition of these beliefs and behaviors.

Individual development and later collective action are linked through similar early social (often preverbal) experiences among mem-

5. The relevance of this work for analyzing social and political processes is addressed in more detail in Ross (1993:51-69). The shift in interest from earlier Freudian stages to the preoedipal period, as well as a significant change in language (and interests) from internal mental processes to ones rooted in social interactions are both very relevant here and very important for making this theory more compatible with the concerns of most social scientists. Relevant work includes that of such object-relations theorists as Winnicott (1953), Guntrip (1968), and Fairbairn (1954); the work of Melanie Klein (1957); and Margaret Mahler (1975). This material is summarized well in Greenberg and Mitchell (1983). For a more recent synthesis of psychoanalytic theorizing with important developmental data on infancy, see Stern (1985), whose work is briefly discussed below.

bers of a group that lead to shared worldviews and a sense of common identity. Early experiences are initially grounded in primary sensations such as smell, taste, and sound which acquire high affective meaning and only later include a more cognitive component. These early experiences are critical in the development of social identity, which draws attention not only to the shared experience of group members but also to the developmental task of incorporating these shared experiences into one's individual identity (Volkan 1988). Group identity formation often overemphasizes what is shared by group members, reinforcing these elements with an ideology of linked fate.[6] The process is perhaps best viewed as a psychocultural "regression to the mean," in that what individuals share is emphasized both affectively and cognitively, whereas deviations from the norm are selectively ignored or negatively reinforced as incompatible with group membership.

Underlying this general developmental pattern are culturally shared interpretations of the self and the social world which, although rooted in early social experiences, are also regularly and widely reinforced through a variety of culturally sanctioned messages and experiences. These experiences provide the basis for the development and reinforcement of internal mental representations that later serve as a template for the interpretation of others' actions as well as a guide to one's own behavior. Dispositions learned early in life are not only relevant on the perceptual level; they are also implicated in specific behavioral patterns which serve one throughout life, such as how to respond to perceived insults, when to use physical aggression, or whom to trust.[7]

Disputants' shared interpretations of the meaning of social action

6. Turner (1988) also has an excellent discussion of the notion of overvaluation of the uniformity within groups.

7. I have increasingly moved away from using the concept of "personality." It communicates a false definitiveness, which the notion of disposition does not. Another concept I decided not to employ is that of "schema," as it has been developed in social psychology in recent years. It overlaps with my notion of interpretations of the world in that each is interested in mental frameworks which individuals and groups use to interpret the actions of others and to guide their own behavior (Nisbett and Ross 1980; Tversky and Kahneman 1980). Schema theory, however, emphasizes cognitive elements and pays far less attention to deeply rooted affective to which I attribute great importance. The debate over modal personalities and national character is not relevant to the argument presented here.

partially explain responses to particular situations. In addition, differences in interpretations are critical in understanding why what seems like a minor issue to an observer may lead to a bitter long-term conflict, and why two conflicts attributed to the same objective cause (livestock theft or job discrimination, for example) can take very different courses. Objective situations alone do not cause overt conflict; the *interpretation* of such situations is central. If the same objective conditions produce different responses, an explanation for conflict behavior requires more than the identification of underlying objective conditions.[8]

Individual and group representations that emphasize a we-they worldview are all too ready to assign malevolent intentions to others while failing to recognize the existence of similarly rooted motives closer to home. Outsiders become ready objects for the externalization, displacement, and projection of a group's most hostile impulses and dreaded fears.[9] Given this pattern, events—including the simplest ones of daily life—can be charged with intense significance as people develop explanations not only for what happened but, more important, why it occurred. The latter issue becomes highly significant for subsequent action. For example, imagine how the attribution of a death to "natural causes" such as a germ or old age is likely to produce a very different response in a community than when witchcraft or poisoning is suspected.

The translation of dispositional tendencies into behavioral patterns occurs on the individual level but is fundamentally a social process; where there is social support for certain types of actions they will be learned and maintained; where they are disapproved of they become less common. From this standpoint, the significance of small differences

8. The term interpretation has been used as a code word for description and story-telling by those who reject systematic comparative analysis. In contrast, I use the term to include people's views of their social worlds, but I also want to understand the connection between "objective" situations and interpretations of them.

9. Herdt's (1987) excellent discussion of gender identity among the Sambia of New Guinea reveals some of these same features in male-female relationships. Male ideology emphasizes their greater power, but, in fact, much of their elaborate ritual activity is aimed at building up their own strength (which is subconsciously quite problematic) and limiting that of females, who are greatly feared. An important element in the complex is, in fact, male-male hostility which is too frightening to be faced directly and is consequently projected on to females.

in early relationships and social learning can be greatly magnified where different courses of action are reinforced. Leaders mobilizing groups for action often produce polarization by emphasizing group differences which are, in fact, quite modest.[10] Perceptions of group identity and differentiation from others facilitate subsequent mobilization. Thus, through a kind of multiplier effect, small objective differences may become magnified through social processes which build on dispositional tendencies and may have important consequences for conflict behavior.[11]

Interpretations of one's own actions and the actions of others bring together individual and collective processes. Examining interpretations can explain why some groups (or individuals) are continually embroiled in disputes while among others they are rare. But an understanding of conflict situations only in terms of the parties' interpretations is inadequate, for there are important questions that psychocultural conflict theory and interpretive mechanisms fail to address. These involve the nature of the individuals or groups likely to oppose each other, the justifications each side articulates (to itself and to third parties) for its actions, and the ways in which disputes, once begun, can end. Interest-based explanations associated with social structure provide an important complement to the interpretations arising from psychocultural dispositions.

Interests, Interpretations, and the Islamic Scarves

Competing interests and divergent interpretations are the basis for different explanations for conflict at the societal level. Similarly, in disputes such as the controversy over the wearing of chadors in French schools, these concepts can offer complementary accounts of the course of a conflict. In the case of the scarves, considering both interests and interpretations helps us understand why the dispute developed in the first place, and, more important, why it escalated as it did, and why it was so difficult to manage constructively.

The conflict over the Muslim girls' scarves was marked by an

10. Volkan (1988) develops this idea building on Freud's idea of "the narcissism of minor differences."

11. This is not incompatible with psychoanalytic processes, as Volkan's attention to the relevance of group identification processes for individual development makes clear.

intensity that is hard to imagine in a nation where dress codes have virtually disappeared, public nudity is seen as a personal matter, and fashions shift quickly. Why did anyone care what fewer than a dozen young teenagers wore on their heads? Why did the story fill newscasts, newspapers, and the covers of the nation's leading magazines day after day and week after week? (Only the fall of the Berlin Wall and Education Minister Lionel Jospin's asking the Conseil d'Etat for a decision gradually moved it off the front pages.) Why were the terms of the debate so extreme, leaving little room for exchange and constructive problem-solving? Consider two possible answers to these questions.

Social Structural Interests As a Source of the Conflict

A structural account of conflict is the story of the interests the main actors pursued. An obvious place to begin is with the prosperity of the French (and European) economy since the 1960s, its need for labor, and the immigration of North Africans (and others) to France during the past two decades. Many entered the country legally; some did not. French public and private employers were glad to find low-cost workers who created few problems (Grillo 1985). Many North Africans saved part of their modest wages and spoke of returning home—to Morocco, Tunisia, or Algeria—when they could afford to do so.

Many, however, stayed in France longer than planned and married and had children. Although their children attend French schools and the families benefit from French social services, the North Africans remain socially, politically, economically, and psychologically segregated in France. Many Maghrebian communities are poor and socially and politically marginal. Many immigrants speak French poorly and participate in the institutions of the wider society only peripherally. They are viewed with widespread suspicion and many of their cultural habits are misunderstood and derided. When the French economy turned downward in the 1980s, the visible North Africans were seen as the cause of the problem (by taking jobs away from the French) and a drain on the economy through their claims for education, health care, and other social services.

It should be noted that the Maghrebian community itself is highly differentiated in several ways. To start, some members are French citizens and some are not; some are French-born and some are not; most, but not all, are Muslims, but even among Muslims there is great variation in religious orientations and practices. Finally, North Africans in France are decentralized politically. Two important implications for conflict follow from this structural situation. One is the absence of effective economic, cultural, or social ties linking the overwhelmingly Muslim North African community to the majority French one. With few overlapping interests to moderate the conflict, the social and political order reinforced a single dominant cleavage which facilitated rapid escalation. If the lines of cleavage had cross-cut each other more and ties among the parties had been better established, the same precipitating incident might have had far less severe consequences.[12] Second, decentralization of the Maghrebians means that there are no obvious leaders or organizations to articulate grievances and negotiate with the government or other groups when conflicts arise.[13] Each factor contributed to the swift escalation of the dispute over the scarves and the inability to find informal or formal mechanisms of conflict management involving the disputants directly.

A structural analysis considers the interests of political groups in the majority community and how they also encouraged escalation of the conflict. The rise of the National Front and its antiforeigner racist agenda made the government uneasy about acting boldly in this area. The opposition, which had played the anti-immigrant and antiforeigner card several times in the past decade, was content to see the high-flying government faced with a difficult problem. The government and opposition were both divided, making it impossible for Jospin, or anyone else, to lower the intensity of the debate over the issue of the scarves within an existing political framework. No coalition for constructive action opposed those calling for clear action against the students. Constituencies who were not pleased with the escalation of the issue remained quiet, hoping the matter would eventually go away.

12. Yngvesson (1978), for example, describes an isolated, factionalized Atlantic fishing community in which taking items belonging to another person is called theft when it is done by an outsider, but borrowing when it is done by a member. In New Guinea, Koch (1974), Meggitt (1977), and others have described the differences in responses to transgressions which occur within the clan, between members of clans of the same phratry, and between phratries.

13. The government would like to see the Muslim community in France better organized for two reasons. First, the presence of groups and leaders offers the possibility of joint problem solving in the future. Second, the Socialists expect to receive the greatest support from the community as its political role increases.

An important factor in the lack of progress toward a constructive solution was the division of the French left on the issue (Beriss 1990). At the same time that many politicians in the Socialist Party were wary of the political risks of appearing to defend the rights of immigrants, the intellectual leaders of the French left, many feminists, and unions (especially the teachers), all spoke out against the wearing of the chadors in school for their own reasons—to preserve the separation of church and state, to protest gender inequality in Islam, or to reassert the authority of the teacher and school. What these groups agreed on with the French right was the threat the large and unintegrated immigrant community represented to French society. In contrast, there were far fewer voices raised to defend the students or the rights of North Africans in general.

Central to a structural explanation for this conflict are interests, arising from the disputants' economic, social, or political positions. Exactly which interests are at stake is not always clear, however. Maghrebian interests include religious freedom as well as concern about the widespread formal and informal social and economic discrimination they encounter in France. For the French majority, the interests at stake were more diverse. For some, the primary interests were economic, and the clash over the scarves pointed up scarce resources—jobs and social services—during economic troubles. For others, however, the critical interests were more cultural in nature and involved public affirmation of core values such as the secular nature of the state, the authority of the schools, or gender equality. For the National Front and opposition, core interests involved gaining popular and electoral support, whereas many socialists feared that any friendly gestures to North Africans would send supporters to the opposition or, worse still, feed the growth of the National Front.

All of these interests, no doubt, played a role in the dispute over the scarves, yet the controversy also raised basic questions about the nature of French society and its cultural diversity. The specific interests the parties raised were real, but they do not completely explain the conflict's intensity. To understand the emotional forces in a dispute, a psychocultural perspective is needed.

Psychocultural Interpretations As a Source of the Conflict

A second answer to the question of why the intensity of the dispute over the scarves was so high is that it brought deep fears and threats to the fore for many people. The interpretations of the parties to the conflict and the public at-large are central in this answer. For many, the critical images were highly emotional and nonnegotiable. Permitting the wearing of scarves in school was returning the country to the cardinals for some and giving it to the Ayatollah for others. For Moslems (a large majority of whom did not even support wearing the chadors in school), the case provided more evidence of French racism and hypocrisy, releasing intense feelings of helplessness and anger.

Why did the girls' wearing of the scarves represent such a basic threat to identity for so many French people and, in different ways, to the immigrants as well? A psychocultural analysis points to the symbolic meanings involved in this highly ambiguous situation, encouraging reliance on fear-laden representations of the world. Underlying the images evoked on many sides in the dispute are perceived threats to a fragile sense of identity. For the French, since the girls wearing the chadors were not themselves a plausible threat, the real responsibility for their actions had to be shifted to their potentially aggressive fundamentalist fathers. Only then could a consensus develop around opposition to the scarves even as those who opposed wearing the chadors disagreed about the nature of the threat they posed.

The political fallout was rapid and left no question as to the dispute's intensity. In early December 1989, two months after the crisis erupted, the National Front received strong support in several local elections, particularly in the south, and won its only seat in the National Assembly. Both the government and opposition concluded that the issue of the scarves had allowed the far right to focus attention on its overtly racist proposals for exclusion of foreigners and a reduction in social services available to them.

Public opinion, in fact, showed that the issue of minorities in French society was potentially explosive. Not only did large majorities oppose the right to wear a chador in school (which 45 percent of Muslims opposed and only 30 percent favored), but in addition, surveys showed that French non-Muslims see Muslims in France as oriented toward the past, and as violent fanatics who repress women (Le Monde, November 30, 1989:15). A majority opposed the idea of a Muslim president or mayor, Islamic political parties or unions, and the right of foreigners to vote in local elections; 25 percent even opposed the right of Muslim parents to give their children Islamic first names (which in France must be registered by the civil authorities). When asked if they favored a policy requiring Muslim immigrants either to become integrated into French society or to leave France, 48 percent of French non-Muslims chose the former and 46 percent chose exclusion (Schneider 1989:73).

A psychocultural account of the conflict emphasizes the importance of disputants' deep-seated interpretations of the conflict, drawing attention to how events arouse culturally shared fears about threats to self-esteem and identity. The approach emphasizes the importance of individuals' definition of their social worlds, identification of key actors (groups and individuals), their goals, interests, and motives. The processing of events, and the emotions, perceptions, and cognitions these events evoke are central. In the controversy over the wearing of the chador in France, on the psychocultural level most members of the majority community transformed the question of religious attire into a threat from fundamentalist Islam; for the minority community, many of whom did not support the wearing of the chador, the hostility and fears of rejection unleashed by the incident were powerful indeed.

Despite the fact that the social structural and psychocultural accounts of this dispute over the scarves differ, both contain compelling elements. One points to threatened concrete interests whereas the other emphasizes the mutually hostile interpretations and the deep-seated fears they evoke. Only when both approaches are taken into account can we understand this dispute and develop strategies for managing it constructively.

Conclusion

My cross-cultural study of conflict shows that psychocultural patterns affect the intensity of conflict in a society, whereas social structural patterns determine the specific ways in which conflict and cooperation are organized. Underlying the social structural and psychocultural patterns are disputants' interests and interpretations, two distinct mechanisms that together account for conflict behavior more effectively than either one alone.

The controversy over the chadors in France showed how both interests and interpretations are relevant to understanding social and political conflict. If interests provide the language participants use to bring their concerns out in the open, interpretations are found at a deeper, often less conscious level. Furthermore, conflict management must address both components in order to be successful. In the French case, where little effort was made to speak to the interests or interpretations of the relevant parties, conflict management failed and tensions between the North Africans and French majority continued to mount.

This kind of outcome is not inevitable, however, and in the next chapter I utilize the concepts of interests and interpretations to develop the concept of constructive conflict management, which can be applied to both the societal and dispute levels. First I consider the institutions and practices in low-conflict societies on the basis of the cross-cultural evidence; then, through a detailed examination of five small-scale low-conflict societies, I describe features of constructive conflict management.

3

The Culture of Constructive Conflict
Management in Low-Conflict Societies

In the popular mind and scholarly literature, crisis situations involving high levels of conflict and violence attract more attention than disputes that are managed peacefully. At first glance this is reasonable, for it is explosive situations that threaten the health and safety of large numbers of people and the communities in which they live. Underlying the focus on high-conflict situations are both an anxiety surrounding the stress and loss associated with conflict and the theoretical assumption that a better understanding of what went wrong in past and present conflicts can help prevent future ones. I develop a different perspective in this chapter, arguing that if peace and constructive conflict management are important, we need to study the development and maintenance of healthy social communities, not just the pathology of violent ones (Ross 1992a). Examining warlike societies may tell us a great deal about the societal conditions associated with violent fighting, but such analyses may often offer only negative data concerning the social and political dynamics of constructive conflict management unlike analyses of communities where high conflict is not a central feature of daily life.

In my cross-cultural study of conflict and violence (Ross 1985, 1986a, 1986c, 1993) I found myself, unintentionally, placing greater emphasis on those societies with high levels of conflict, in part because it is easier to account for the presence of something than its absence. Yet low-conflict communities are not simply characterized by the absence of features possessed by high-conflict societies. The low-conflict society and its patterns of cooperation can and should be described and discussed in terms of its own practices and internal dynamics.

The goal of describing the culture of conflict in low-conflict societies is both theoretical and political. The theoretical goal is to understand better the institutions, practices, and worldviews found in low-conflict communities, particularly the dynamics of their conflict management practices. The political goal, related to my interest in ethnic conflict and peacemaking, is to increase discussion of low-conflict communities in a world where high-conflict societies get the lion's share of attention. By discussing low-conflict societies and situations where different groups live together peacefully I hope to counter the sense that severe conflict is inevitable and to suggest distinctive institutions and practices found in low-conflict settings which may have relevance elsewhere (Ross 1992a, 1992b). I hope to provide a more complex and nuanced notion of successful conflict management as well as a vocabulary to discuss it (Kriesberg 1992).

In this chapter I introduce the concept of the constructive conflict society, extending Deutsch's (1973) dispute-level concept of constructive conflict management to the societal level. I begin with a description of the low-conflict society derived from my cross-cultural analysis, which emphasizes two components: the distinctive psychocultural dispositions found in societies with low levels of internal conflict, which produce shared interpretations of the world and facilitate the management of differences without resort to violence; and strong cross-cutting ties, which prevent the development of localized power groups and exclusive interests. I then examine conflict management in five low-conflict societies —the !Kung, the Senoi Semai, the Tikopia, the Papago, and modern Norway—describing how their psychocultural interpretations and social structural interests enhance the likelihood of resolving substantive differences in constructive ways. The final section analyzes the seven key cultural features of constructive conflict management societies: psychocultural dispositions associated with low expression of conflict and violence, a strong linkage between individual and community interests, a preference for leaving ultimate control over decisions in the hands of the disputants, the availability of third parties (sometimes in the form of the entire community) to facilitate conflict management, a concern with the restoration of peace that at least equals concern with the substantive issues in a dispute, and possibility of exit when parties are unable to resolve differences peacefully, and specific conflict avoidance strategies.

Constructive Conflict Management[1]

The low-conflict society is not without disputes and differences; rather, the differences which arise are managed in such a way that avoids extreme rancor, polarization, and outright violence.[2] The cross-cultural evidence shows that the low-conflict society is distinctive in terms of both its psychocultural features and the interests that arise from a society's social organization, permitting the development of institutions and practices for handling disputes constructively (Ross 1985, 1986a, 1993).[3]

Low-conflict societies have a psychocultural environment that is affectionate, warm, low in overt aggression, and relatively untroubled by male gender-identity conflicts. Dispositions established in life's earliest relationships build worldviews that foster the peaceful management of disputes. These dispositions engender a low level of overt conflict, so that there are few models of violent action and reinforcing the idea that nonviolent action can be efficacious. Interpersonal and social trust tied to a secure self-identity are crucial dispositions in the low-conflict society. Secure, trusting individuals are less likely to interpret developing conflict situations in extreme terms, increasing the likelihood of moderate, less escalatory responses to events. Greater trust of others means less sense of isolation, less fear of abandonment, and a stronger belief that effective action can be taken to make things right. The tendency not to view conflict situations in intensely personal terms facilitates third-party involvement in developing solutions and satisfactory compromises. Finally, empathy with (if not necessarily acceptance

1. Ross (1993:chapter 11) presents a more complete statement of the argument.

2. The concept of the low-conflict society is more useful than that of the peaceful society for several reasons. It suggests the notion of a continuum rather than a dichotomy, that all societies have at least some conflicts, and that peace is just one feature, albeit an important one, of low-conflict societies.

3. Many claims about low- versus high-conflict societies have a tautological character. For example, high conflict is often explained in terms of cultural or ethnic diversity, ignoring other cases where the same diversity exists but the level of conflict is far lower. An example discussed further in chapter 7 is Northern Ireland, where the high level of conflict is explained in terms of differences between Catholics and Protestants, despite the many nations in Europe (and elsewhere) where the incidence of overt Protestant-Catholic violent conflict is far lower.

of) the concerns of an opponent makes it easier to work with others toward mutually acceptable solutions.

Of course these characteristics are relative, not absolute. Disputes in low-conflict societies can be intense and bitter, but they are less likely to escalate into violence and destruction, which make constructive solutions harder to achieve. Certainly anger and frustration may be accompanied by displacement, projection, and externalization. But, in the end, these emotions are less intense because conflicts are not felt as threats to the fundamental existence of oneself or the group.

Low-conflict societies have fewer common structural features than psychocultural characteristics (Ross 1985, 1993). Low-conflict societies do not simply have less wealth and hence less reason for people to fight; there is little relationship between overall conflict and wealth or complexity in preindustrial societies; nor is there one mode of production which is favored. Low-conflict societies are not more likely to be centralized powerful states capable of limiting internal fighting, although this is the case with the preindustrial Buganda and the Aztecs (and even the former Soviet Union). While Koch (1974) says that conflicts can easily escalate when there are no authoritative third parties to step between the disputants, the cross-cultural analysis finds many low-conflict societies lacking such third parties and cases of high levels of conflict despite their existence.[4]

The most distinctive structural feature of societies with low levels of internal conflict is their integration through extensive cross-cutting ties, which can effectively limit the escalation of bitter disputes, as discussed in the previous chapter.[5] Turner (1957) provides a dramatic but

4. Fabbro (1978), using seven societies to develop a model of peaceful societies, finds that these societies have small face-to-face communities with a basically egalitarian social structure without patterns of ranking and stratification. By selecting only peaceful societies, Fabbro fails to recognize that there are also many small-scale, nonhierarchical societies where the level of internal conflict is high and complex ones where it is not. Howell and Willis (1989b:24) make the same argument. The systematic cross-cultural examination of these hypotheses, however, provides little support, especially with respect to levels of internal conflict (Ross 1986a, 1993).

5. Internal conflict and violence are given more attention than external conflict in the description of constructive conflict management developed here because internal interactions almost always outnumber external interactions so that internal disputes assume a greater role in defining a society's overall style of

apt example of this phenomenon, describing how the Ndembu of Zambia respond to the periodic stress rooted in the conflicting principles of postmarital virilocal residence (a preference for living with the husband's kin) and matrilineality through intense ritual activity which unites previously divided individuals and groups. North American Plains groups also use intense ritual activities at crucial times, such as just prior to the hunting season, to bring together kinship-based and other groups who would otherwise come into conflict during the upcoming months. Although strong cross-cutting ties may limit internal conflict they may embolden (to the point of foolishness) a society facing an external enemy.[6]

The Constructive Conflict Management Society

To the quantitative label "low-conflict society" I now want to add a qualitative characterization of a society's conflict management style in order to explain the process of conflict management, not just its level of conflict. Deutsch (1973) uses the concept of constructive (versus destructive) conflict to characterize individual disputes (Deutsch and Shichman 1986). This concept can be fruitfully extended to describe the extent to which societies' styles of conflict management produce constructive or destructive outcomes for their members. It encourages investigation of the institutions, practices, and worldviews found in such settings, and consideration of how features of constructive conflict management can be developed in communities where they are not common at present.

Constructive conflict management develops creative solutions

---

conflict management. In discussing the internal and external conflict, it would be useful to have some sense of the relative role of each in the thoughts and considerations of individuals in their social interactions and in conflict situations. In the only data on this question I am aware of, Robarchek (1992:194) reports Yost's calculation that among the Waorani, where warfare has accounted for more than 60 percent of adult deaths over the past five generations, 44 percent of adult deaths came from internal feuding and 17 percent from external raiding.

6. Murphy's (1957) classic description of the internally peaceful yet externally fierce matrilocal Mundurucu is a well-known example of this phenomenon. See also LeVine (1965).

which benefit all parties. Deutsch (1973) characterizes the concept of constructive (he also uses the term productive) conflict in terms of cooperative processes, not just attention to outcomes. He focuses on the need for cooperative problem solving involving effective communication among disputants and addressing the concerns of each party (Deutsch 1973:362–364). Constructive processes help disputants develop mutually benevolent perceptions, define shared interests, and search for innovative, integrative solutions in which all parties are better off than they would be without an agreement.

Positive interpretations of the opponent's motives are, in effect, a prerequisite for effectively addressing substantive differences. The cooperative process helps alter disputants' interpretations of each other and of demands and encourages the participants to view interest differences as more bridgeable than before. Exchanges and the openness necessary for creative problem solving are far more likely to develop when the prevailing interpretations of adversaries are nuanced rather than simplistic, and where images of effective cooperative action prevail over those of a life-and-death struggle.

Constructive conflict management, according to Deutsch, is more likely when the power of the parties is relatively equal, although he does offer a number of suggestions about how weaker parties can bolster their positions in certain situations (Deutsch 1973:393–399; see also Fisher 1983). Deutsch also suggests that third parties may be crucial in developing cooperative conflict procedures and in helping parties to reach constructive outcomes.

High-conflict situations are rarely constructive because the effective communication needed for creative problem solving is difficult to start or maintain. Instead, high-conflict settings are often characterized by escalation of hostile actions, a polarized community, radicalized leaders, and little middle ground (Coleman 1957; Pruitt and Rubin 1986:7). Substantive differences, on which disputants might have shown flexibility at first, are then easily transformed into differences of principle, making any concession feel like defeat. In such situations there are few constraints on the actions of disputants and force is readily used.

Low-conflict societies are the most likely places to find constructive conflict management because there the psychocultural dispositions are most conducive to creative joint problem solving and open communication. But this is not inevitably the case. There are some low-conflict

settings where conflict management is not constructive, partially because low levels of conflict can occur when one party is more powerful
than the other and the weaker party is unable to press its case effectively.
There is little reason to believe, for example, that constructive conflict
management as Deutsch describes it is found in hierarchical preindustrial
states, such as the Buganda or Aztec, or modern authoritarian regimes.
The intense ethnic rivalries and open fighting in the former Soviet Union,
Yugoslavia, and other areas of eastern Europe are testimony to how during many years of authoritarian rule these societies failed to address
these fundamental differences constructively.

Constructive conflict management is also not present in low-
conflict societies such as the Cayapa of highland Ecuador and Colombia
(Altschuler 1965) and the Utke Eskimo (Briggs 1975), where people are
so fearful of interaction that they avoid the exchanges and sharing needed
for creative problem solving. Altschuler (1965) describes the Cayapa as
extremely anxious about social relationships and highly suspicious of
others. This mistrust results in extreme social withdrawal and a high
incidence of alcohol dependency as a coping strategy. Organized conflict
is low because the collective actions needed in order for it to occur are
absent, rather than because of the presence of constructive conflict management. The pattern is not common, but has been noted elsewhere.
Briggs (1975) describes the Utke as so overwhelmed by what first appears to be high maternal nurturance (really a powerful combination of
affection and aggression) that few adults are capable of expressing strong
emotions in significant relationships. Overall conflict levels among the
Utke are very low, but as with the Cayapa, this is true not because conflict
is managed constructively but because it is so assiduously avoided.

Applying Deutsch's concept of constructive conflict to the societal level points not to isolated techniques but to the institutions, practices, and worldviews comprising the culture of conflict management
(Deutsch 1973; Deutsch and Shichman 1986). Examination of particular
cases, however, reveals important stylistic differences among constructive conflict societies as well as shared characteristics. A common pattern is that the goals of conflict management are often quite diffuse and
subjective. Even while disputants are in conflict, they seem to have a
strong sense of linked fate. As a result, conflict management often develops a strong orientation toward the future in which parties do not emphasize short-term concerns as much as long-term relationships. In fact,

these societies seem to resist focusing exclusively on the narrow substance of a dispute and instead to pay attention to the larger social context in which it is embedded. This provides a way to avoid responding to hostile actions of others with reciprocal, mutually hostile acts that set off escalatory spirals.

In contrast to bargaining or strategic models of conflict management, such as Axelrod's (1984) strategy of Tit-for-Tat or Fisher and Ury's (1982) proposed use of principled negotiation, which focus exclusively on the interests not the personalities involved, here I argue that parties may best deal with the substantive issues when they develop interpretations of the conflict which incorporate (or even create) concerns about the larger social context and potential future relationships. These interpretations, then, help broaden the concerns of the parties and increase the chances of finding a basis for agreement. Just as Fisher and Ury (1981) warn that personality differences may inhibit the search for interest-based agreements, the obverse may also be the case: that when interest differences seem unbridgeable, the presence of interpersonal trust and a valued link among participants may pave the way toward agreements not otherwise possible (Rothman 1989).

Five Low-Conflict Societies

The five low-conflict societies examined below—!Kung bushmen (southern Africa), Senoi Semai (Malaysia), Tikopia (Polynesia), Papago (North America), and modern Norwegians[7]—come from all over the world and exhibit a range of constructive conflict management styles. Here and in later chapters the account is presented in the ethnographic present, although many of the patterns described are no longer found today.[8]

7. Two other societies that might have been included are the Mbuti of the Zaire rainforest (Turnbull 1961, 1978) and the Lepcha (Gorer 1938), which are discussed in Ross (1993). For additional examples of low-conflict societies see Montagu (1978), Fabbro (1978), and Howell and Willis (1989a).

8. Although the present circumstances vary from case to case, the emphasis is on the preindustrial period when colonial and western influences were relatively weak (except in the Norwegian case). This in no way means that these societies were necessarily homogeneous nor that there was no contact with outsiders or change that resulted from it. Rather, my emphasis is on the ethnographic record at a point in time prior to the influx of western, industrial values.

Interpersonal contact is sometimes very intense in these societies, and in fact at least two ethnographers who studied them reported that they had trouble adjusting to the lack of privacy (Dentan 1979; Lee 1979). This social density may give rise to many disputes and quarrels in the course of daily life (although among the Papago and Norwegians this seems less common), but only rarely do these disputes turn violent. Among the !Kung and Tikopia, intense verbal exchanges are common but exchanging blows is not, whereas among the Semai or Papago the same words and tone would disrupt the social calm and provoke a crisis. Despite their differences, these societies, when compared with the high-conflict cases, share certain psychocultural dispositions, although the five societies discussed here show important variations. The high level of sociality of many low-conflict societies (Howell and Willis 1989b) is rooted in early developmental processes and links individuals to their communities socially and emotionally. Children not only seek cooperation, Trevarthen and Logotheti (1989) argue, but also need and develop powerful bonds to others that can be reinforced by cultural practices like generalized sharing, a widespread pattern in the low-conflict societies examined below and in those discussed in Howell and Willis (1989a).

!Kung

Both social structural and psychocultural features help explain one of the best-known ethnographic examples of a low-conflict society, the !Kung bushmen of southern Africa.[9] Located in the sparsely popu-lated Kalahari Desert, these hunter-gatherers live in small nomadic bands

---

In many of these cases, however, there was significant external influence prior to the period under study.

The five societies all have low levels of internal conflict. The Papago are the only case presented here whose external conflict score is not well below the sample mean in the cross-cultural study.

9. There has been a certain amount of discussion in recent years about how peaceful the !Kung actually are. The issue of the !Kung homicide rate is discussed in Lee (1979) and Knauft (1987); see also Eibl-Eibesfeldt (1979). I am not persuaded by the argument that the per capita rate is high since 40 percent of the killings Lee reports in a 28-year period stemmed from one feud. More important, overall conflict is not just a function of homicide but also depends on the broader complex of cultural beliefs and behaviors (Draper 1978).

with shifting composition.[10] They have frequent lively verbal quarrels but no internal or external warfare; organized violence is virtually unknown. Marshall (1961), for example, describes nearby bushmen's aversion to overt fighting and the use of long, often elaborate discussions involving all who are present. Lee says that the !Kung "do not fight much, but they do talk a great deal" (1979:372), often following accusations of improper meat distribution, gift exchange, laziness, and stinginess. Bickering is common, tempers can flare, and fights often seem imminent but rarely occur. As Marshall says:

All these ways of talking, I believe, aid the !Kung in maintaining their peaceful social relations. Getting things out in words keeps everyone in touch with what others are thinking and feeling, releases tensions, and prevents pressures from building up until they burst out in aggressive acts. (1976:293)

Two features of !Kung conflict management are worth noting: the speed with which those present can and often do join a conflict, and the use of community fission as a mechanism of conflict management. Although the addition of many new participants to a conflict could simply polarize the community, among the !Kung it communicates that antisocial behavior is everyone's concern and helps all move toward an acceptable solution (Draper 1978).

Although the population density of the Kalahari region is very low, within their camps the !Kung live nearly on top of each other (at least by American standards). Private discussion is virtually impossible, and any hostile exchange immediately has a wide audience whose members feel free to add their own thoughts or take corrective measures quickly (Draper 1978). Often in the ensuing discussion the issue is

---

10. A recent debate has developed concerning the relationship between the !Kung and other groups in southern Africa. Wilmsen (1989) and Wilmsen and Denbow (1990) argue that the portrait of the !Kung as self-sufficient foragers offered by Lee and other members of the Harvard Kalahari project is a product of particular historical circumstances that ignores important material in the archaeological record. Lee (1990) and Solway and Lee (1990) respond that Wilmsen's assertions far outrun his evidence and that many of his claims do not hold for the specific areas Lee and his co-workers studied. I am in no position to decide who is right in the larger sense, but it seems that each side is answering somewhat different questions. Even if Wilmsen is correct, this would not affect my argument here, which examines the internal dynamics of !Kung society from the mid-1950s until the mid-1970s, the period studied by Lee and others.

redefined away from the concerns of the original parties toward finding common ground so that social peace can be restored. But sometimes tempers stay hot and one person, feeling particularly aggrieved, leaves to sulk for a time; withdrawal, not physical aggression, is the culturally appropriate consequence of anger (Draper 1978). When violence begins or even seems likely, women and old men step between the disputants and sometimes are injured, Lee reports. In the majority of the 22 homicides he documents from 1920 to 1955, the victim was not a principal in the verbal conflict that led up to the actual killing (Lee 1979:392).

Physical separation of disputants resulting in the splitting of a camp, with each principal party and his or her supporters going their separate ways for a time, is likely when neither side is clearly right or wrong (Draper 1978:43). This is possible because of the low density of the region's population and a social system in which the !Kung have widespread social ties and where movement between camps is common. The use of the exit option recognizes that the restoration of personal relationships—the dominant concern of the community—cannot be achieved immediately.

!Kung conflict management, as in !Kung culture in general, stresses a fundamental equality among all members of the camp. Fresh meat, for example, is shared; one of the most serious grounds for verbal attack is taking more than one is entitled to. Individuals are safest when they blend in and most vulnerable when they seek special treatment or act arrogant, boastful, or proud. Public verbal taunting reinforces the norm of equality and provides an enforcement mechanism (Draper 1978). Sensitivity to the moods and needs of others is highly developed, and informal social controls are readily invoked in a setting where all are aware of the interdependence of group members and fearful of violent or unpredictable persons who threaten it.[11]

!Kung psychocultural dispositions help explain why their internal and external conflict levels are among the lowest in my cross-cultural study. Draper describes the !Kung as "extraordinarily successful in discouraging harmful and malicious behavior in young people" (1978:48) and argues that early social relationships produce dispositions associated with low conflict. Children are treated warmly and with affection

11. Draper speculates that in the past !Kung communities may have killed individual troublemakers who proved to be incorrigible (1978:40) but does not suggest that this happened very often.

and build strong attachments to those around them (Konner 1982:301–307). There is little harsh treatment, and socialization for aggression and male gender-identity conflict are low. !Kung children have no aggressive models to imitate; rather, they are quickly integrated into the affectionate and intense social life of the band and invariably have multiple affectionate caretakers. Although females perform more child care than males do, the !Kung have far less gender differentiation in interactions with children than most societies. Children are rarely alone, and when they get into conflict situations, they are often removed but not punished in any other way.

When two small children quarrel and begin to fight, adults don't punish them or lecture them; they separate them and physically carry each child off in an opposite direction. The adult tries to soothe and distract the child and get him interested in other things. The strategy is to interrupt misbehavior before it gets out of hand. For older children, adults use the same interventionist technique. (Draper 1978:36)

!Kung children certainly have angry outbursts, but when no one is directly threatened, the preferred way to deal with them is to ignore the tantrum until the anger is spent.

!Kung social organization, as well as psychocultural environment, promotes low levels of conflict and violence (Draper 1978:32; Lee 1979). The !Kung have significant social ties extending beyond the local community, and their bilateral descent system provides a significant number of kinship links throughout the region. Localized power groups with interests in accumulating and defending material resources do not develop. In fact, !Kung bands do not have much private property that needs to be defended from outsiders, and even water holes that are acknowledged as belonging to certain individuals are available to any member of the band, and to outsiders provided they ask permission in advance. Finally, Lee suggests that the remoteness and harshness of the !Kung territory has severely limited contact with other groups (until recent years) and partially explains their low external conflict level.

Senoi Semai

The Senoi Semai, swidden (slash-and-burn) horticulturalists of Malaysia, live in politically autonomous bands with shifting membership. The Semai are a low-conflict society with a very different cultural style than the !Kung. Where the !Kung are boisterous and expressive, the Semai are meek and even fearful, especially with outsiders. They go to great lengths to resolve internal disputes without violence, placing the maintenance of peaceful interpersonal relations above material gain (Robarchek 1990). When confronted by outside aggression, the Semai prefer to flee rather than fight (Dentan 1978). While the Semai generalize low violence across domains, they are strong differentiators psychologically, distinguishing between the members of the band one can trust (sources of nurturance and support) and the outside world of unremitting danger and hostility (Robarchek 1989a:911).[12]

The concept of *punan* or *pehunan* (a state of being unsatisfied from a strongly felt want that can make someone sick or prone to accidents) is placed at the center of their explanations for Semai nonviolence by both Dentan (1968) and Robarchek (1989a). This state is most likely to occur as a result of the actions (or inaction) of others in one's community; the voicing of wants turns individual needs into group responsibilities. Robarchek argues that needs are psychological and cultural constructions and that individuals are dependent upon the community for their fulfillment (1989a:910).

Because individuals are so sensitive to the needs of others, conflict avoidance is a major Semai method of conflict management. When disagreements cannot be resolved, one party often moves to a neighboring band (Dentan 1968:80). Systems for sharing food and other resources are highly developed. Yet quarrels and disputes do occur and sometimes physical violence is threatened (Dentan 1978:98). The Semai have no overarching authorities to impose binding decisions on unwilling parties. Elders are approached and listened to out of respect. Conflict resolution may become a public matter involving a large proportion of the community, even though most people are reluctant to be involved in

---

12. In Ross (1993:chapter 7) I distinguish between generalizing and differentiating societies. The former are cases where there is a strong correspondence between the levels and styles of internal and external conflict behavior suggesting that particular modes of action are generalized across domains; in contrast, differentiating societies are those in which internal and external conflict behavior differ sharply. The data show that while there are more generalizers and differentiators among the preindustrial societies I examined, both patterns are present. The important issue of when and why generalization and differentiation develop remains a topic requiring further study.

anything that threatens the foundations of their personal security, as any conflict might (Robarchek 1979a:105).

On certain occasions a formal proceeding, the bcaraa', brings together the disputants and their respective ego-centered kindreds (each person's kin, defined individually, not through group affiliations).[13] The bcaraa' begins with long, formal affirmations of the interdependence of group members and the necessity of maintaining group unity prior to any consideration of the particular dispute. When the dispute is finally addressed, there is great attention to motives underlying action, and although people participate as advocates not witnesses, overt anger and other emotions are rare. The discussion ends when no one has anything more to say, at which point the headman voices what he understands to be the group's consensus; he sometimes assesses a small fine, some of which is later returned to the guilty party as a symbol of reconciliation. The elders from each side and the headman then reaffirm the interdependence of the group and the need for unity (Robarchek 1979a:106–111). Robarchek interprets the long discussion as a process of desensitization which "provides an institutionalized procedure that drains the emotion out of conflict situation" (1979a:112) in a society where fear of emotional arousal is high, thus facilitating the resolution of the substantive issues at hand. The positive reintegration of the wrongdoer(s) into the group is symbolized by the return of the fine, the acceptance once again of the nurturance of the group (1979a:113).

In one dispute Robarchek describes, a man who planted trees on land traditionally belonging to others. An assembly was called but few members of the accused man's kindred attended. After many hours of discussion—during which there was a clear recognition by all that the trees were planted on land belonging to others—there was much admonition about the dangers of fighting, the importance of respecting the rights of others, and the need to avoid quarreling. In the end it was decided that the man could keep the trees he had planted but must not plant any more. Robarchek's discussion with the disputants afterwards made it clear to him that the restoration of personal relations and the fear of violence if this was not achieved were more important than material interests. "Lack of harmony within the band was seen

13. As these are not corporate or formal groups, all members of the community would have slightly different kindreds, and in any dispute it is almost inevitable that some people would be kin of both disputants (Robarchek 1979a).

in terms of its potential for producing the war of each against all. Constantly affirmed were the necessary unity, mutual aid, and support of the band, and the responsibility of each for the others" (Robarchek 1989a:915).

Dentan suggests that there is very little Semai violence because they consider it so terrifying. Yet because there are no institutional controls governing use of aggression, the Semai must rely on internal ones (1968:59). He describes Semai socialization as indulgent toward infants, involving little performance pressure, and making them the focus of much emotional and ritual attention. However, there is an abrupt transition to early childhood which is much less nurturant and affectionate (Dentan 1978:126). Fear is instilled to protect children from strangers, as adults "scare" children with threats of evil spirits, strangers, and thunder squalls to keep them from doing bad or dangerous things (Dentan 1978:128; Robarchek 1979b). Sometimes adults threaten to hit children (although they almost never do). Children, Dentan says, "come to fear their own aggressive impulses" (1968:60), although there are virtually no aggressive adult models available and no overt punishment of aggression. Adults and older children generally ignore the quarrels of younger children, and fearfulness is probably felt when a child resorts to violence and is abruptly removed from it.[14]

The psychocultural dynamics underlying the low level of Semai violence are only partially consistent with the model of the low-conflict society derived from the cross-cultural study. Socialization is certainly not physically harsh and there is little evidence of serious gender-identity conflict in males. However, whereas the cross-cultural evidence identifies trust, secure identity, and attachment as crucial psychological constructs in the worldviews found in low-conflict societies, the Semai case differs in two significant ways. First, trust, security, and attachment are less generalized and come to be more exclusively associated with in-group members than my analysis suggest they should be (Robarchek 1979b,

14. Dentan adds that the child is doubtless impressed with the seriousness of the parental response of physical removal "because adults are usually indifferent to children's activities" (1968:61). He notes in a later work, "Social psychologists contend that this situation, in which ignorance of violence combines with parents' not expecting children to become violent, not punishing it with violence, and not permitting it to occur is one maximally geared to producing nonviolence" (1978:132).

1986). Robarchek (1989b:34) says that fear and an intense sense of personal isolation are also involved, and identification with others is poorly developed (1989b:41).[15] Second, the absence of aggressive models and the widespread cultural rejection and fear of violence may keep overt conflict low but may also make constructive conflict resolution difficult, especially in disputes involving outsiders. The conflict management process Robarchek describes helps the community to address disputes and to maintain peaceful personal relationships over time. At the same time, I should note that of the low-conflict societies discussed here, the Semai practices are the most difficult to describe as constructive. Dentan and Robarchek's material makes it clear that conflict arouses very high levels of anxiety and that constructive processes such as the bcaraa' are used more as mechanisms of last resort than they might be in a setting where conflict does not evoke such strong fears.[16]

Dentan (1978:133) argues that psychocultural factors alone cannot explain Semai nonviolence; social structural factors are also important. Localized power groups with exclusive interests are not present. Strong cross-cutting ties exist among the Semai of different communities, and there are no fraternal interest groups that might promote internal conflict between communities. Thus the Semai "do not have segmentary social groupings like clans and hierarchies, which combat violence by freezing the threat of counter-violence in perpetuity" (1978:134). Instead, the kinship system, patterns of mobility between communities, and shared ritual experiences linking people in different communities work against the development of permanent cleavages in Semai society. Finally, Dentan (1992) argues that the existence of refuge areas to which people may flee from community or interethnic quarrels has meant that leaving has always been a viable alternative to fighting.

15. Howell (1989) attributes the limitation of violence among the Chewong, a nearby Malaysian people, to fear, suggesting that timidity is considered a normal human condition and bravery is not. Also see Gregor (1990) for a discussion of fear of witchcraft among the peaceful Xingu of Brazil.

16. Robarchek (1979b) offers a good discussion of the concept of fearfulness among the Semai and argues for its strong associations with thunderstorms and strangers.

Tikopia

The !Kung and Semai show low levels of conflict in egalitarian bands; the Tikopia illustrate low levels of conflict in a chiefdom. The Tikopia live on a small, isolated Polynesian island with a certain number of quarrels, scandals, and private feuds, but few escalate into serious violence. External conflict is rare (perhaps due to their isolation), chiefs and other leaders are shown great respect and deference, but conflict management is considered the responsibility of everyone.

Firth (1949, 1963) says that maintaining order is a chief's responsibility, yet the most common response to hearing about a quarrel is to order the parties to resolve it themselves, perhaps with the help of their kin. In land disputes, according to Firth, though chiefs may put in their two cents like any other member of the community and men of rank may try to reconcile the parties or even suggest a settlement, the closest a chief usually comes to involvement is letting the parties know that if a solution is not found he may take the land for himself (1949:174–175).

Although the chief's authority should never be directly contradicted, Firth describes a variety of ways in which the chief's sons, men of rank, and even the general population can get chiefs to change their minds, provided they do not challenge his authority directly. In one case he reports that a chief became furious when some men violated the prohibition on fishing in a certain area he had ordered as part of mourning the death of a man of high rank. First the chief screamed at the transgressors and then, in a rage, went home to get a weapon. His sons sought to restrain him.

In dealing with an angry chief every care and tact is used, since his power is absolute, and there is, for the time being, no appeal beyond him. His sons grasped the weapon and held it respectfully but firmly while they talked soothingly to him, adjuring him not to do damage to his people nor to cherish his anger. The old man sat silent, his whole form quivering with wrath, his eyes glaring, his face working. From time to time he ejaculated merely, "May their fathers eat filth," and spat emphatically into the fireplace. At last, yielding to the continued exhortations of his sons, he allowed the gun to be drawn from his grasp . . . After sitting for a time he rose to his feet, seized an old sabre [and went outside] . . . Standing up to his full height he began to stride purposefully down to the beach, brandishing the weapon over his head, his grey locks streaming out, an impressive, even awe-inspiring figure . . . At his side and behind him came his sons and their wives, endeavoring to restrain him with placatory words, but not interfering immediately with his progress. When he reached the beach, however, one of the wives, a woman of rank of another clan, stopped close and grasped his sword arm. A young man also from another clan, and of *maru* status [men of rank], ran in and clasped him round the knees, making the *songi*, the salutation of respect to a superior, by pressing his nose to them. Thus impeded the old man stood still. Again he began to shout in fury . . . Mingled with the conventional *forua* [high-pitched shrieks] were curses heaped on the heads of the offenders and their progenitors. This exhibition lasted for several minutes while more and more folk assembled from their houses and came to soothe the chief by tactful words. At last the old man ceased to rage. His frenzy had spent itself. Yielding up the sword he walked back to the house, silent, but stiff and dignified, with his sons and villagers in train. No further action was taken by him against the offenders. (1949:181–182)

Firth adds that such a series of events is spontaneous yet follows a well-defined course. Not only does the chief express his indignation at the breach of norms but the people in the process of restraining him also express their support for him. As for the culprits, they remain in seclusion for some time and then bring the chief a gift of food. "The whole course of events, then, including the protest of the chief and the efforts of the people to pacify him, is a customary mechanism in which the behavior of all parties is based on real emotions but expressed itself according to traditional rules" (Firth 1949:182).

Like the !Kung, the Tikopia engage in much shouting and verbal abuse, but physical force between parties is rare. New parties may be drawn into conflicts easily, but often they try to reconcile the disputants and find a mutually acceptable solution. Chiefly authority is powerful but not unchecked, and public opinion and the actions of other men of rank can modify chiefly authority without confronting it directly (Firth 1949).

Tikopia psychocultural dispositions are similar to those in other low-conflict societies: much affection and warmth and little harshness, and low gender-identity conflict. These dispositions promote trusting and secure relationships and strong social attachments and their consequences are seen in Tikopia conflict management in several ways. One is the expectation that disputants can, and will, resolve disputes without resort to chiefly authority. This provides a model of constructive conflict management using joint problem solving. The attachment of the Tikopia to their cultural system is grounded in a secure sense of self and group identity. Only secure and trusting individuals (no matter how high their rank) would dare place themselves in front of a raging chief whose authority is never questioned directly. Tikopia society provides few models of violent, aggressive individuals, and in addition its low emphasis on aggression in socialization and low gender-identity conflict provide little basis for subsequent stress and violence.

The social structure of Tikopia society is also an important reason why conflicts are not severe and violent. According to Firth, the society has a common social and cultural system marked by important crosscutting ties rooted in the kinship system, and although he adds that there are some tensions between the two sides of the island, intermarriage and other social ties prevent the development of localized kinbased power groups who fight with each other. Instead, although villages tend to have a dominant clan, clans are dispersed throughout the island. Furthermore, even though the Tikopia are patrilineal and patrilocal, Firth describes affinal ties (kin ties acquired through marriage) as important both materially and emotionally. Political loyalties and ritual activities also link all members of the society. Finally, the hierarchy of Tikopian society does not promote peaceful conflict management through the threat of force. Rather, Firth suggests that the leaders' legitimacy is well established and connected to strong identification with the community and acceptance of its norms.

Papago

The Papago of southern Arizona and northwestern Mexico are a particularly interesting case of a society made up of a loose conglomeration of groups speaking the same language. They have a good deal of conflict with a neighboring society but little internal conflict. The Papago are regularly raided by the Apache but maintain peaceful relations with other neighbors, clearly differentiating actions and attitudes directed toward Apache and toward non-enemy outsiders. For the Papago, war is not a source of glory, only a necessity. They do not take booty, fearing the evil magic associated with the enemy (Underhill 1946:165). Internal peace, ethnographic accounts suggest, is not simply a response to external aggression but is rooted more fundamentally in Papago psychocultural processes.

The Papago live in partially dispersed settlements, organized for defense against the Apache, although on occasions they retreat into more rugged areas rather than stand and fight. Like other peoples in the semi-arid region, they were affected by the arrival of the Spanish and the introduction of the horse which they adopted and used in defending themselves against Apache attacks between 1700 and 1870. The Papago practice both agriculture and animal husbandry and rotate settlements seasonally (Joseph, Spicer, and Chesky 1949). Local communities, the key social unit among the Papago, are exogamous, inheritance is bilateral, and there are no organized ancestor groups. All of these structural arrangements build links across the society and inhibit the development of localized power groups with exclusive interests.

The Papago have no history of central authority and are divided into dialect groups which maintain a certain level of mutual distrust but do not engage in open fighting. When necessary, neighboring groups cooperate with one another (Underhill 1939). Each village has a ceremonial leader, and others lead particular activities, but there is no elaborate political hierarchy, for within each community there is a minimum of formal authority and decisions are made by mutual consent. The men meet daily to discuss important matters (Underhill 1939). The village council apportions land for use and organizes cooperative livestock rearing, brush clearing, and fence repair (Joseph, Spicer, and Chesky 1949:61).

Internal peace is central to the Papago.[17] Open quarreling and the expression of anger is strongly disapproved and people avoid harsh words and overt disagreement. Moral suasion is used against transgressors more often than punishment. Underhill (1939) reports individuals' extreme sensitivity to being spoken about negatively by others and a deep fear of

17. While the data which Joseph, Spicer, and Chesky (1949), Underhill (1939), and others present on the Papago come from a time well after contact with white society and outside conquest of the region, there is the clear implication that both the socialization practices and value on internal peacefulness are in no way new to this society. The Papago have been affected by world-system processes for many centuries. Focusing on their internal dynamics does not deny this reality in this case or in that of other tribal peoples. For a provocative discussion of this issue more generally see Ferguson (1992). In my cross-cultural investigation I distinguish between understanding patterns of conflict in preindustrial societies, which I think can be done, and studying these societies in a precontact period prior to any outside influence, which I do not think is possible. See chapter 5 of Ross (1993).

witchcraft and magic. This trepidation in conjunction with public opinion controls most people's actions. Although admonition, banishment, and supernatural vengeance are possible threats, they are seldom needed.

Hard work and cooperation within the family are highly valued, and significant gift exchanges mark relationships among relatives. The local community is important and pressure for group approval leads to conformity in the household and village: "The person who fails to conform to these standards is made aware of the disapproval of others by criticism, ridicule, or denial of privileges . . . 'People will talk' is an ever present and powerful inducement to live up to economic and social obligations" (Joseph, Spicer, and Chesky 1949:53). Within the family there is a moral obligation to settle disputes amicably. For example, Joseph, Spicer, and Chesky (1949:55) report a case of a suit over land among relatives which others said never should have been brought to the community for settlement. Grievances are rarely expressed overtly but may be aired via gossip or out of fear of witchcraft.

Joseph, Spicer, and Chesky (1949) and Underhill (1939) assign a prominent role to socialization in explaining low levels of conflict in Papago society.[18] "Training in peaceableness begins in childhood," according to Underhill (1939:113). Child rearing is informal and leisurely. Children are indulged and the Papago believe they should be happy at all times. Joseph, Spicer, and Chesky report that the Papago are taught not to be angry from an early age (1949:9). There is great affection towards children, even from men who are usually reserved. Children are seldom struck or punished, but they learn obedience early (1949:51). The warm, supportive family environment allows the child to follow his or her own pace. Working hard and getting along with others are emphasized. A misbehaving child is separated and excluded but not physically punished, but there is usually little quarreling in play groups, and play is rarely violent.

Task training begins early as children learn about family and com-

18. I recognize that the child-rearing observations come from a period well after pacification of the region and the end to fighting between the Apache and Papago. The discussion in the ethnographic material, however, suggests that the pattern of Papago peacefulness and their socialization style is of much longer duration, but more precise data would be useful here. The issue reminds us how cultural patterns change over time in reaction to changing patterns of contact, ecological and technological circumstances, and political relationships, questions relevant to the discussion of postcolonial New Guinea in chapter 7.

munity needs. Public opinion is a powerful force, sanctioning those who deviate from the rules, which apply to all. Personal achievement is disapproved. Papago supernatural sanctions like those of the Semai enforce responsibility to the group (Joseph, Spicer, and Chesky 1949:166–167). Again like the Semai, the evocation of external enemies is used to control behavior. From a very early age the threat of illness caused by a displeased animal spirit or ghost is very real.

The Papago is admonished constantly to avoid quarreling and becoming angry but he is also threatened with illness if he thinks badly of another or holds a grudge. Since there is scarcely anything that could stimulate a Papago to respect the feelings of his associates more effectively than his great fear of sickness, the Desert People evade situations which give rise to angry sentiments. (167)

Joseph, Spicer, and Chesky describe a Papago tendency to use escape as a survival strategy. "As the Papago evade enemy attacks, so they try to avoid the unmanageable dangers of daily life" (218).[19] The ethnographic material does not contain much detail on dispute management, however, making it difficult to understand this process in detail. What is striking, however, is that despite the need to train men to fight the Apache and defend the community, the Papago accord the warrior no special status or privilege. The definition of war as an evil necessity caused by outside forces allows the Papago to emphasize community and cooperation, which are rooted in early relationships, reinforced through the threat of the supernatural, and consistent with the absence of localized power groups within Papago society.

Norway

Although Norway is not a preindustrial society, it offers a good example of a small, low-conflict society whose conflict management techniques share a number of features with the other cases already discussed.[20]

19. Joseph, Spicer, and Chesky (1949) suggest that Papago affection and support in the family produce little anxiety or inhibition, a strong fantasy life, and some hostility toward siblings.

20. Although Norway is larger than most of the small-scale preindustrial societies I have examined, its population of just four million makes it small among industrial nation-states. Much of the discussion that follows is taken from chapter 9 in Ross (1993).

The quality of life in contemporary Norway is often at or near the top of national rankings using a variety of measures (Naroll 1983). Of particular relevance here is the fact that conflict levels in Norway are very low and that even when Viking warriors were feared throughout Europe the domestic society was relatively peaceful (Eckstein 1966:115).[21] Norwegian popular culture offers few aggressive models (Bolton 1984).

An important Norwegian strategy for dealing with aggression is to avoid creating situations where it might be inadvertently expressed. In the rural community Hollos (1974) studied, family roles are highly structured in order to separate individuals where tensions might develop. In the typical three-generation household, mother-in-law and daughter-in-law stay out of each other's way; father and adult son often engage in the same job but in different locations, for example chopping wood on opposite sides of the house. Outside the family, potential disputants avoid each other (Barth 1952; Ramsøy 1974). Because the norm against aggression is so strong, people who do not actually like each other sometimes appear together in public and proceed with task performance (Hollos 1974:40). Withdrawal and isolation are learned as appropriate ways to handle hostility.

Some authors connect the low levels of Norwegian conflict to a deep collective sense of responsibility (Ramsøy 1974:219–224). Eckstein emphasizes the noneconomic aspects of relationships as part of the strong sense of community (1966:80–92). The sense of social responsibility is expressed in a variety of ways: a strong emphasis on equality and leveling, attentiveness to community norms, a great degree of conformity, and a high level of participation even without necessarily high personal commitment (Hollos 1974:40). There is, simultaneously, a profound concern for the welfare of others and a certain emotional reserve in personal relations. Tremendous care is taken not to hurt the feelings of others. Directness in interpersonal relations is rare, but cooperation occurs because of mutual attentiveness, somewhat like among the Semai (Castberg 1954). Hollos describes the use of indirect signals and nonverbal cues to avoid direct commands, even to children. Friendships are highly valued, and Gullestad (1984) describes the mutual responsiveness and awareness present in friendship groups.

21. Suicide rates in Scandinavia generally are high, yet Norway has one of the lowest suicide rates in Europe.

Despite their interpersonal sensitivity and reserve, however, Eckstein (1966) says Norwegians have little suspicion of public or quasi-public authority and they do not believe that others will take advantage of them. Rather, the community is there for all, if and when it is needed. Decision making and the exercise of authority in Norway are intended to keep overt conflict low. Local decision making often involves extensive private discussion to reach consensus prior to public consideration (Hollos 1974). Broad-based coalitions are valued and regularly sought, and when consensus cannot be reached, matters are often dropped. Conciliation councils—local community institutions in which three citizens serve four-year terms—hear civil cases before they go to court to see if simple mediation might yield a solution (Aubert 1969). Connary reports that in this way more than a third of the cases are quickly resolved (1966:186). Finally, Eckstein makes much of Norwegian legalism and formalism as a way of removing an issue from controversy by standardizing the ways in which tasks are performed (1966:171–172).

Social structural factors in Norwegian society clearly contribute to its low level of overt conflict and violence. An obvious starting point is Norway's social homogeneity.[22] In addition, although Norwegians value individual independence, they possess what Naroll (1983) calls large moralnets, by which he means the existence of many people who can provide support to individuals in times of need. This can take the form of a rich extended family life or numerous available friends and neighbors. Hollos (1974), for example, describes a rural community made up of isolated farms in which there is exchange labor when it is required. Although social interactions among neighbors are infrequent and not highly affective, people know they can count on others in times of need (see also Barth 1952). Extensive involvement in voluntary associations (often characterized by attachments that are more instrumental than emotional) and overlapping networks make it difficult for communities to divide into permanent factions (Eckstein 1966).

Norwegian psychocultural patterns contribute to the society's low

22. The Lapps are the most visible minority in Norway, and although conflict between the two groups has not been severe in recent years, there certainly has been tension at times (Eidheim 1969). In addition, although most outsiders emphasize Norway's social homogeneity, through the nineteenth and early twentieth centuries Norwegians emphasized regional differences within the nation and frequently described them in racial (i.e., biological) terms.

conflict level as they do in the preindustrial societies. Norwegian child rearing is described as warm and indulgent and stresses kindness; there is little use of physical punishment (Barth 1952, 1960; Eckstein 1966:160–161). Hollos (1974) says there is a very high level of maternal nurturance and supervision, with little emphasis on discipline or control. Little is demanded of young children and they engage in a great deal of self-initiated play and exploration of their immediate environment. There is little parental verbal instruction and strong emotions are not expressed. From observations in a more urban setting, Bolton (1984) says there is often much involvement of fathers, a strong emphasis on peer culture, and little performance pressure on children. In both rural and urban settings, emotional self-control especially over negative feelings is stressed (Bolton 1984; Hollos 1974). This norm carries over into adulthood and, consequently, at times much adult interaction is highly stylized and superficial.

The emphasis on a low level of overt aggression and strict self-control which both Bolton and Hollos report is consistent with Sears, Maccoby, and Levin's (1958) findings that a low level of aggression is promoted by both low permissiveness and low punishment of children. It is clear to Norwegians even at an early age that aggression or even direct confrontation of others is unacceptable. Social conformity apparently makes punishment unnecessary, for individuals and groups often monitor themselves.

Noteworthy Features of Constructive Conflict Societies

The low-conflict societies discussed here are, for the most part, also constructive conflict societies. Their conflict management styles involve strong norms against physical violence and emphasize cooperative processes to deal with disputes among community members, although in no two cases are the strategies exactly alike. At the most general level, these societies point to seven characteristics that are important in constructive conflict management: psychocultural practices which build security and trust; a strong linkage between individual and community interests and high identification with the community so that individuals and groups in conflict trust that its interests are their own; a preference for joint problem solving which leaves ultimate control over decisions in the hands of the disputants; available third parties (sometimes in the form of the entire community) to facilitate conflict management; an emphasis on the restoration of social harmony that is often at least as strong as the concern with the substantive issues in a dispute; the possibility of exit as a viable option; and strategies of conflict avoidance. Each of these is discussed briefly below.

Psychocultural practices. In none of the constructive conflict societies explored here is socialization harsh; warm and affectionate child rearing is common, contributing to feelings of security and trust. Similarly, these societies have relatively little overt gender-based conflict, as in the peaceful societies presented in Howell and Willis (1989a). Male and female socialization is commonly relatively parallel, especially in the early years, and the view that male and female natures are similar is widely held (Howell and Willis 1989b). Lack of gender differentiation and extensive affection contribute to the avoidance of overt expression of hostility and foster the constructive management of disputes. The psychocultural processes of these low-conflict societies also help develop strong identification with others in the community. Konner (1982), for example, describes how the nurturant mothers and other band members facilitate strong attachment and confidence in others among !Kung children. Even among the Semai, fear may be a central mechanism of socialization, but it is always associated with outsiders or natural forces, never with other people in one's community.

Linked individual and community interests. In constructive conflict societies interests are frequently defined in inclusive rather than exclusive terms, and strong localized power groups do not easily develop. In these societies the common western distinction between the needs of the individual and those of the society seems inappropriate. Instead, there is strong identification with the wider community, accompanied by the view that individuals prosper only when relations within the group are harmonious and that the community is the source of individual strength and fulfillment. Although such constructions are often found in authoritarian regimes, the dynamic here differs in a crucial way: the authoritarian state removes all power for autonomous action, imposing decisions on individuals, whereas the constructive conflict society leaves the final choice to the disputing parties. The societies discussed here push people to participate and take responsibility for their own lives. Both the authoritarian state and the constructive conflict society claim to nurture citizens, but in one case this is achieved through forced dependency, while in the other it is through responsibility.

When individual and community interests are equated, interests are easily defined in inclusive terms. This linkage between interpretations of the world and conceptualization of interests means the community can serve as an important source of individual nurturance and support. Individual interests are not opposed to those of the community, but instead are often met through cooperation with others. This is seen in a conflict among the Mbuti of Zaire (a peaceful society not described here) involving Cephu, an Mbuti man who set up his hunting nets in front of everyone else and not in coordination with them. Upon returning to the camp after the hunt, everyone (including the children) began to heap abuse upon him; he received no food for some time and soon began to whimper. The removal of all social support was far more powerful than any fine or physical punishment might have been and within twenty-four hours Cephu was reintegrated into the group, painfully reminded that life outside the community is precarious indeed (Turnbull 1961).

The emphasis on the community in each of these societies is seen in the pattern of "generalized reciprocity,"a key element of a peaceful society identified by Fabbro (1978) and also mentioned by a number of the contributors to Howell and Willis' (1989a) volume on peaceful societies. Available resources are to be shared and refusing to do so is grounds for either open criticism or covert, perhaps supernatural, retribution. Not only are individuals responsive to requests for assistance from others, but there are also mechanisms which make it easy to anticipate a need and respond to it before problems develop.

The social structure of these low-conflict societies makes them inclined to define interests inclusively and this conceptualization of interests promotes the development of constructive solutions to conflicts. Dentan (1978) describes in the Semai what my cross-cultural data analysis found more generally: that the absence of geographically based corporate interests makes it likely that the level of internal conflict will be low. An inclusive notion of interests goes beyond one's immediate material concerns to include the welfare of others and the harmony of the community. For example, the notion that individuals can cause misfortune for others by failing to respond to their needs is particularly explicit among the Semai but has elements seen in many other cultures as well.

This is in marked contrast with social psychologists' approach to interests and cooperation. For example, one of the major findings from Sherif's Robbers Cave experiment was that the presence of superordinate goals facilitates cooperative actions among previously hostile groups (Sherif et al. 1988). Social psychologists argue that the existence of common goals (or an outside enemy for that matter) unites former opponents by emphasizing their linked fate and stress how the achievement of superordinate goals brings obvious (and often immediate) advantages to all previously disputing parties. In many constructive conflict societies, however, short-run gains are much less obvious, less concrete, and perhaps less significant to the parties. Whereas the social psychological literature on cooperation growing out of the Sherif tradition emphasizes concrete gains achieved through cooperation, conflict management in constructive conflict societies identifies goals that are much more diffuse, subjective, and less immediate.

An even clearer difference is found if we contrast self-interest as a motive for cooperation with the more diffuse motives found in constructive conflict societies. Axelrod's (1984) discussion of cooperation in situations without overarching authority (such as in stateless societies or the present international system) identifies a strategy (Tit-for-Tat) which produces the greatest long-run collective gains.[23] In a few important ways, the pattern of constructive conflict management in low-conflict societies resembles Axelrod's Tit-for-Tat: in both, success in the long run is premised on groups or individuals acting in ways that do not necessarily produce the greatest individual short-term (material) gain. Axelrod talks about "the long shadow of the future"; so too the Semai disputants worry less about the short-term gain from the trees planted where they did not belong than about the restoration of community harmony and affirmation of its norms. But at another level, the two processes are strikingly different. Tit-for-Tat says stop cooperating (for one move in Axelrod's game) as soon as an opponent does, whereas the Semai or !Kung are taught to resist defection through "benevolent misperception"

23. Axelrod's (1984) analysis of Tit-for-Tat as an effective strategy for cooperation is based on two prisoner's dilemma computer tournaments that he ran, which were won by the simplest program, Tit-for-Tat, only four statements long. The strategy involved cooperating on the first move and then reciprocating on each move thereafter. The findings and his discussion of them are quite provocative and suggest important questions about the impact of culture on strategies of conflict and cooperation (Ross 1993:27–31).

and other strategies which permit parties to express their anger without threatening the groups' integration.[24]

Joint problem solving. Although there is a good deal of variation in how much autonomy the original disputants retain, in all of the societies examined there is a reluctance to completely remove final decisions from the hands of the parties. Disputes are effectively managed by calling upon informal practices to supplement formal institutions, as the cases in Nader and Todd (1978) also show. Among the Tikopia, disputants are strongly encouraged to work out differences on their own, as are the Papago in the case of family disputes; among the Semai, the community hears cases that people cannot resolve on their own, but there is fear that the expression of underlying emotions will shatter the perhaps fragile harmony of the community. In Norway, although the sophisticated legal system can render binding decisions, there are many procedures, both formal and informal, that parties can use to avoid a dispute altogether or to settle it prior to resorting to legal avenues. As a result, there is more modest expansion of the legal system in Norway than we have come to expect in other industrial nations since the mid-nineteenth century (Aubert 1969). In contrast, another style is found among the !Kung (and Mbuti), which first might appear to be an exception. Other community members become involved in disputes so quickly that it seems fair to say that the boundary between private and public is virtually nonexistent. At the same time, the original disputants remain part of the dispute, have a say in any outcome, and may leave a camp if they dislike what others say and do.

Third-party assistance. Third parties play a significant role in constructive conflict management, although in the cases examined here this is not because they offer binding decisions. Often their involvement facilitates communication among the disputants or helps redefine the conflict in terms which make it easier to find solutions. In other situations third parties articulate the interests of the community in such a way that the disputants are able to put their conflict in a wider perspective, allowing the disputants to develop a solution themselves. At other times individuals mediate, arbitrate, or help the disputants negotiate a solution. Sometimes, as with the !Kung and many other peoples, the

---

24. Many other cultural assumptions about Tit-for-Tat turn Axelrod's question about cooperation in the absence of centralized authority into an interesting cross-cultural question. For additional discussion of some of these matters see Ross (1993:chapter 2).

entire community constitutes the third party, hearing and discussing a dispute either on the spot or at an announced meeting. Effective third-party involvement, in short, does not necessarily mean offering authoritative settlements in the form of judicial or administrative decisions.

Harmonious social relationships. There is support for the idea that conflict management in low-conflict societies places a greater emphasis on the reestablishment of harmonious social relations through the equation of group and individual interests than on the punishment of wrongdoers for past transgressions. Gluckman (1955) and Nader and Todd (1978) suggest this is most likely where social relations are multiplex rather than simplex (meaning that disputants are related in a number of continuing ways). The analysis here supports their argument but also identifies the psychocultural, not just social, dimension of multiplex relations which emphasizes the group as a source of nurturance.

In the societies discussed here the social density of community life tends to be very high, social harmony is highly valued, and those who threaten it are severely chastised in a variety of informal ways. Social anticipation—a sensitivity to others and their needs—is one of the earliest and strongest messages a child learns. Conflict management in these settings emphasizes the restoration of social relations within the community. To do this effectively, as Robarchek (1979a) suggests, it is often necessary to separate the emotions underlying a conflict from the substantive issues involved.[25]

Viable exit option. When successful conflict resolution is not possible, all of these societies use physical separation of the disputants as a viable option, at least to some degree.[26] Against external enemies, flight means migration, often to more marginal ecological areas. In internal conflicts, community fission or at least the movement of one or more parties to different communities of the society is possible (see Howell 1989).[27]

25. This is similar to but not exactly the same as Fisher and Ury's (1981) suggestion that separating the people from the problems is the crucial first step in conflict resolution.

26. Fabbro (1978) also finds separation of opposing parties important in his analysis of peaceful societies.

27. Ember, Ember, and Russett (1992) suggest that the generalizability of this finding may be limited. Only under particular circumstances does fission serve this function. They find, using the same sample and many of the same codes I do, that internal warfare is, in fact, positively related to the frequency of fission; my results examining the internal conflict agree.

Movement is facilitated by the existence of kin (and sometimes other) ties in neighboring settlements and by the absence of exclusive, corporate, geographically concentrated groups. Fission is also easier in societies where resources are more mobile and where political control of individuals is weak. Interestingly, these characteristics may be prevalent among foragers, some pastoralists, and in modern industrial societies.[28]

Fission can halt interpersonal feuds and allow parties to save face to avoid violence. As Lee writes:

People get on each other's nerves, and as the situation tightens this leads to heightened irritability and a lowered threshold of conflict. As food becomes harder to provide, it becomes more important that everyone do his fair share of the work. In this atmosphere even small disagreements may erupt into conflict, and this conflict usually results in one or both parties splitting off to seek greener pastures. Hunters say "to hell with it" . . . Unlike farming or city peoples, foragers have a great deal of latitude to vote with their feet, to walk out of an unpleasant situation. And they do so, not when their food supply is exhausted, but well before that point, only when their patience is exhausted. (1979:367)

Conflict avoidance strategies. The availability of exit is a mechanism for separating disputants that limits escalation. Moving to another community is not always a feasible option, however, and in some cases severing relations with certain groups and individuals is an important mechanism for avoiding violence (O'Nell 1989).

Constructive conflict societies make widespread efforts to avoid conflict in the first place so that matters which might become a source of intense controversy in another society often lead to no dispute whatsoever.

In the case of Norway and among the Semai, individuals feel particular responsibility to be sensitive to the needs of others. This anticipation of needs prevents potential differences from arising. In addition, potential disputants make an effort in certain situations to demonstrate that they can appear and even work together in public in spite of latent differences.

Another mechanism of conflict avoidance involves cultural prohibition on the expression of strong emotions, especially in public settings. Again both Norwegians and the Semai fit this pattern and it is

28. For a broader discussion of the question of political uses of fission see Ross (1991a).

clear that adults are expected not to display strong feelings which might threaten the social order (also see Gregor 1990). Fear of the fragility of the social order, not just strong interpersonal attachments, may be important here (Robarchek 1979b; Howell 1989). While one view of this cultural prohibition on the expression of emotion would suggest that high frustration would produce subsequent aggression (possibly against safe external targets), the data from the Papago, the Semai, and Norwegians provide little support for this argument, at least in these cases. Perhaps one case which does is the Xingu of Brazil, a peaceful society in which there is high fear of witchcraft (Gregor 1990).

The Intersocietal Context

The discussion above has focused almost exclusively on internal rather than external conflict, in contrast to the view of international relations scholars (for example, Waltz 1959, Midlarsky 1975, Zinnes 1980), who explain conflict and cooperation in terms of the properties of the system not of individual states. The system-oriented view needs to be taken seriously in thinking about low and constructive conflict societies, for a prosperous society living with aggressive neighbors in a hard-to-defend environment is likely to find itself under attack at some point no matter what its internal characteristics. The fact that societies are aware of and affected by the activities of their neighbors has led D. White (1989) and others (for example, Divale 1974) to examine a society's interactions with other societies in general, and patterns of external conflict in particular, as a cause of internal conflict and changes in internal social organization.[29] Low-conflict societies, from this perspective, are likely only in certain settings. They need either to have relatively peaceful neighbors (as part of a local security system), or to be located in an environment where they are not vulnerable to attack or from which flight is a viable option, or, of course, to be so much stronger than their neighbors that no one dares attack them (Gregor 1990).

In the low-conflict societies considered here, the extent to which

29. I was unable to replicate D. White's (1989) finding using his data as well as my own. Although the hypothesis that external conflict is related to contact with other societies is a plausible one, none of White's world-system measures, including location in the world system (scored from the core to periphery), is related to either of my composite measures of internal and external conflict.

constructive approaches also characterize the management of external conflict is uncertain. In quantitative terms, all but the Papago are considerably below the sample mean on external conflict in the cross-cultural study (and these societies clearly separate war from other domains of life and accord little glory to warriors). In the case of the Tikopia and !Kung their relative isolation from outsiders is no doubt important. The Semai and !Kung are now embedded in larger states and there is evidence that since they have served in military units, their participation in organized state violence has increased.[30] For the Semai, the Lepcha described by Gorer (1938), and to some extent the Mbuti and !Kung, avoidance or flight is a viable option and therefore often selected over conflict. Were this option to be removed, however, Dentan (1978) asserts that the Semai would fight rather than yield. Norway, like the Papago, certainly has more external than internal conflict. The Norse Vikings were once feared throughout western Europe, and Norway has been involved in recent European wars and security arrangements. In considering the management of external conflict, power inequalities between the opposing parties are probably crucial, especially since the normative constraints that operate in some internal conflicts where the opposing parties are unequal in strength will rarely be as powerful in an external conflict. When a party confronts a far stronger opponent, Dentan (1992) points out how flight can be a rational option; facing a more equal opponent, the disputant may select another strategy.

My cross-cultural study found that societal complexity is associated with greater external (but not internal) conflict. A potentially useful corollary may be that with increased complexity comes a greater capacity to develop enduring links within and between societies. Strong cross-cutting ties lower internal conflict; strong ties between groups in different

30. The debate around the Semai case is particularly complicated. Robarchek and Dentan (1987) attack a large number of people who used Dentan's (1968) ethnographic account in support of the argument that humans are naturally aggressive. Dentan's original account, taken with his 1978 article on Semai nonviolence, seems most consistent with the conclusion that by nature the Semai are neither more nor less aggressive than other people. Rather, their culture and social organization offer no encouragement for aggression, but in other settings such as the army, aggression is higher and this suggests a biological urge to be aggressive, as Konner (1982) claims. Clearly this conclusion was not Dentan's intention, but the language he used in his original text, I think, encouraged others to draw conclusions he saw as inappropriate.

societies can have the same effect. Weakening within-society ties is no solution, but building significant ties between societies is often both possible and useful. This argument, of course, is very similar to that of Haas (1964) and other functionalists who saw this as the route to European integration. While it is now clear that functional linkages among societies alone are insufficient to build constructive conflict relations, they can be a crucial ingredient when accompanied by relative equality between the parties, appropriate political leadership (Lindberg and Scheingold 1970), and a conducive psychocultural environment.[31]

Conclusion

The argument developed here is a call for better description and analysis of more low-conflict communities and cases of constructive conflict management (for example, Gregor 1990). From such cases we can learn how institutions and practices associated with constructive conflict management can be developed in communities where they do not now exist (Ross 1992b). The notion that a high level of human conflict is unavoidable is a product of our beliefs more than of our experience. We cannot counter this widely held notion on moral grounds alone; we also need to understand particular communities in which high levels of destructive conflict are not inevitable and borrow ways in which they manage conflicts in order to improve approaches in modern industrial societies.

31. Interaction between groups does not necessarily improve intergroup relations. Under conditions of perceived scarce resources, threat, and inequality, for example, interaction can raise, not lower tension (Brewer and Miller 1984). The most positive changes occur when members of different groups see themselves as pursuing a superordinate goal (Sherif et al. 1988).

4

The Conflict Management Process:
Changing Interests and Interpretations

In chapters 2 and 3 I focused on conflict at the societal level. Here I shall examine the sequence of events in individual disputes, suggesting how the concepts of interests and interpretations offer a language to describe conflict in a way that links analyses at the societal and dispute levels. I use a controversy over public housing in New York City that came to a head in 1972 in order to illustrate general conflict issues. Two points are central throughout this chapter. The first is that, although a societal analysis of conflict stresses the continuities of interests and interpretations, at the dispute level the capacity of interests and interpretations to shift and be transformed is at the heart of conflict and conflict management processes.

The second key point is the need to develop a more complex and nuanced view of the process of conflict. It is common to begin with the statement that two parties, X and Y, got into a fight over Z, a scarce resource. Then there might be a discussion of what each side did to try to control Z, a summary of the outcome (meaning who got how much of Z), and the cost to each of the parties. Such descriptions are fundamentally misleading.

The errors of omission in such a presentation involve a failure to recognize changes and uncertainties in the course of a conflict. As a result, our everyday accounts emphasize a clear link between initial grievances and outcomes when the connections are frequently complicated and subtle. Too often the way we recount individual conflicts makes the outcomes, and many of their key elements, seem far clearer in hindsight than they were at the time. In many disputes, who the opposing parties are, what they seek, and what actions they choose are far more problematic than most post hoc recounting suggests. Complex social conflicts are not a straightforward story with parties and goals set at the outset; they are more accurately characterized as follows: tensions develop among several parties; each party cites specific concerns although the grievances are often general; some key players may be present from the outset, but the composition of opposing groups shifts during a dispute; the goals each disputant pursues change as the aims are continually sharpened and redefined in the course of a conflict; parties often have a vague sense at the outset of how they will pursue particular goals; and frequently action strategies are developed as a response to the deeds of allies and adversaries. In short, conflict behavior involves a series of interactive sequences, the outcome of each often being far more complex and uncertain than is suggested by most after-the-fact accounts. Finally, an outcome is most often best viewed as a settlement of a specific controversy, not a resolution to the underlying conflict. In the dispute over wearing the chador in French schools, the administrative process yielded an outcome, but the process hardly resolved the deeper rift between North Africans and the French majority. The controversy over public housing in New York City described in this chapter illustrates the same point.

Public Housing in Forest Hills

By the mid-1960s New York, like most large American cities, had decided to cease building large public housing developments in its poorest areas. Instead, it planned to invest in "scatter-site" housing, meaning smaller projects located in a variety of neighborhoods. The switch made good sense given the widespread criticism of existing densely populated, high-rise projects and the goal at the time of many city administrations and the courts in attacking urban segregation. What occurred in New York and many other cities as a result, however, was not the effective implementation of the new policy but bitter, public conflict over individual proposals. The location and size of the buildings, the class and ethnic composition of the projected residents, and the effects on existing neighborhoods were sources of controversy. One particularly well-publicized conflict involved a proposed project consisting of three 24-story buildings (840 units) intended to house lower-income (meaning minority) residents to be built in the predominantly middle-class Jewish neighborhood of Forest Hills in the borough of Queens.

Initially, a somewhat smaller project had been proposed for nearby Corona, a working-class Italian community, but when grumbling was heard there, the city's site selection board agreed in late 1967 to a proposal to place a high school on the Corona site and to locate the housing on a vacant area in Forest Hills. Five years later, as the city began work on the project, Forest Hills community, business, and political leaders and residents organized highly publicized opposition to Mayor John Lindsay's administration's housing project—involving loud and bitter demonstrations and a good deal of racially inflammatory rhetoric. Concerned about polarizing Jews and blacks[1] and seeking to limit the political fallout, the administration asked a young lawyer and law professor, Mario Cuomo—who had successfully represented the Corona community in its earlier legal battle with the city—to serve as an independent third party empowered to report to the mayor on "possible revisions in the Forest Hills housing project and the overall planning for low-income housing in Queens" which could serve as the basis for modifying the project and for easing the tension surrounding it (Cuomo 1974).

Cuomo's detailed diary covering his thoughts, meetings, and discussions concerning the dispute from May to October 1972 shows both the complexity of such conflicts and how they change over time. He describes a shift in how the issue is considered, in the specific parties central to the dispute, and most important, in the disputants' relationship and the nature of their communication. At the time Cuomo entered the fray, the city insisted it would build the project as proposed while community protesters countered with cries of "No project, no way." In a short period of time, other options emerged between these two incompatible positions. Beneath objections to the project, Cuomo saw the issue of middle-class white fears of a lower-class black influx into the community, whereas for black politicians and white liberals the issue was symbolically important in terms of the city's commitment to social change

1. In a bitter New York teachers' strike in 1968, a central issue was the demand by local communities, particularly black areas like Ocean Hill-Brownsville, for greater local control over educational policy and its implementation. This was strongly resisted by the United Federation of Teachers and its primarily Jewish membership. During the course of the strike there were bitter exchanges involving charges of racism and anti–Semitism that left many Jews and blacks uneasy and disturbed the working coalition that had existed between these two ethnic groups. On the strike and its ethnic aspects see Berobe and Gittell (1969) and Ravitch, *The Great School Wars* (1974).

and justice. The key was fashioning a proposal that addressed both concerns. In addition, Cuomo sought a solution which would prove viable and would not encourage white flight from the area. For Cuomo and the city the issue was never whether or not to build the project; he never wavered in his support of the legal and moral obligation of the city to provide housing for the poor and minorities. However, Cuomo's appreciation of the fears of community residents led him to explore various project modifications—increasing the proportion of elderly inhabitants, altering the mix of low- and middle-income residents, decreasing the number of units, allocating a proportion of the units to Vietnam veterans, shifting units to other areas in Queens, and making some units available on a purchase or cooperative basis.

The identity of the parties engaged in the dispute changed during the period Cuomo was involved, in great part due to his ability to redefine the issue in terms of project specifics.[2] Crucial here was Cuomo's recognition that the Forest Hills community, which to many outsiders seemed uniformly opposed to the proposed housing, did not speak with a single voice. Cuomo succeeded in identifying multiple community leaders and interests rather than assuming that they all had identical goals. At the same time, the proponents of the housing plan were difficult to identify at times and were not organized in the way opponents were (Cuomo 1974:28). City Housing Commissioner Simeon Golar strongly supported the project but other backers were not involved in the intense, continual manner that some Forest Hills residents were, in part because they did not live in the area and their daily lives would not be affected by the project. Other parties included Mayor John Lindsay (who had national political aspirations at the time), other city and state political figures and groups, and the elected officials from Forest Hills and the rest of the city who would be involved in the decision. Finally, Cuomo himself developed interests in particular proposals and his reputation became linked to his ability to fashion a viable agreement.

After nine weeks of discussions and meetings in which Cuomo partially defined to whom, and more important, the terms under which he would talk, he proposed to the mayor modifications that would scale

2. A court ruling that refused to block the project and a primary election defeat for Jerry Birbach (outspoken leader of the Forest Hills Residents Association and project opponent) clearly affected the course of the dispute and the public role that parties were willing to play (Cuomo 1974).

down the project to three twelve-story buildings (432 units), 40 percent of which would be allocated to the low-income elderly. Cuomo believed that the changes were significant enough to win over a number of political and other community leaders while still gaining the support of the mayor and other officials who needed to approve any revisions. Initially there was strong opposition from both Jerry Birbach, an outspoken community opponent, and Housing Commissioner Golar, but others, including many Jewish moderates and Forest Hills leaders, endorsed it as did the city's papers and other media. After waiting three weeks, so did Mayor Lindsay, who brought Golar along. Three sets of hearings over the next few months abounded in rhetoric from opponents in Forest Hills and from liberals who saw the changes as a retreat. Then, once the city approved the proposal, the issue quickly disappeared from the agenda and it received little media attention, although the larger issue of black-white relations and the question of segregation and social inequities was in no sense resolved.

In fashioning a specific proposal, Cuomo came to appreciate how each of the major actors had somewhat different interests in the outcome and he skillfully used these differences to put together a package which he believed both members of the community and the city housing commissioner, as well as the mayor, would accept. Cuomo, a third party, was accepted in part because he came with no strings attached. His power came from his ability to recommend changes in the initial proposal, tempered by the fact that the mayor and his administration were not necessarily committed to following Cuomo's recommendations. Therefore he needed to craft a proposal which could attract a broad basis of support. To do this Cuomo spent the bulk of his time talking with as many parties as possible to get a sense not only of the specifics of the housing proposals being bantered about but also some of the disputants' underlying needs and fears.

The Cuomo proposal allowed the project, in modified form, to go forward. It failed, however, to do much about deteriorating race relations in the city or the larger issue of segregated neighborhoods and racial inequality. Within a short time the federal government, the major public funder, put urban public housing lower and lower on its agenda. Forest Hills, such a potent symbol of polarization for a short time, soon faded from memory as New York and other large cities turned their attention away from housing and toward law and order and other issues. The dispute in Forest Hills, I suggest, was managed more or less constructively, but the inability of the city and the country to address the more profound and pervasive issues of race and social justice leads to a more negative judgment concerning management of the larger conflict.

The Process of Conflict and Conflict Management
Conflict as Process

The conflicts of interest here, like the Forest Hills housing controversy, are collective behaviors that occur as parties act because of perceived divergent interests or incompatible goals among them and are aimed at obtaining scarce resources, either tangible or symbolic, and in so doing deny them to others.[3] Although sometimes hard to adhere to, the distinction between a dispute—meaning a particular issue or event being contested—and conflict—the underlying deeper differences among parties—is useful. In this sense, disputes may be resolved more frequently and easily than conflicts. In Forest Hills, the conflict erupted over a building project, but it also involved community control, intense fears on the part of blacks who felt that their interests were being ignored, and worry on the part of middle-class whites about increased crime, personal security, and property values. The dispute over housing was part of a larger conflict involving race relations and social justice. While recognizing that settlement of a dispute does not usually resolve the underlying conflict, we should also note that an escalating dispute

3. Conflict is variously defined in terms of incompatible behaviors (e.g., Deutsch 1973) or divergent perceptions (Pruitt and Rubin 1986). Each definition has a different utility. Focusing on what people actually do certainly has a greater methodological simplicity, allowing us to avoid the subjective states which precede action. It also emphasizes something that needs to be understood—how people behave. The perceptual approach, by suggesting that differences in interest are perceptual, leaves open the question of how incompatible interests actually are, pointing out an important mechanism by which conflicts that seem intractable at one time may be resolved at another. Considering perceptions emphasizes that conflict is a process, not a static condition, and that the change in subjective understandings over the course of a dispute is an important element. Defining conflict in terms of both behavioral and perceptual elements is useful, especially for the purposes of this inquiry into conflict management. Considering behaviors without perceptions ignores the motivations underlying an action, whereas examining only goals and perceptions does not distinguish among situations where similar perceptions lead to divergent behaviors.

can worsen and prolong a conflict. Just as conflicts can have future consequences, so can partial agreements (Kriesberg 1992). Constructive conflict management occurs when a large conflict can be progressively de-escalated through the successive settlement of a series of component disputes.

In and of itself, conflict is neither desirable nor undesirable. Just as there are cases where the costs of conflict to the individuals involved and the wider society are too high, there are situations where the absence of conflict is similarly costly. Judgments about any conflict are complicated and involve not only considering the goals each side seeks, but also asking if there might have been alternative, less costly ways to achieve them, or if the short-term effects outweigh long-term effects.

Descriptions that focus only on individuals and their motives miss the fundamental social nature of conflict. Some conflicts readily involve preexisting groups, but in many controversies groups form and old identities change as disputes unfold. Conflict, in fact, should be seen as intimately related to a fundamental human propensity to form and identify with groups readily. Strong support for this notion comes from small-group research and studies like the Robbers Cave experiment, in which eleven-year-old boys with no prior relationship to each other form named groups which engage in cohesive action and exhibit strong in-group identity and out-group hostility (Sherif et al. 1988).[4] Although Sherif's results involved preadolescent white Protestant American males in the 1950s, few people who read the results fail to believe that the ease with which in-group solidarity and out-group hostility develop is widespread across age and sex groups, cultures, and historical periods. Equally striking evidence for a readiness to form groups is found in the minimal group experiments of Henri Tajfel and his colleagues (Brown 1986; Tajfel 1981; Tajfel and Turner 1986). In these experiments, individuals are assigned to groups on the basis of arbitrary and unimportant reasons, such as whether they preferred a painting by Klee or one by Kandinsky. Despite the fact that they never meet others with whom they share the

4. This study is thought-provoking in the interesting questions it raises but does not answer. For example, how might the pattern of in-group formation and out-group hostility followed by cross-group cooperation have been similar (or different) if the participants in the experiment had been female instead of male, adults rather than eleven-year-olds, racially and ethnically heterogeneous, non–Americans, and so on.

group label, the subjects in these studies systematically make in-group-biased judgments in the allocation of points to tasks supposedly accomplished by members of one group or the other.

In-group identification is an adaptive social-cognitive process that makes possible pro-social relations such as social cohesion, cooperation, and influence (Turner 1988:67). Groups are the central mechanism for providing individuals with their identity; rather than thinking about individuals "sacrificing" part of their identity when they become part of a group, Turner (1988) (whose perspective I adopt here) sees individual identity as possible only in the context of secure group attachments. This explains why social ostracism can be so effective as a mechanism of social control (Gruter and Masters 1986); expulsion or exclusion from the group and its activities is terrifying not because of a physical threat to individual security but because emotional separation is intolerable. As seen in the cases of the chadors in French schools and the Forest Hills housing controversy, any analysis of conflict must consider social groups, and not just the individuals involved. The notion of individuals apart from groups, I suggest, is a product of western thought, not the human experience.

The Paradox of Conflict: Instrument of Change Versus Instrument of Control

At many levels it is easy to imagine ways in which conflict enhances a person's well-being, sense of satisfaction, and quality of life. Even in infancy there is evidence that tension stimulates physiological and psychological development (Lichtenberg 1983; Stern 1985). Intrapsychic conflict is often a necessary component for individuals to resolve personal dilemmas and make effective choices. Intergenerational conflict within families, organizations, and nations provides a vehicle for establishing competence and autonomy. Conflict can clarify and limit the capricious exercise of authority in a community. It can push individuals and groups to articulate and commit themselves to goals and strategies to achieve them. And, as Coser (1956) reminds us, conflict processes can be crucial in building bonds among groups and individuals and securing needed social change.

Conflict can also be frightening, inhibiting, limiting, and controlling. Severe psychic conflict produces diminished capacity for action.

Bitter conflicts between groups produce hatred, loss of property, injury, and loss of life. People caught in the midst of intense conflicts, like Lebanon, Northern Ireland, South Africa, and the Middle East, show signs of severe stress and a weakened capacity to act effectively, to sustain relationships with others, and to live rewarding lives.

Conflict is paradoxical because we can only evaluate its occurrence if we know something about its context. Conflict can variously serve as an instrument of social and political change or social control; in either case, our evaluation ultimately depends upon our judgments about who is engaged in the conflict and what is achieved. Often these evaluations are complicated, highly subjective, and based on a good deal of inference. In the end, deciding whether more or less conflict is good or bad is a very context bound judgment and one easy to make only for the extreme situations. In addition, judgments may differ when we ask about the effects of conflict on individuals, on social groups, or on the wider society.

For disadvantaged groups and individuals, the ability to threaten, initiate, and maintain a conflict with those who are more powerful can be critical in achieving a redistribution of resources or a change in the organization of a community. Obvious examples are the civil rights movement in the United States in the 1960s, third-world anticolonial movements, and the union movement in industrial nations in the first half of the twentieth century. In each of these cases, those in power had little interest in listening or responding to the grievances of the disadvantaged. Only the ability of the less powerful to initiate independent action in the form of escalating conflict led to a process whereby their demands were addressed and changes were made.

The ability of power-holders to suppress conflict is a reminder that the absence of conflict is not necessarily more desirable than its presence. Authoritarian regimes, for example, frequently point to their social order and absence of strife as evidence of success, when, in fact, these characteristics represent order based on fear and repression not the expression of popular sentiment from below. Industrial disputes were surely far less frequent in Nazi Germany and Stalinist Russia than in any other industrial nations at the time, but we can hardly take the absence of conflict in these regimes as evidence for fewer worker grievances and better working conditions.

The Stages of Conflict

Many social science discussions of conflict behavior identify stages through which disputes pass, drawing attention to the interactive nature of conflict processes, in which the actions of one party during one period are crucial in shaping the subsequent behaviors of other parties (for example, Coleman 1957; Gulliver 1979; Pruitt and Rubin 1986; Swartz, Turner, and Tuden 1966). Although the number of stages identified and the names they are given vary (often depending on the goals of individual theorists), the formulations almost all pay attention to the following stages (in varying degrees of detail): a build-up or preconflict stage where initial goals are articulated and strategies considered; an escalation or confrontation stage where opposing parties openly challenge each other and pursue their goals vis-à-vis others; a de-escalation or preresolution stage where the parties begin to move toward a settlement; a settlement stage in which specifics of a solution are worked out; and the final outcome.[5] Stage models of conflict are not necessarily sophisticated, but they correctly emphasize how prior events influence subsequent ones and how the actions of parties in a dispute are responses to prior steps of others.

Scope, intensity, and visibility can describe the specific changes that occur in individual disputes (Schattschneider 1960). *Scope* refers to the number of actors involved in a dispute; *intensity* is how strongly they feel about the matter and the resources they are willing to commit to it; and *visibility* describes the degree to which nonparticipants are aware of a conflict, a first step to being drawn into it (what Schattschneider calls the audience). His view is that conflict is inherently expansive, and the losing side is inevitably pushed to draw in new parties (from the audience) in hope of altering the outcome.[6] Sometimes this is achieved by

5. The distinctions between the phases are analytic, not chronological, and, as in any complex dispute processes, elements best described in different stages may occur at the same time (Gulliver 1979). Second, while the language here suggests that conflicts have clear boundaries with a beginning, middle, and end, in practice this is rarely the case. Third, the term "conflict resolution" suggests that conflicts can be "completed," but, as Moore (1975) notes, they do not "end" in that disputants remember them and previous conflicts may affect how subsequent ones are handled. For this reason I use the term "conflict management," which suggests less finality, rather than "conflict resolution."

6. Sometimes losing parties try to reduce the scope of a conflict, recognizing that with fewer people involved they may fare better. A good example of

simply appealing to the uninvolved. Crucial to the expansion process, however, is the *redefinition* of a conflict in increasingly general terms to provide incentives for the audience to join the fray. Control over the definition of a controversy, Schattschneider argues, is the ultimate source of political power (what he calls the mobilization of bias). Redefinition means that not only do the critical participants change, but the substantive focus of the dispute as well (Edelman 1964; Mather and Yngvesson 1981).

In Forest Hills, the scope, intensity, and visibility of the conflict all increased. The issue attracted widespread attention both in the city and nation; the controversy soon included many more individuals than the city housing officials and community residents directly affected by the project; and the feelings of many of the actors were strong. Political allegiances, ethnic loyalties, and ideological concerns drew in many people who knew little about the community or the specifics of what the city planned to build. Strong ethnic identities—already polarized following the black–Jewish division surrounding the bitter teacher's strike a few years earlier—meant it was not easy to find common ground. Only when Cuomo redefined the issue around the details of the project and not its existence did a coalition develop which supported his proposed changes and lowered the intensity of the dispute.

In this case as in many others, conflicts are expansive and difficult to reverse once they are launched on an escalatory trajectory (Coleman 1957; Pruitt and Rubin 1986). The polarization of a community, according to Coleman (1957), involves a redefinition of disagreements from the specific to the general, the formation of partisan organizations, the emergence of new leaders who typically have weak ties to the community to replace local moderate leaders, and the emergence of new and different issues. In the end:

The process may be said to create a "Gresham's Law of Conflict": the harmful and dangerous elements drive out those which would keep the conflict within bounds. Reckless, unrestrained leaders head the attack; combat organizations arise to replace the milder, more restrained pre-existing organizations;

---

this less common strategy is President Nixon's behavior at the time of the Watergate scandal. He (probably correctly) believed that he would be more likely to remain in office the less Congress and the public were involved and the more the issues could be restricted to technical concerns in the courts.

derogatory and scurrilous charges replace dispassionate issues, antagonism replaces disagreement; and a drive to ruin the opponent takes the place of the initial will to win. In other words, all the forces put into effect by the initiation of conflict act to drive out the conciliatory elements, replacing them with those better equipped for combat. (Coleman 1957:14)

Not all conflicts continue to expand, however, and there are important forces that can keep conflicts from leading to mutual destruction and produce settlements. Coleman refers to the third force which "preserves the community from division and acts as a 'governor' to keep all controversies below a certain intensity" (1957:14). Among these forces are cross-pressured groups and individuals having important ties to both sides, community norms legitimating certain actions but not others, identification with the community itself, mobilization of community elites in favor of a settlement, and cooptation of dissident forces.

In Forest Hills, Cuomo served as a force for containment both in his redefinition of the conflict around the specifics of the project, and in his identification of parties who would support an alternative plan. He effectively isolated Birbach and other outspoken community opponents while empowering those leaders who would support the modifications he proposed. Similarly, he worked with Golar and other black leaders (as did the mayor) to make a clear commitment both to the larger goals of public housing for the poor, and to provide the number of units originally planned by proposing that they be built in other parts of Queens.

Conflict Management

Conflict management is the steps disputants or third parties take in order to direct disputes toward certain outcomes which may or may not produce an end to the conflict and may or may not be peaceful, positive, creative, conciliatory, or aggressive. Conflict management can involve self-help, joint problem solving (with or without third-party help) or third-party decision making—each of which is discussed in greater detail in the next chapter. For now I shall emphasize conflict management as a series of actions and reactions between disputants and other parties. A process-oriented approach to conflict management addresses communication patterns (including behaviors) of the disputants and how they affect interests and interpretations of the conflict. Gulliver (1979) points out that adversaries need information to make decisions about what to ask for and what to offer and often the only way to obtain this information is, in effect, by providing an adversary with information about one's own situation. Certain conditions, however, hold more incentive than others for parties to communicate accurate information (Raiffa 1982). Subjectively, the question of the relation between messages one party sends and those the other hears is critical, for the higher the tension in a situation and the greater the differences between the disputants, the lower the likelihood that the message intended is the one received (Deutsch 1973; Jervis 1976). Sometimes effective communication among disputants can occur only through a trusted third party.

Often accounts of conflict management emphasize either changes in interests or psychocultural interpretations. The strength of interest-based approaches is their focus on integrative (positive-sum) outcomes in situations that initially look like they can produce only zero-sum solutions. In doing this, the analysis begins with the recognition that, at the outset, parties see interests as fixed—there may be a defined amount of arable land in a community, a fixed amount of money to be divided among inheritors, or a limited number of political offices to be distributed. Fixed interests are mutually exclusive in that the more one party obtains, the less there is for others. Such interest differences can be addressed in several ways. One is through a zero-sum solution, such as a compromise, in which each party receives what it and others consider to be a fair share of the limited pie. Another focuses on how strategic considerations affect the outcomes parties achieve (Pruitt and Rubin 1986). For example, Tit-for-Tat, according to Axelrod (1984), is a viable strategy because in protecting his or her own interest, a party also increases the size of the pie in the long run for all parties.

One way integrative solutions become possible is when the concept of interests is extended to less exclusively individual concerns. This may involve common interests like peace and tranquility, which may be best obtained when they are widely shared, not just enjoyed by one party. Any path to integrative solutions depends on the fact that opposing parties in a dispute rarely have exactly the same interests and that these differences may be used to build integrative solutions giving each side at least part of what is most important to it (Raiffa 1982). Cuomo clearly used this notion in fashioning his proposal. More generally, this same idea underlies Fisher and Ury's (1981) four suggestions aimed at helping negotiators arrive at viable and fair agreements: separate people from the problem; focus on interests not positions; invent options for mutual gain while brainstorming—not negotiating—because it works better when tension is low; and insist on using objective criteria for evaluation. Their notion of each party constructing a best alternative to a negotiated agreement (BATNA), is aimed at getting disputants to compare alternatives rather than viewing proposals in isolation during joint problem solving. When the opponents in Forest Hills did this, they realized that remaining intransigent could mean that the city would build the project as originally proposed, while the proponents of the housing project were afraid that total rejection of compromise could kill the project altogether. When there is a sense that an integrative outcome is possible, parties are often able to devise creative solutions, even in complex public disputes, especially if they involve distributive rather than moral issues (Susskind and Cruikshank 1988).[7]

Effective conflict management also needs to address disputants' divergent psychocultural interpretations. Hurt feelings and severe misunderstandings indicate significant barriers to reaching a settlement. A graphic example is found in Kelman and Cohen's (1986) description of Israelis and Palestinians talking for the first time in problem-solving workshops, where minor, unintentionally hurtful remarks are made. Until there is at least some mutual understanding of what transpired, further discussion is limited. Learning something about each other's fears and the metaphors associated with them is a necessary step toward discussing substantive differences and frameworks for dealing with them. Until disputants are able to communicate their concerns and fears effectively to their opponents, basic information needed to construct creative settlements is lacking.[8]

The Stages of Conflict Management

Successful management of disputes is often complicated because so many different pieces need to come together, leading some analysts to

7. Although one can criticize the idea of integrative problem solving for failing to address intense conflicts where no joint problem solving has started, or complex multi-issue, multiparty disputes, it is also important to recognize the analytic insights it offers in situations where the concept does apply.

8. It is not necessary to personally like or to feel very comfortable with an adversary for this to take place. Some level of basic trust or empathy may be necessary, however (White 1984). This question is considered in more detail in chapter 8.

Figure 4.1
A Developmental Model of Negotiation

1. Search for an arena
2. Composition of agenda and definition of issues
3. Establishing maximal limits to issues in dispute
4. Narrowing the differences
5. Preliminaries to final bargaining
6. Final bargaining
7. Ritual affirmation
8. Execution of the agreement

Source: Gulliver (1979)

propose particular stages in the process where the components might fruitfully occur (Kriesberg 1992).[9] Process models of dispute management emphasize how certain questions are the focus of attention in particular phases, and they can show how failed conflict management efforts differ, depending on where the process was halted. Too often, however, named phases are more descriptive (for example, outset of the dispute, intensification, resolution) than analytic (as in Kriesberg 1982; Swartz, Turner, and Tuden 1966).

One notable exception is Gulliver's (1979) developmental model of the negotiation process, what I call joint problem solving in the next chapter (figure 4.1). He is particularly helpful in describing the full range of substantive tasks associated with different phases of negotiation and their interrelation. His broad theory is especially sensitive to the way the interests of disputants and their psychocultural interpretations of the situation affect conflict management outcomes at each phase of the process. Central to this process is the emergence of new patterns of communication and new relationship among the parties. In the Forest Hills controversy, for example, the different parties no longer only squared off in the public arena but also channeled communications through Cuomo, the third party working to fashion a solution.

Gulliver notes that the stages do not always occur in the order listed; his phases are organized conceptually, not empirically. Several steps may occur together in actual disputes, and sometimes parties return to earlier phases while dealing with issues associated with later ones, as in revising the agenda (1979:121). He also observes a regular

9. The presence of multiple issues, multiple parties, and lack of unity within most parties is a reality of most social conflicts (Gulliver 1979; Raiffa 1982).

cyclical movement within each phase as the parties come together and move apart. This movement comes about as disputants learn more about their own positions as well as those of the other parties. Rather than a uniform movement from antagonism toward coordination, Gulliver describes a rise and fall in tension as the problems of each phase are addressed (1979:181), noting a general decrease in the intensity of the successive alternations when negotiations are on a successful path.[10]

Although Gulliver does not use the terms interests and interpretations, each of his stages focuses on interests embodied in the specific task of that stage and on interpretations in the ebb and flow of tensions between the disputants. As each task is set aside (sometimes temporarily) and a new one addressed, there is a change in the dominant dispositions that characterize the disputants' interactions (1979:184). What Gulliver means is that there is a movement from antagonism to coordination within a stage, a cycle repeated during each stage in successful joint decision making.

Interests and Interpretations in Conflict Management at the Dispute Level

A societal level analysis of conflict focuses on dispositional and structural explanatory factors in their most general form, but in order to examine individual disputes, it is necessary to identify more proximate manifestations of interests and interpretations. Unless this is done, an explanation for a dispute will invoke factors that are too remote, mechanical, and often reductionistic. Neither social structural interests nor psychocultural interpretations defined at the societal level provide efficient explanations for the course of single disputes such as the Forest Hills controversy, nor do they answer such questions as: Why was a particular target selected? Why did a dispute escalate at the time it did? Why were certain incompatible demands made by each side? Why were certain dispute management methods used and with what effect? How did the interests and interpretations of disputants change in the course

10. Quandt's (1986) detailed description of the Egypt-Israel peace negotiations (discussed in chapter 6) clearly reveals cycles of approach and avoidance on the part of the three principals—Carter, Begin, and Sadat—which Quandt variously attributes to political and strategic considerations, mood, or apparently random factors.

of a conflict? How could the conflict have been managed better than it was? Explaining the course of particular conflicts means identifying the specific interests and interpretations involved and trying to understand how they connect to more general forces.

Applying the concepts of interests and psychocultural interpretations to the dispute level involves more than just invoking more specific factors. It also requires a transformation in thinking, because dispute-level analyses answer different questions than societal level ones. Dispute-level analysis of conflict pays particular attention to the process by which conflicts unfold, trying to understand their origin, development, and management. This approach examines changes within a specific dispute, whereas the societal level analysis focuses on continuities among disputes in a society. One question which then follows is how interests and interpretations, which are seen as relatively unchanging at the societal level, can change at the dispute level.

Changes in Interests

If interests are seen only in terms of the social structural conditions that produce them, then suggesting adjustment in interests during conflict management seems to be a contradiction, or involves an idealistic request that parties set their interests aside in order to achieve agreement. Yet all actors have multiple interests, and any disputant almost never chooses between getting everything or sharing it with others. Rather, the options are what can be obtained by engaging in different forms of conflict management. Following Fisher and Ury (1981), parties' development of a best alternative to a negotiated agreement (BATNA) helps disputants to frame this choice; in the process they often find that by doing this, they prefer engaging in some joint problem-solving process rather than self-help (including doing nothing). Change and mutual adjustment may occur as each party comes to understand what others seek and clarifies its own goals. An agreement is only possible, however, if the ranges of what each party is willing to accept partially overlap (Gulliver 1979; Pruitt and Rubin 1986; Raiffa 1982).[11] In this way, social structural conditions broadly shape interests, but more proximate events modify,

11. Raiffa calls this the "zone of agreement"; Gulliver talks about a "viable range"; for Pruitt and Rubin, it is the "perceived common ground."

reorganize, and prioritize them and in so doing affect the course and outcomes of disputes. In addition, often the overlap of interests among disputants is greater than initially recognized because parties have different priorities even when a set of common items is contested.

General grievances and specific demands. General grievances are frequently all that each party articulates in the early phases of a conflict. For constructive conflict management to occur, however, these broad concerns need to be translated into specific demands which can be acted upon. Factory workers, for example, may complain that working conditions are unsatisfactory, but when they sit down with management or with a third party, they need to be able to say whether they want higher wages, improved safety conditions, clearer grievance procedures, better fringe benefits, or reorganization of work. In many disputes, parties begin with general grievances and it is only when obliged to spell out in detail what they want that they become aware of what their specific demands are.[12] When conflict management is going badly, the reverse process may occur, as Coleman (1957) points out: the failure of parties to resolve specific differences of interest can lead to a more generalized antagonism and polarization. In Forest Hills, the "build-as-planned" versus "don't build" focus was not amenable to mutual adjustment. Only when participants began discussing details of the project could progress toward a settlement be made.

Ranking of interests. Most disputes are complicated by multiple issues and multiple parties (Gulliver 1979; Raiffa 1982). An important indicator of change occurs when each party gets to a point where it (sometimes implicitly) prioritizes its interests. In Forest Hills, Cuomo decided that opponents of the project were most concerned about its size and the composition of the residents, while the proponents' highest priority was the affirmation of the principle of scatter-site public housing. Ranking can create opportunities for integrative solutions. Focusing resources on achieving certain goals means that other aims are either discarded, set aside for later, or traded away as part of an agreement.

12. It is often the case that groups in a dispute consist of individuals or subgroups which differ in the specific aspects of the general grievances which concern them the most. A common example from labor negotiations is that older workers are especially concerned with health benefits and pensions while younger workers care more about wages.

Identification of common interests. The key to developing integrative outcomes is the extent to which the parties see their changing interests as having common, or at least compatible, elements around which a mutually acceptable outcome may be built. In polarized conflicts, common interests become harder to define, whereas in constructive conflict situations, they are increasingly apparent to disputants. In Forest Hills, common interests emerged most clearly for many of the politicians who wanted to limit the escalation of the conflict and its accompanying racial polarization.[13]

Changing interests in Forest Hills. At one level the conflicting interests of New York's blacks and Jews are rooted in the social structure of the city (Gans 1969). Identification of these interest differences, however, tells us little about the specific course that conflict takes in any given dispute. Black mobility increased conflict with Jews who had arrived in the middle class in the previous generation. Differences were not only racial, however, and as Cuomo correctly understood, class interests also came into play and to some extent cut across ethnic lines.

Racial tensions, which had increased since the mid-1960s (especially during the teachers' strike in 1968), contributed to the polarization in Forest Hills and the articulation of general demands—"build as planned" versus "don't build"—with little middle ground. Only through the specific efforts of Cuomo, the third party, were interests redefined to produce a constructive outcome. Proposals for specific modifications in the project, the ranking of interests, and the identification of some common interests led to an acceptable proposal. It turned out that opponents of the project were less concerned with the city's providing housing than with who lived in it and how this would affect personal safety and property values. Small apartments for the elderly were, from their perspective, very different from larger units for younger households. Proponents of the project had less clearly articulated interests. Many were middle-class blacks and liberals who would never live in the housing themselves. The poor and ill-housed, as Cuomo (1974) noted at several points, were relatively uninvolved, in part because of their traditional lack of organization and also because it was not yet clear who would

13. There was a clear sense that some political figures sought to exploit the racial differences. Cuomo mentions several: Birbach, who was defeated in a primary for state senator, and others who were not powerful figures in the city at the time.

actually live in the new housing. The political figures' interests in continuing electoral success and fear of racial polarization entered into their calculations as they maneuvered on the issue and lined up on Cuomo's proposal. Finally, Cuomo's suggestion for another project not far from Forest Hills with about the same number of units helped to legitimate the changes to supporters and assuage the fears of skeptics.

Changes in Interpretations

Although disputants' interpretations of conflict situations might ultimately be linked to dispositions rooted in early socialization, this does not mean that dispositions fully determine interpretations. Psychocultural data more proximate than socialization experiences are highly relevant in considering specific conflicts, such as the disputes over the wearing of the chador in French schools or building public housing in Forest Hills. An adequate account must begin with data on beliefs and behaviors most clearly associated with the events to be explained. Even if good data on child rearing for major actors were available, this would not be where we would turn first. Also important is explaining how culturally shared interpretations of people and events shape action. Psychocultural dispositions help us to make sense of conflict and conflict management, and though the cross-cultural theory of conflict ultimately links these interpretations back to early developmental experiences, more proximate evidence is relevant for understanding parties' interpretations of specific disputes.

In contrast to psychotherapy, there is no effort in conflict management to alter underlying dispositions; rather, the approach recognizes their relevance in managing conflict constructively. In order to succeed, such strategies build on the analogies, metaphors, and other connections linking early experiences and images to later experiences. Rather than altering psychocultural dispositions, however, strategies can selectively emphasize the particular interpretations certain dispositions give rise to, and linkages among interpretations can be reorganized as part of the conflict management process. In settings where there is a strong predisposition to define in- and out-groups in dramatically different terms, to see the actions of others as threatening and provocative, or to identify with few outside one's inner circle, conflict management cannot realistically try to alter the inner psychic structures; it can, however, provide alternative, psychoculturally appropriate analogies, metaphors, and images which may be more compatible with constructive conflict management.

Here I draw on the principle of psychocultural complexity and the notion that the organization of dispositions is as important as the existence of any particular disposition.[14] Therefore, although groups and individuals tend to emphasize certain dispositions, there are also possibilities for reorganization and changes in emphasis. To incorporate psychocultural dispositions and interpretations into conflict management does not require changing the fundamental worldviews of all parties in a short time—a most unrealistic goal to say the least. It does mean aiming for both affective and cognitive reorganization of some kind. This may involve an expansion of who is understood as "we," may emphasize metaphors associated with past joint successes, or may offer a vision of mutual gain that effectively challenges a current pattern of animosity. When disputants have a long history of hostility, this is difficult, and skilled third parties can be especially helpful. Altering participants' interpretations of a situation can be achieved without directly addressing their childhood experiences but not without considering how their culture selectively reinforces dispositions developed at that stage.

This is fully compatible with psychoanalytic thinking, although this is not my focus here. Strong dispositions often indicate the presence of important unresolved issues. One popular but useful statement of this viewpoint is Erikson's (1950) stage theory of development. According to Erikson, certain developmental tasks are critical at particular stages of life, but each of the eight issues he identifies has some relevance for every stage, and developmental tasks that are inadequately resolved during the stage when they are the central focus may have ramifications long afterward.

Consider a situation where there are strong psychocultural dispositions emphasizing independence in addition to interpretations of a conflict in which independence plays a significant role. Here we are likely to find unresolved issues linking independence to the question of nurturance. It is reasonable to suggest that there may be a strong desire for nurturance along with an even stronger fear that it will be oppressive (or that if sought it will not be provided). Inability to resolve the dilemma

14. The focus is on the system of interacting dispositions in the same way that family systems therapy focuses on the interactions among members of a social system, rather than the characteristics of any single member in isolation (Bowen 1978).

results in a strong emphasis on behaviors and beliefs emphasizing independence accompanied by a less visible yearning for nurturance, which can produce feelings of being threatened. The conflict management consequences of this pattern are significant. This dilemma may first be associated with a preference for self-help out of fear of loss of autonomy. It also can explain why a party engaging in apparently successful joint problem solving may suddenly break off discussions. For example, as parties move to an agreement (which in many cases involves increased interdependence) the process might evoke a high level of anxiety arising from a sudden fear of loss of autonomy. Eventual success may depend on emphasizing how an agreement will not lead to oppressive interdependence and may even enhance autonomy because the antagonists would no longer be preoccupied by an ongoing dispute.

Herdt's (1987) discussion of gender identity issues among the Sambia of New Guinea suggests how another common dilemma affects conflict management. "The Sambia are preoccupied with the differences between maleness and femaleness," Herdt writes (1987:6), and this creates two worlds, two cultures, two systems of behaviors: the male and the female. Sambia males are close to their mothers and have little to do with their fathers in their early years. Suddenly, between age seven and ten they are literally pulled away from their mothers and their aggressive, harsh, and painful socialization into the world of men begins. Yet throughout the long and arduous process of becoming a culturally acceptable male, boys and young men experience both a fear and a jealousy of what is female. For example, women's menstrual blood is highly threatening; but as if males are trying both to rid themselves of what is female and to show that they possess female powers, men periodically engage in ritual nose-bleeding which is identified with menstruation. "It is a traumatic but very effective means of channeling bachelors' sexual impulses away from women and toward younger initiates. Here is where ritual beliefs about the deadly pollution of women's bodies rationalize bachelors' fears and avoidance of women" (1987:185). Women are denigrated and devalued while at the same time there is tremendous envy of their birth-giving and breast-feeding powers (1987:176).[15]

15. Another powerful connection Herdt describes is the equation of mother's breast milk with semen. Although the former is believed to be produced naturally, the latter can only be produced if boys ingest sufficient amounts of older boys' semen in fellatio during initiation.

In fact, Herdt says, male identity "is fragile and needs firm ritual boundaries and social supports" (1987:171). Male behavior is continually directed at asserting their identity which, in fact, remains problematic. The men's secret society remains one bulwark against the world of women. Another is the institution of warfare through which men can achieve external validation of their maleness.[16]

Masculinity is purchased through war exploits, including the defense of one's hamlet guarding the innocent. Even today men are the more suspicious of Sambia citizens. In both group situations and individual relationships a wrong or an insult (imagined or real) can provoke quick violence. Without written laws, policemen, or courts, men must rely on their own might and their supporters in defending themselves. (Herdt 1987:26)

Successful conflict management in such a setting must take into account this fragility of male identity, and alternatives to violence must be presented in ways that validate rather than threaten it.

There is rarely a one-to-one correspondence between dispositions and interpretations; rather, a range of interpretations tends to be compatible with a given set of dispositions. Because altering dispositions is not possible in many conflict situations, conflict management needs to develop solutions which recognize existing dispositions and evoke alternative interpretations compatible with them.

As a conflict unfolds there can be important transformations in how the parties interpret events. Although groups and individuals tend to emphasize certain interpretations, possibilities for reorganization and changes in emphasis associated with new interpretations are relevant for conflict management. The specific shifts in interpretations will vary according to the conflict, but important changes would include: the extent to which the parties develop some degree of linked fate, perhaps in the form of empathy (but not necessarily sympathy) for the other(s) (White 1984);[17] the degree to which each side can accept the existence of

16. Herdt views warfare as the root of Sambia socialization practices. My perspective reverses the causal sequence.

17. Empathy does not necessarily involve agreement with an adversary, but rather the sense of why the other party thinks as it does. White (1984) talks about realistic empathy as a key element in conflict management. Rothman (1992) uses the term "analytic empathy" to emphasize an understanding of what an opponent is saying without necessarily agreeing with the opponent or sharing the opponent's feelings.

an opponent (rather than simply wanting to see it annihilated or removed from the territory); the extent to which members of each community can conceptualize how they would be better off if they cooperated, as opposed to continuing the conflict; and the extent to which each community believes that its opponents understand and accept its core needs. We also want to know the extent to which an adversary threatens a party's core sense of identity, for many conflicts evoke deeply held fears involving threats to group identity, self-esteem, and legitimacy (Horowitz 1985; Northrup 1989; Turner 1988).

Changes in interpretations, which affect adversaries' chances of managing a conflict constructively, are most likely to come about when there is a shift in the salience of key dispositions or a reorganization among existing elements rather than through abandonment of long-held dispositions, for this rarely occurs. While disputants are often only partially aware of adjustments in interpretations of the conflict situation, specific shifts in language can be particularly good tip-offs. We should be particularly attentive to the way leaders as well as the public talk about their own groups and their opponents. Is there a shift in the adjectives used over time? Do the metaphors used to discuss the conflict and express grievances change? Is there any modulation in the expression of fear or threat? What about the degree of empathy and acceptance of the other side's basic needs?[18] The adjectives and metaphors used to talk about a dispute reflect and also frame the disputants' understanding of the situation. Changes in communication patterns (both verbal and nonverbal) are critical in development of constructive outcomes to disputes involving mutually hostile interpretations.

In Forest Hills, the intensity of emotions (especially on the part of the opponents of the project) and polarized interpretations of the situation were a critical aspect of the dispute; these elements provide strong evidence that the substantive demands were linked to threats to identity and concerns about group legitimation (Horowitz 1985; Northrup 1989). Successful conflict management rested on Mario Cuomo's ability to modify the polarized interpretations associated with the initial definition of the issue and thereby lower the associated emotional intensity. To succeed, a solution needed to acknowledge and affirm the central concerns

18. Some psychoanalytic theorists argue that these changes can only occur when there is a genuine reconciliation in which each side acknowledges the other side's hurts and fears (Montville 1991a; Moses 1991).

of both sides—accepting the goals of the strategy of scatter-site housing and addressing the legitimate fears of the local community. Decreasing the size of the project, reserving a high proportion of the units for the elderly, and holding out the possibility of managing the project as a cooperative softened the threat posed to local residents. As a result, several political and community leaders were willing to support the proposal publicly and the media endorsed it. To assuage the fears of the proponents of the original project, Cuomo strongly endorsed the city's commitment to public housing for the poor, recommended that the units not built in Forest Hills be located elsewhere in Queens, and considered additional future public policy options to deal with segregated housing and urban poverty.

Although many rejected Cuomo's solution as either too much or little, public debate of the issue surrounding Cuomo's report provided richer and more nuanced terms for discussing the issue and encouraged an interpretation that helped build support for his proposal. At the same time, the outcome had only few long-term effects on housing policy in the city or nation. The future role of community involvement in deci- sions over housing and other matters remained unclear. Similarly, while the outcome included a restatement of support for public housing for the poor, the intensity of this controversy made it clear to public officials in New York and elsewhere that bitter, destructive conflict would probably follow any proposal to house the poor in middle-class communities. In the end, although the solution was somewhat successful, and it probably had a positive effect on race relations in this city, the most important lesson for most political figures may have been the political inviability of public housing as a vehicle for achieving racial integration.

In the dispute over wearing the scarves in French schools, the deeper concerns of the disputants were hardly addressed; in Forest Hills, Cuomo's conflict management did so. At the same time, however, just as the French controversy was followed by a period of increased antiforeigner sentiment and political support for the ultra-nationalist right, so too did racial polarization increase in New York in particular, and in the United States more generally, particularly in ways which increased class differ- ences in the black community (Wilson 1980). This is not to say that Cuomo's intervention was a failure. In fact, without it, race relations in the city might have deteriorated significantly. There was no way to know at the time how weak the commitment to public policy in the housing area would be in the following twenty years. Constructive conflict management of particular disputes may occur, but only when it is followed by efforts to address the deeper conflict is it effective in any larger sense.

Conclusion

Changes in interests and interpretations are critical elements of the conflict management process. Chances for constructive conflict management are most likely to occur where there is a partial identification of common interests which adversaries share, and some shift in interpretations of an adversary's motives and needs which permits effective communication among the disputants (even if it is through an intermediate party). In addition, interest changes on several critical dimensions can promote constructive conflict management. There can be a transformation of general grievances into specific demands which can be acted upon. Another shift involves the clarification of each party's interests such that they can be ranked and weighted, at least qualitatively. Through clearer specification of grievances, parties may also identify common and compatible interests and make progress toward a mutually acceptable outcome.

Although changes in interests are crucial to reaching solutions, constructive conflict management also requires attention to interpretations of the conflict situation. Successful management of social conflicts rarely alters deep-seated dispositions; however, it can address possibilities for altering hostile interpretation through reorganizing the connections among dispositions, shifting the emphasis on particular ones, and making new linkages among existing dispositions which may enhance the chances of producing a viable agreement among adversaries. Many of these are reflected in the changing language disputants employ as the conflict unfolds and moves toward a settlement. In this chapter I indicate that changes in interests and interpretations are a necessary part of constructive conflict management. How these can be achieved is the main question of the next chapter, in which I consider specific methods of conflict management and how each addresses disputants' interests and psychocultural interpretations.

5

The Sources of Conflict and Strategies of Conflict Management

Examination of the conflict management process at the dispute level reveals the importance of the transformation of interests and psychocultural interpretations during a dispute. Now I want to address specific conflict management strategies at this level that affect the content of these transformations by considering how each strategy addresses different sources of conflict.

Implicit in any strategy of conflict management, but rarely spelled out, are hypotheses about the causes of conflict. In order to understand patterns of usage and effectiveness of self-help, joint problem solving, and third-party decision making—my focus here—what I explore is how any strategy of conflict management is a function of both the actual interests at stake in the context in which the dispute occurs and participants' interpretations of events.[1] Underlying my analysis here is the hypothesis that the effective use of dispute management procedures is related to ways in which the procedures incorporate assumptions about both the structure of interests and the psychocultural sources of a conflict.

Successful conflict management must address the underlying sources of conflict but how to achieve this is not necessarily obvious. Two critical steps in managing conflict constructively—the development of shared interests among disputants and the transformation of disputants' interpretations of each others' motives and needs—were discussed

1. Conflict refers to the deep underlying differences between parties, whereas disputes are the specific differences that emerge on particular occasions. In practice as well as common usage the boundaries between the two are not precise and they are often used interchangeably, partly to avoid using the same word endlessly.

in the previous chapter. Here I suggest a third step, the use of procedures that give disputants a sense of control over the process and the solutions it produces. Recent literature on conflict resolution emphasizes joint problem solving as the most likely way to achieve these goals and produce constructive conflict management. Although these arguments have merit, it is also important to consider the limitations to the use of joint problem solving and to understand how self-help tactics and third-party decision making can contribute to constructive outcomes. Effective conflict management strategies must be consistent with existing cultural norms and practices and cannot import methods that are successful in other settings without paying attention to their application in local contexts.

Sources of Conflict

Social structural and psychocultural theories of conflict identify very different sources of conflict. Social structural theory emphasizes the competing interests of groups as prime motivators of conflict. Actions of others, according to this theory, create real threats which promote in-group solidarity and collective responses against opponents. The key mechanism is the link between threat from outside the group and ethnocentric feelings and actions which result in increased in-group identity, less frequent defection, and greater punishment of deviants (LeVine and Campbell 1972:31–33). The structure of cross-cutting ties determines to what extent such interests are defined in society-wide or more localized ways and to what extent inhibitions on the actions may be taken in pursuit of these interests. Effects of complexity focus on macro-structural differences among societies, identifying interests and ways they are defended that are associated with the organization of production (Harris 1979; Fried 1967).

Psychocultural conflict theory explains conflict in terms of psychological and cultural forces that frame beliefs about the self, others, and behavior. These dispositions, which constitute the inner worlds of a group and its members, are used to make sense of external events and the behavior of others. Early socialization and relationships with others are particularly important in forming psychocultural dispositions, but later experiences continue to reinforce and modify them at other stages of the life cycle (Ross 1993). Psychocultural dispositions serve as a template for fashioning interpretations of particular groups both within and outside one's society and determine the actions taken in disputes between one's own group and others.

Because social structural and psychocultural theories attribute the primary source of conflict to different forces, each leads to distinct methods for managing conflict successfully. Structural theory gives a primary role to conflict management strategies involving altering incentives, payoffs, or—most fundamentally—the organization of society. Divergent interests, in this view, are difficult to bridge and result in either unilateral action or third party involvement to step between disputants. In contrast, psychocultural conflict theory focuses on the processes that alter perceptions or the affective relationships between key parties; according to this theory, interests are more subjective and changeable than in the structural view. It is useful to discuss methods of conflict management in some detail and to consider how it addresses each source of conflict and contributes to constructive conflict management.

Strategies of Conflict Management

In discussing conflict management the distinction between actions where the locus of action is one party, two parties, or multiparty is commonly used (Gulliver 1979; Nader and Todd 1978). *Self-help* strategies, ranging from the use of physical force to withdrawal, are the actions individuals or groups take to advance their own interests in the absence of coordination with others. *Joint problem solving* involves the principal disputants acting together to resolve a dispute; it can involve direct bargaining between the parties as well as decision making through third-party assistance such as mediation, arbitration, or negotiation. *Third-party decision making*, such as adjudication, occurs when third parties, as representatives of the wider community, make decisions which are binding on the disputants through reference to shared norms. Many complex conflicts, such as the Forest Hills housing controversy or those described in chapters 6 and 7, involve all three strategies.

Although what constitutes the core of each strategy is clear, at the edges (and in practice) they blend into one another (Gulliver 1979). For example, before undertaking unitary action a party might let it be known what it is planning, either as a signal to another to begin discussions or as a call for third-party assistance. If either of these is forthcoming, then the message is the first step in a two- or three-party communications process; if not, then it remains a unilateral action. When we look at particular disputes, it is most often the case that several strategies are used, even at the same time.

In many societies an aggrieved party often has some choice about how to handle a dispute. Nader and Todd (1978), for example, present a series of case studies showing the existence of parallel informal and formal dispute management procedures in many communities. Often the choice of which one to use is tied to the disputants' position in the social system. There is often a preference for more informal joint problem solving, yet the success of such efforts is related to the relationship between the parties. The same dispute may be treated on occasion in both the informal and formal domains, sometimes with different outcomes.

One-, two-, and multiparty conflict management strategies all address differences in the interests and interpretations of disputants.

Self-Help

Self-help strategies are often viewed solely as one party taking unilateral retaliatory actions against another, which can be devastating or even self-destructive. Unilateral actions sometimes take the form of a strong party imposing its will on others who are weaker. But self-help can also be a useful and constructive strategy in the forms of withdrawal, noncompliance, avoidance, or independent action, where self-help offers an important option for the weaker party in situations of power inequality. Where such options are viable, the bargaining power or legitimacy of weaker parties can be enhanced to increase the likelihood that joint problem solving or third-party decision making can then be used to develop constructive solutions.

By themselves, however, self-help actions are rarely viewed as constructive. Self-help is often action which is one-sided and invites reciprocal, potentially escalatory responses which can make constructive solutions difficult to achieve. But this is not always the case. We should consider the context of options from which self-help actions are selected and distinguish among the different forms self-help can take. Finally, although self-help in isolation may seem destructive, when it is seen as a step toward the use of other strategies or as part of an effort by a weaker party to strengthen its situation or call in potential allies, the assessment is often more balanced.

Exit, when it is possible, is a particularly effective self-help action for strengthening weaker parties facing strong opponents. Hirschman's (1970) analysis shows how the presence of a viable exit option makes it more likely that weaker parties can gain "voice" (meaning a say in outcomes.) He argues that weakening exit options can weaken voice. His hypothesis is borne out in my analysis of political participation in preindustrial societies (Ross 1988). Political involvement of community members, the data show, decreases as the society's political complexity increases. In more complex systems participation can be limited in two ways, both of which involve restricting exit options. First is the increasing concentration of power into fewer hands and the concomitant development of institutions which directly affect people's lives. Second, greater limits on individual mobility exist in more complex preindustrial societies where economic resources are larger and less mobile, land is less available, and group boundaries are more permanent.

The likelihood of community fission (meaning the movement of dissatisfied persons following disputes) is a societal level indicator of the availability of exit. Fission is used more frequently in less complex societies, as may be expected, and increases with the level of political involvement.[2] So despite the fact that exit and voice are alternative mechanisms, as Hirschman argues, they are not simply mirror images; under certain conditions they simultaneously strengthen or weaken each other. The viability of exit thus enhances the level of participation, whereas closing off the possibility of exit weakens voice.

Having a voice in conflict management can forestall departure when it is a feasible option. When political power is not concentrated, political involvement becomes a strategy for dealing with important matters such as warfare, migration, or violation of community norms. In societies with limited and unstable resources, political power is less likely to be concentrated (Ross 1981), but participation becomes a critical mechanism for achieving compliance with decisions (Ross 1988). In communities with easy means of exit, a person with the ability to inspire confidence by making individuals feel that their interests are being served and their views considered is most likely to remain a leader (Levi-Strauss

2. The correlation is .21 ($N = 59$).

1944). In contrast, regimes where power is more concentrated can more easily resist pressures for widespread political involvement. Here leaders have little reason to promote or even tolerate dissent and are likely to limit participation when they can.

Avoidance, or what Nader and Todd (1978) call "lumping it," is a self-help strategy which involves not raising an issue when faced with a stronger opponent or a potentially hostile community. From the point of view of an interest-based calculation, it means that the costs of actions are greater than any possible returns, not that the aggrieved party is satisfied with a situation. Avoidance may be used because of power differences between the parties and the sense that the weaker one will get nowhere if a matter is contested; at other times avoidance may occur because a matter is unimportant enough to a party that the effort of doing something about it is not worth the cost.

Noncompliance is one party refusing to do something others expect it to do. In the Semai dispute discussed in chapter 3, where the man accused of planting the trees on land that was not his own could persuade only four supporters to attend the meeting to discuss the issue, this was a powerful statement of lack of community support. Noncompliance often signals disapproval and may be costly in situations where the constraints on authorities are few and power is highly concentrated in their hands. Even in such situations, Sharp (1990) argues, this strategy may be very effective, not necessarily in getting others (such as the authorities) to act differently but at least in raising the costs of their actions. In cases where a society is internally divided, noncompliance can be especially useful in drawing attention to a problem, in mobilizing supporters, and as a first step to using joint problem solving or third-party decision-making strategies, as in the civil rights movement in the United States in the 1960s.[3]

3. There are important limits to the effectiveness of noncompliance. Consider, for example, how much more quickly American society responded to civil rights demands than did whites in South Africa. One hypothesis explains the difference in terms of the relative power and threat of each community. Another is that whites in America were much more divided on the questions of race and change than their counterparts were in South Africa. Israel is another place where noncompliance produced only small changes in government policy between the onset of the *intifada* in December 1987 and the 1992 electoral defeat of the Likud government, although there is evidence of much larger change among the population as a whole, which was affirmed in the June 1992 vote.

Unilateral action involves one party taking steps to further what it views as its interests. Mae Enga clans try to seize the lands of their neighbors; Yanomamo groups try to capture women from each other; young Somali take unprotected livestock. In all of these examples unilateral action involves at least possible violence. Not all unilateral actions are violent, however, although they are often part of an escalatory sequence that can end in violence. Moving boundary markers, denouncing others publicly, diverting water supplies, or raising the costs of using a waterway or road, for example, are not overtly violent but may invite a violent response.

A serious limitation to self-help is that the meaning of the actions is ambiguous and the response from an adversary is not necessarily what was expected or intended. Unilateral action, even when accompanied by clear communications of intentions, is easily subject to misinterpretation. Much of the recent critique of deterrence as a strategy, and of Tit-for-Tat in particular, is based on the argument that actions that appear to be clear to one side are often perceived very differently by others (Jervis, Lebow, and Stein 1985; Lebow and Stein 1987; Gowa 1986; Keohane 1986; Larson 1988). These limitations are why self-help actions, by themselves, rarely lead to constructive conflict management outcomes. In some cases, however, either the possibility of their use or their actual utilization as a step toward other procedures may contribute to constructive results.

Joint Problem Solving

Joint problem solving leaves the control over dispute outcomes with the parties, even when it involves third-party assistance. In Hirschman's terms, joint problem solving is voice as disputants have a say in the final outcome. A class prototypical example of joint problem solving is two-party economic decision making in a competitive market where direct communication is, in fact, minimal. Sellers offer products and services; buyers choose among them and in the process drive the prices for some goods up and others down. Underlying these exchanges are two core assumptions of the economic decision-making model: first, an implicit acceptance of the legitimacy of the rules underlying the transactions, and second, a drive to maximize individual self-interest, which, it is argued, benefits the community through its efficiency. These provide the basis for a wide range of laboratory explorations of joint problem solving. Best known is the prisoner's dilemma game, but there is a myriad of other experimental games designed to explore how and when parties make joint decisions.[4] This type of joint decision-making situation is described as *distributive*, meaning that the parties' strictly opposing interests can be expressed in terms of single standard like money (Raiffa 1982) and the gains for one side equal the losses for the other.

Many students of conflict resolution despair at the limitations of the lessons from distributive two-party bargaining for settling complex social or political disputes constructively. They are more interested in *integrative* decisions, those involving multiple issues in which the outcomes leave all parties better off, or in the language of game theory, where the gains of each of the parties are greater than their losses.[5] Social situations are far more complex in a number of ways than those described in simple one-product economic models (Raiffa 1982). Most important, the majority of social situations do not possess the clear standard of valuation that economic situations do, and this leads to additional problems which must be addressed in developing integrative solutions.

Identification of interests. Unlike market models, where interests of any party are clear, identification of interests in social and political disputes can be quite complex. Consider a simple dispute between two neighbors over the location of the boundary between their properties or the use and maintenance of a common access road. Although an overt dispute might develop over one of these concerns, it is quite likely that an investigation into the matter would quickly reveal a number of additional grievances, some precise and some quite vague. For example, Gulliver presents the case of two Arusha farmers who contested the vacant land between their farms. His summary of the agenda for the negotiations that eventually took place between them listed sixteen items, several of which started out only as general concerns.[6]

4. An excellent discussion of this material is found in Raiffa (1982). He provides not only a highly readable overview containing excellent examples of the kinds of studies which have been conducted from this framework but also an excellent introduction to the central principles of this research tradition.

5. Integrative decisions are the product of what Deutsch (1973) calls productive conflict processes. Whereas many discussions of integrative decisions focus on the outcome, Deutsch pays attention to the sequence of events leading up to it as well.

6. This case is dealt with in detail in chapter 7.

One of the serious obstacles to conflict resolution is the common inability of parties to translate vague grievances into concrete demands that another party can understand and to which they can respond (Susskind and Cruikshank 1988). Perceptions of threat, abuse, or exploitation are common in group conflicts, as in those between ethnic communities, but until the parties convert these grievances into concrete demands, the chances for effective processing of the concerns are very low. A significant barrier here is affective: the aggrieved party believes that its wants should be obvious and it perceives the refusal to recognize its grievances as a personal rejection.

Weighting interests. Even when explicit interests are identified, each party may attach a very different value to each one. This can be especially helpful in facilitating integrative solutions (Raiffa 1982). Consider another simple dispute over land where two parties, L and W, are fighting over a common boundary but soon realize that their dispute is also about rights to water from a spring in the area. For L, enclosing the largest amount of land on his side of the border may be most important because he intends to use the land for grazing, whereas for W, access to the water may be her real concern. Knowledge of what matters most to each disputant makes the development of a mutually advantageous solution more feasible.

When preference rankings of the disputants' interests differ it becomes possible to construct integrative outcomes. For example, the boundary could be drawn to provide L with more land while granting W the portion that provides access to water. Although integrative outcomes may often be constructed in social and political conflicts, identifying the relative importance of interests for each party and constructing acceptable tradeoffs are often critical but far from obvious (Susskind and Cruikshank 1988). As Raiffa says:

The potential of finding joint win-win situations depends on the exploitation of differences between beliefs, between probabilistic projections, between tradeoffs, between discount rates (a special case of intertemporal tradeoffs), and between risk preferences. (Raiffa 1982:286)

After acceptable solutions are arranged, it is easy in retrospect to see them as rational and even obvious. This ignores how hard it often is to effectively speak to both the substantive issues at hand and the emotional threats that the conflict poses to each party. Exploring alternative interpretations of a situation is often extremely difficult, as the open communication and trust needed are frequently lacking and it should not be assumed that problem solving can easily overcome this barrier.

Third-party assistance and support. The process of constructing acceptable resolutions to conflicts can be highly complex. In negotiations over questions like the Law of the Sea, which lasted more than a decade, there were many parties and many issues (Raiffa 1982). In other situations, such as classic community feuds, the issues ostensibly seem simpler but feelings are so intense that all efforts to find solutions are thwarted.

Parties in conflict frequently need the help of a third party who can provide a setting where disputants can meet as well as legitimate each disputant and his or her demands. A third party may facilitate communication (sometimes by serving as the messenger between the disputants), make proposals about procedure, translate grievances into concrete demands, help parties define the relative importance of different concerns, set an agenda, make suggestions about substantive issues, and suggest integrative packages (Deutsch 1973; Pruitt and Rubin 1986; Raiffa 1982).[7]

Although third parties may facilitate the development of integrative solutions, the power to accept or reject outcomes always rests with the disputants in joint problem solving. Consequently, interveners need to learn to do only what is necessary, no more, and to withdraw as soon as possible. When and if a time to withdraw arises depends in large part on the nature of communication between the disputants and the level of trust and empathy they develop. The goal of third parties is not simply to help construct a workable solution but to do it in such a way that the disputants feel the solution is theirs and not that of the third party.[8]

Effective communication. Parties locked in a dispute need not

7. Distinctions between kinds of third-party interventions—assisted negotiation, mediation, and arbitration—are not my focus here.

8. I mention some additional questions often raised about third parties: Should the third party be weak or powerful? Should the party try to intervene actively or simply facilitate discussions? How are "neutral" third parties different from those who have substantive interests in an outcome or those who can have resources that can be used to compel one or more parties to accept a solution? A theory of third-party action would need to explain how third parties function under a series of contingent conditions (Princen 1992).

talk directly to one another to reach a solution, but they must communicate effectively. For example, no officials of the Iranian or U. S. governments met face-to-face to discuss the release of the American hostages in Tehran in 1980–81, but the Algerians talked to both parties, relaying vital messages needed to construct an acceptable deal. In fact, later news reports indicated that almost no significant communications between Iran and the United States took place for the entire hostage period. A critical problem was that Iranian demands were so general that the United States was hard pressed to know how to respond to them, whereas U.S. proposals were too vague for the Iranians to know what was actually offered. Only in the last six weeks of the fourteen-month crisis were there any serious negotiations, and these occurred only after the Iranians understood that the United States would consider releasing hundreds of millions of dollars of frozen Iranian assets as part of any package.

Effective communication involves the exchange of information needed for the disputants to construct an integrative solution,[9] including one's own position and that of the other party regarding the issue(s) in dispute. But effective communication has other elements as well, involving the exchange of information on matters that may not at first seem relevant to the dispute but that may contribute to an integrative decision. For example, consider again the boundary dispute between L and W. A third party trying to mediate this dispute might well despair at first upon learning the history of claims and counterclaims over the disputed area; both sides could be making reasonable but not fully substantiated claims. More important, there may be no clear principle to be invoked to dictate a single outcome. When discussions between the parties reveal that L is particularly concerned about using the land for grazing and W wants access to the water source, however, the basis for a settlement of their dispute became clear. Such additional information at first does not seem relevant to the question of which party's historical claim is more appropriate, but it does increase the chances of finding a mutually satisfactory outcome.

Effective communication expands the issues considered by enabling the parties "to go beneath the manifest to the underlying issues involved in the conflict and, thereby, to facilitate the meaningful and

9. Of course, in most disputes more than one integrative solution is possible. However, I do not worry here about whether a solution is the best possible one in a given situation or simply good enough to be accepted.

accurate definition of the problems they are confronting together"
(Deutsch 1973:363). Perceived injustices and hurt feelings need to be
aired as much as substantive demands. Deutsch (1973:364) also suggests
that effective communication involves a certain amount of "benevolent
misperception," a tendency to minimize differences and believe in the
opponent's good intentions.

More diffuse information about the other party's intentions and
trustworthiness is often exchanged and may facilitate the development
of integrative solutions. Raiffa (1982) reports several laboratory experiments where disputants communicating face-to-face achieve more satisfactory outcomes than those who exchange information in other ways.
The explanation seems to be that direct exchanges transmit more information relevant to the dispute than the issues ostensibly being discussed.
Of course, in many situations face-to-face discussion is counterproduc-
tive because of what the parties say or perceive. A striking example,
considered in the next chapter, is the Camp David Accords, an example
of successful joint problem solving with third-party assistance. From the
start, the personal tension between Anwar Sadat and Menachem Begin
was so high that little effective communication took place between them.
Both men trusted Jimmy Carter, however, and he was able to relay messages between the two which led to significant information exchange
and an eventual agreement (Carter 1982; Quandt 1986).

Trust that an adversary will keep an agreement. Disputants do
not have to like their adversaries, but they must believe that viable
settlements can be made with them. One way in which this can be
accomplished is via a structure of penalties to be paid if either side
reneges on an agreement. The money could be held in escrow by a
third party. For example, trust between Iran and the United States in
early 1981 was so low that an elaborate scheme involving international
actors was worked out to simultaneously verify that the plane carry-
ing the hostages cleared Iranian air space and release the frozen Iranian
funds held by U.S. banks. Rarely are such elaborate procedures needed
or used, but their value should not be discounted. Progress in arms
agreements, for example, has been significantly aided by the availability of advanced spy satellites that verify that parties are abiding by
agreements.

Informal penalties also are widely used. In small communities,
parties that fail to follow through on publicly made agreements may be

subject to social ostracism and gossip.[10] Oathing ceremonies or other ritual actions can effectively bind parties to joint agreements. Agreements made face to face often are kept because of the moral force that links people who have established a personal relationship. Sometimes it is one party's concern for its reputation and how this may affect future dealings which matters most. In other situations, the penalties for violation are contained in a commonly jointly accepted decision rule, such as "I cut; you choose."

A second approach is to create a situation where the mutual benefits for continued cooperation are high enough that neither party seriously considers breaking an agreement. Deutsch calls this "cooperative commitment," meaning that "past investments, already established facilities, procedures and institutions, obligations to third parties, and situational pressures may operate to bind one to a cooperative relationship. This is so even when the emotional attachments to the other and the perceived utility of the relationship do not by themselves warrant its continuation" (1973:364). Western Europeans waged war against each other about once a generation over several centuries; in the almost fifty years since World War II there has been no war in western Europe, and no hint of one between the Germans, French, British, and Italians, all former adversaries. Why? One answer is that the presence of the Soviet bloc precluded any fighting among these countries. While this certainly mattered, the explanation ignores the significant effects, particularly in recent years, of European community institutions and the joint benefits they offer to all.[11]

The literature about joint problem solving gives a great deal of attention to the need to develop effective communication and trust that a viable agreement is possible (Deutsch 1973; Fisher and Ury 1981; Gulliver 1979; Pruitt and Rubin 1986). Another prerequisite for addressing substantive differences raised by White (1984) is the need for empathy—but not necessarily acceptance, of the other side's point of view—and its role in facilitating agreements with opponents whose aggression is defensively motivated. When empathy develops, exchanges are more ef-

10. Many of the essays in Nader and Todd (1978), especially Todd's, show how informal and formal systems of conflict management can complement each other, but also how informal measures may have limited effectiveness for groups or individuals who are marginal in a community.

11. One measure of change is that despite the tension between Germany and others over unification in 1990, there was no talk of military solutions, only intense political discussions and subsequent agreements.

fective, parties are more open to a range of options that speak to each party's interests, and viable agreements become more attractive to all.

Successful joint problem solving is difficult to achieve but most likely to result in constructive conflict management. In order to alter their images of the situation and of other actors, parties need to engage in the open communication and search for creative solutions that Deutsch (1973) sees as critical. Because the parties maintain control over the disputes, they develop an investment in the achievement of a successful outcome. Unlike adversarial procedures where there is an incentive to emphasize how evil an opponent is, joint decision making relies on the need for exchange and tempered language to modify substantive positions and develop creative solutions (Susskind and Cruikshank 1988). However, just because joint problem solving can produce such outcomes does not mean that it always does so.

Third-Party Decision Making

In third-party decision making, control over decisions no longer rests with the disputants. Probably the most common third-party decisions are those of administrators, applying an apparently clear decision rule in order to dictate a certain outcome. Conflict management literature, however, focuses more on third-party adjudication as part of a legal process. Here an aggrieved party—an individual, group, or community —brings a dispute to a third party who renders a binding decision.

Of course, in practice the process is not so simple. For one thing simply threatening to "see you in court!" or taking the initial steps to do so can provoke unilateral action or facilitate joint problem solving. In fact, in the United States, as elsewhere, only a small proportion of civil cases brought to court are actually heard (Yngvesson and Mather 1983:61–63).

Third parties can be effective conflict managers for several reasons. In some cases they have special knowledge or expertise. Yngvesson and Mather (1983) describe how the Azande oracle, like the American administrative judge, "by virtue of his special training and esoteric language . . . [is able] to provide a general framework for dispute definition . . . [and] through his performance . . . to proselytize for a client's cause, to pay the piper and lead his client's co-residents towards a consensus of support for one man against another of the same community" (1983:70).

Third parties, as either administrators or adjudicators, represent community norms in dispute settlement. In some very small societies the entire community hears a case and offers a decision (Gibbs, 1963). More commonly, selected members of the community hear a dispute and offer a decision in the name of the community. For example, in Talea, a Zapotec community in Mexico, leaders elected yearly are expected to settle disputes in ways consistent with the community's "harmony ideology," meaning that they emphasize restoring the peace and keeping outsiders out of local affairs (Nader 1990).

Third party effectiveness is also attributed to the formal and informal coercive power of the community that underpins their decisions. Although community enforcement of a decision is not always spelled out, a crucial element in third-party decisions is not only that such coercion is legitimate but that it will occur in the case of noncompliance.

No wonder Felsteiner (1974–75), Newman (1983), and Schwartz and Miller (1964) find that the likelihood of a society using adjudication increases with societal complexity and the existence of coercive power. Yngvesson and Mather (1983), however, remind us that the use of adjudication involves other factors as well, and that in more complex societies, other methods of dispute management are probably used more often than adjudication. It is better, Yngvesson and Mather suggest, to consider the combination of methods used in any society than to think that it uses only a single method.

Even when adjudication is employed to manage disputes, Abel (1973–74) notes that there can be wide variation in third-party role differentiation. His theory of the dispute process examines "changes in the role differentiation of the intervener as a possible explanation for the characteristics of the dispute process" (1973–74:251). Third parties, he observes, can differ widely in the basis of their authority, their training, as well as in their structural differentiation, and there is great variation in the specifics of the dispute process across societies.[12]

Why are third-party decisions accepted? In addition to the coercive power of the community, the legitimacy of the process and its underlying norms often produce compliance, even in the absence of coercion. Milgram's (1974) obedience experiments show that compliance

12. Abel offers a comprehensive discussion of structural and processual variables which could be used to compare dispute processing across contexts (1973–74:251–284). Newman's (1983) cross-cultural study of legal behavior also suggests important dimensions of variation.

with the demands of an apparent authority, even when no element of physical coercion is present, is often very high. Finally, it is important to recognize that third-party decisions may be accepted because they provide a vehicle for disputants to terminate their conflict in an honorable manner. When disputants accept the legitimacy of third-party decisions, the outcomes tend to be more constructive than when they are simply viewed as coercive. The dilemma is that the procedures involved in many forms of third-party decision making, such as adjudication, polarize the disputants by emphasizing opposing grievances and claims while offering little incentive for compromise or creative problem solving. This does not have to be the case, however, and authoritative third parties can certainly use specific procedures which address participants' interests and interpretations and contribute to constructive outcomes. In Talea, Nader (1990) describes third-party decisions focused on maintaining a balance within the community as part of a strategy to preserve local autonomy within the Mexican state, an important motivation for complying with decisions.

Limitations to Constructive Conflict Management
Inequality

There is no doubt that equality between the parties and egalitarian social settings promote constructive conflict management (see, for example, Deutsch 1973 and Raiffa 1982). Yet the question remains how far the parties can deviate from an egalitarian situation and still produce constructive decisions.

The most obvious way in which egalitarian situations facilitate constructive conflict management is by removing the possibility of one party imposing a solution on another, thereby substituting coercion for mutual agreement. Knowing that they have a final veto over any proposed solution and/or the ability to leave the community if one cannot be found encourages disputants to act responsibly and efficaciously. When no disputant can force another to act against their will, the conflict management process must ensure that all points of view are considered in arriving at a settlement. For example, Robarchek (1979a) presents a dispute between two Semai brothers which no one in the community took very seriously and everyone hoped could be resolved quickly. However, when the younger brother proved very reticent to speak at the *bcaraa'*, the headman was obliged to resist terminating the meeting, knowing that important underlying concerns had not been expressed and that a quick solution would fail to address these deeper issues and could unravel. He then, in effect, forced continued consideration of the concerns for several hours until he was convinced that they had all been aired in a way that could contribute to an enduring agreement.

Evaluating the degree of equality between two parties is often difficult. Parties may possess different forms of power (for example, population versus money) which are hard to compare. While it is important to consider the actual resources (numbers, material goods, and so on) of the disputants, their perceptions of the situation also matter (Fisher 1983). If a party sees itself as weak and unequal, its ability to show sufficient trust in the conflict management process is likely to be severely impaired. Ironically, both because the resources of each side are almost never identical and because perceptions are selective, in many situations all parties see themselves as a vulnerable minority, and these conflicts are difficult to manage constructively. A particularly clear example is the Middle East, where Palestinians are often incredulous to hear that Israelis, the region's strongest military power, describe themselves as vulnerable; likewise, Israelis do not understand how Palestinians can see themselves as an oppressed minority given the Arab majority in the region's population.

Apparent inequalities do not necessarily forestall the development of creative, constructive solutions (Fisher 1983). In the case of the Tikopia chief discussed in chapter 3, though the chief's formal authority could never be directly questioned, the actions of his sons, their wives, and the wider community constrained his behavior while upholding the norms the chief felt had been violated. The norm which had been broken was not the only one that came into play; by invoking additional, equally important norms, the behavior of the supposedly all-powerful chief was significantly modified. The inequality of the parties was offset by a widespread consensus that additional norms were relevant, which alerts us to be concerned not only with the question of equality but also the wider context in which decisions are made.

Self-help actions which establish a party's commitment and capacity for efficacious action sometimes go a long way toward bringing another party to the negotiating table and launching joint problem solving. Threatened lawsuits and other actions which involve additional outside parties may also have this goal. In this sense, perceived (and real) inequality at the bargaining table can sometimes be countered by resorting to other strategies that can raise a party's effective power or its perceived legitimacy.

Cultural Limitations

There are often limitations to what conflict management procedures and institutions can accomplish. Effective conflict management institutions have to be at least partially consistent with a culture's practices and dispositions in other domains. For example, if moral and material success in a society are achieved through physical exploits in interpersonal encounters, compromises arising out of third-party mediation can easily feel like failures. When the social structural and psychocultural dispositions in a society fail to reinforce the results produced by conflict management institutions, conflict management is less likely to be effective. The challenge to practitioners in such situations is to try to build on whatever elements are present, however meager they may be.

Conflict management procedures that are at odds with the dominant metaphors and values in a culture are not likely to become easily institutionalized. In cases where a method is criticized as inconsistent with a deep-seated disposition, it may become important to emphasize ways it is consistent with a different disposition or to suggest why the first linkage is inappropriate. For example, if an opponent is viewed as inhuman, thus legitimating behaviors which might not otherwise be used, one conflict management strategy is to emphasize ways in which the two sides share some common concerns and have common human needs.[13] If the question of linkage between psychocultural dispositions and interpretations is not addressed, the chances of legitimating particular procedures, no matter how highly regarded they may be, are not good. Culture is hardly a unitary phenomenon, however, and it changes over time, often in reaction to contact and exchanges with other groups. Cultural complexity means that the reorganization of linkages among key elements is often possible but that the legitimation of effective conflict management methods may require attention to this question.

---

13. This question is addressed at greater length in chapters 8 and 9.

Figure 5.1.
The Relevance of Sources of Conflict to Dispute Management Strategies

	Sources of Conflict	
Dispute Management Strategies	Social Structural (Interests)	Psychocultural (Interpretations)
Self-help	Views interests as the primary shapers of behavior (exit, avoidance, noncompliance, or unilateral action) and as responses to differences in resources	Considers psychocultural interpretations implicitly in that demands of opponents are seen as fixed, often insatiable; hence, cooperative joint action is rarely seen as fruitful
Joint Problem Solving	Assumes that stated interests are not necessarily the prime source of conflict and can be redefined in order to produce integrative outcomes	Focuses on mutual images and low trust as crucial sources of conflict and the need to create a climate where open exchange and creative problem solving can occur
Third-Party Decision Making	Views interests as crucial to a dispute; the third party decides among them by reference to common norms or authoritative rules	Considers psychocultural interpretations only in so far as they are tied to interests or concern about the dispute resolution procedures themselves

Partial Linkage

All three conflict management strategies draw on the social structural and psychocultural conflict theories selectively and in different ways.[14] Making the connections explicit helps us understand the underlying assumptions in each conflict management method and how it, implicitly, views certain causes of conflict as more important than others (figure 5.1).

Self-help strategies emphasize competing interests as prime shapers of action and suggest that groups or individuals who do not defend

14. Kriesberg (1992) argues that three views of the international system —statism, populism, and pluralism—lead to distinct analyses of the nature of conflict and to very different steps in negotiating a settlement of the differences.

or pursue their own interests will suffer. The success of self-help, particularly as it is spelled out in game theory, depends on strategic considerations and resource maximization. Choices among unilateral action, exit, noncompliance, and avoidance are made on the basis of costs and benefits at a given time. There is an implicit notion that interests are clear to parties at a specific time, and maybe even over time. Finally, this perspective implies a limited (or fixed) resource view of the world and the presence of opponents with insatiable demands and rigid, mutually antagonistic perceptions.[15]

Joint problem solving, in contrast, emphasizes the role of perceptions and interpretations (like threats to identity) in creating conflicts and the need to alter these subjective elements in order to create a climate in which integrative problem solving can occur. Differences in interests are not denied, but joint problem solving approaches often encourage disputants to see them as less important, as surface manifestations of the more basic conflict, or as the result of a dispute as much as the cause. In addition, the distinction between the interests parties have in resolving past differences and their future interests in living together in harmony comes into play with more emphasis on the latter. Interests, then, are seen as somewhat flexible and subject to redefinition so that settling differences hinges, in great part, on how the parties view each other and themselves. From this perspective, if antagonistic perceptions rooted in deep-seated worldviews can be altered, bridging differences in interests may follow, producing integrative outcomes.

Third-party decision making works on the assumption that differences in interests are real and less flexible than joint problem solving approaches suggest, and that self-help strategies too easily exacerbate differences without resolving them. Third-party decision making is less concerned with how the disputants view each other than joint decision making because outside parties, representing the community's authority

---

15. The issue of the nature of opponents' demands is an important theoretical issue. Jervis (1976) points out how deterrence theory assumes that opponents have insatiable interests and prefer large relative gains vis-à-vis opponents, whereas conflict spiral theory, which does not make this assumption, suggests that absolute gains are of primary importance. Snidal (1991) contains a useful general discussion of the consequences of assuming that parties pursue relative versus absolute gains.

which all parties accept, decide among competing claims and back such judgments with threats of force. As a method it focuses on past behavior more than future action (although this is sometimes involved), and it primarily addresses the substantive differences among the parties rather than the more subjective elements of the conflict.

Each method is biased in that it addresses certain sources of conflict more readily than others. Self-help strategies emphasize each party's interests but nearly ignores joint interests. They pay scant attention to the role of subjective interpretations of action because there is little sense they are relevant to interest-motivated behavior. Joint problem solving often fails to see the essential role that differences in interests play in a conflict and overemphasizes the importance of intergroups perceptions created between disputants through interpersonal contact, especially when large communities are involved.[16] Third-party decision making is sometimes inadequate because of its failure to address underlying psychocultural realities and because it may provide "solutions" to a dispute without addressing the underlying conflict (as in the case of the *chadors* in French schools).

Clear assumptions about the psychocultural aspects of conflict are embedded in self-help and third-party dispute management strategies, as are assumptions about interests in joint problem solving. What is striking, however, is how poorly developed each of these is and how they differ from the assumptions made about the same factors in the context of the other dispute management strategies. In some cases, assumptions made about sources of conflict that underlie different procedures appear to contradict each other; in other cases, they are not contradictory, but the emphasis is quite different. The analysis here suggests the need for a more comprehensive view which identifies both structural and psychocultural roots in almost all serious conflicts; therefore, constructive dispute management procedures must address both the interests and interpretations to produce constructive outcomes.

The crucial resulting hypothesis is that the effective use of any

16. Rothman (1992) and Kelman (1987) argue that in intense ethnic disputes, as in the Middle East, establishing personal ties among the parties is not an appropriate goal of joint problem solving. Although mutual perceptions and needs should be addressed, Rothman emphasizes the development of skills that help the disputants resolve differences effectively rather than the development of personal bonds. For more on this question see chapter 8.

method of dispute management is linked to incorporation of procedural elements that address the assumptions made about both structural and psychocultural causes of that dispute. When dispute management strategies address only one root of conflict, or when the underlying assumptions are incorrect, failure is more likely.

Conclusion

The main argument in this chapter is that each conflict management strategy—self-help, joint problem solving, and third-party decision making—addresses either the structural or psychocultural causes of a dispute differently, often leaving the other untouched. My major hypothesis is that conflict management is most effective when both the actual interests and the psychocultural interpretations of disputants are addressed, making enduring, mutually acceptable solutions possible.

In the previous chapter I argued that two elements are crucial: addressing interest differences among disputants, by paying attention to future relationships as well as past events and to common needs shared by even the most antagonistic disputants, as well as transforming disputants' interpretations of each other's needs and motives to increase the likelihood of managing the conflict constructively. The focus on conflict management strategies in this chapter leads to a third element: the need to find ways to get disputants to accept the outcomes of conflict management through their ownership of the process. One hypothesis is that disputants' increased participation in dispute management should lead to increased identification with and ownership of outcomes.

To the dispute management professional, the problem of addressing these three elements is partly strategic. How can any (or all) of these processes be advanced so that constructive conflict management can get a toehold where it was previously weak? In situations where groups and individuals have long-standing suspicions about each other or the organization of power and the distribution of rewards in a community, the challenge is formidable. Communities whose institutions have been used to maintain the power and privilege that is itself being contested will not be likely candidates for constructive conflict management.

This discussion has raised general issues about the linkage between interests and interpretations as sources of conflict and the specific conflict management strategies that address them. In the next two chapters I address this question by discussing specific conflict management successes and failures, examining how interests and interpretations were or were not adequately addressed, and I then consider how the specific cultural context shaped the strategies used and their effectiveness.

6

Successful Conflict Management

Given the amount of violence in the world and the intolerance some contending groups display toward each other, it is easy to become discouraged about our ability to manage conflict constructively. As a result, there is widespread acceptance of the inevitability of severe conflict and our ability to affect the outcomes of many disputes. The acceptance of these assumptions is troublesome, because one consequence is that both social scientists and practitioners pay too little attention to ways in which the course of conflicts can be altered. Many people reach the conclusion that conflicts are unmanageable due to our strong propensity to focus on the most intense disputes, which have the greatest chances to remain unresolved, while denying ourselves the lessons from those situations where conflict management is more effective. As a result, we do little to counter the pervasive view that disputes somehow take on a life of their own and an unalterable course.[1] In this chapter I challenge this view by examining conflict management successes, emphasizing those which occur in situations where they were not anticipated. Success is not just the absence of failure; it needs to be studied on its own terms.

Our lack of understanding of conflict management success is partially due to the insufficiently nuanced language we use, which often communicates no more than the dichotomy between success and failure.

1. This is particularly true in ethnic conflict, an area where both popular images and scholarship treat severe conflict as somehow natural or inevitable. For discussion of this general issue with respect to ethnic conflict see Ross (1992a) and in terms of the issue of successful ethnic conflict management see Ross (forthcoming).

Building models of conflict management success requires identifying degrees and kinds of success. Most important, we need to stop focusing exclusively on the question of whether or not the resolution of a conflict is ideal, and instead ask whether or not a particular conflict management strategy made things better: Is there a discernable improvement in a situation, and does this enhance the possibility of producing more such changes in the future?

In this chapter I first offer criteria that can be used for judging the degree of success and failure in conflict management, and I then distinguish between relative and absolute success. A critical element to consider may be how hard a conflict is to manage in the first place. The cases of conflict management success introduced throughout the chapter— ranging from a land dispute among Arusha neighbors in Tanzania to the Camp David accords—have in common the fact that both the substantive interests and disputants' interpretations are addressed, although participants are not always fully aware of this. In the constructive conflict management efforts considered here (and other successes we can identify) viable outcomes are rarely imposed on the parties, opponents usually have important internal differences (if not divisions), and third parties of many sorts often assist the disputants. Most often joint problem solving is important in this process, although self-help actions and third-party decision making may also play a role as part of a larger conflict management process.

Evaluating Success and Failure in Conflict Management

Determining the success of a particular conflict management effort involves a series of comparisons, often implicit, that may yield different answers. The most severe, but not necessarily unfair, criterion of success, considers the outbreak of conflict, particularly when it is violent, as evidence of failure. The best conflict management, this point of view suggests, heads off severe conflict before it begins. I adopted this perspective in chapter 3 when I identified a range of practices found in low- and constructive conflict societies which work to limit the outbreak of severe conflict.

The perspective I take here is somewhat different. It begins with the assumption that in some situations severe conflict is not always avoidable. I ask what happens once such a conflict begins. How are we to decide if the conflict management methods used were successful or not? Conceptually, two counterfactual comparisons may be made. The first asks what outcome would have occurred if nothing had been done, if the conflict management methods had not been tried. This is not just a rhetorical question, for there are more than a few cases, such as the conflict between MOVE and the city of Philadelphia discussed in the next chapter, where it is plausible to suggest that doing nothing would have been better than what was done. This does not mean, however, that doing nothing would have been the best course of action. Second, how would the outcome have been changed if a different action had been taken? Although foolproof answers to this question are not possible, its consideration may suggest possible future alternatives for action.

These counterfactual comparisons are analytically useful, but they are hypothetical and cannot help us consider the success and failure of the conflict management strategies actually used in a particular conflict. To make such an evaluation, three criteria—acceptance, duration, and changed relationships—seem reasonable (Deutsch 1973; Pruitt and Rubin 1986; Susskind and Cruikshank 1988; Ury, Brett, and Goldberg 1988):[2]

1. *Acceptance*: the degree to which a solution is accepted by the parties to a dispute. Parties accept a solution for two reasons: because they like its substance or because they consider the process through which it was arrived at to be fair. The case where a party does not oppose a solution because it lacks the power to act is not acceptance, but resignation, although acceptance sometimes comes later.[3]

2. *Duration*: the degree to which a solution is enduring. Longer term solutions, especially when combined with mutual acceptance, are better than ones that work only for a short time. One caveat, however, is that a solution may be excellent from a variety of points of view but collapse because of exogenous forces over which none of the parties have any control.

3. *Changed relationships*: the degree to which interaction between the disputants differs (in a positive way) before and after the dispute settlement.

2. These criteria focus on the dispute itself as do those in Ury, Brett, and Goldberg (1988). Other criteria evaluate success in terms of societal concerns as well. Just because a dispute is managed successfully in terms of the criteria listed here does not mean that it is being managed constructively in terms of the concerns of the society. For example, labor and management may come to an agreement that excludes or discriminates against certain classes of workers or consumers.

3. Cases in which a party does not approve of an outcome but does nothing because the matter is relatively unimportant are not considered here.

The best conflict management, much of the literature suggests, transforms the relationship between the disputants in such a way that the relationship itself becomes more rewarding to each party, greater efforts are made to maintain it, and more positive affect is associated with it.

Although it is tempting to suggest that these criteria be arranged in a hierarchy, this is not always the case. It is most useful to view each as a continuum with individual cases revealing different combinations and to note that changes in any one may have important consequences for the others. For example, as a conflict management outcome becomes more enduring, there is an increased likelihood that relationships between members of each group will change, especially with new generations, who never experienced the original dispute first-hand. The most successful conflict management produces solutions that are not only mutually acceptable and enduring but that also alter the relations between the parties, transforming the dynamic that produced the threats and mutual fears. One model of such conflict management comes from psychotherapy, where a mutually acceptable solution tends to endure when it is linked to changes in self-image and different behavior. To evaluate conflict management success, I suggest, we need to be aware of small shifts, not just large jumps.

An upper limit to this definition of success is that in social disputes large-scale changes in group relations are rarely achieved quickly and usually involve several generations. Similarly, few successes in complex social disputes are total. More often, as is discussed in the next section, outcomes represent relative improvements over a prior situation, with considerable room remaining for further progress. It is critical, however, not to confuse the absence of complete resolution of differences with an absence of any progress whatsoever. Rothman's (1992) term "pieces of peace" is very useful here.

Specific Examples

Examining specific conflict management successes shows that some are more limited than others, and that in some cases where the level of overall success is quite similar, the changes in specific dimensions of success may vary widely. There are many possibilities between the lowest level of success—where both parties accept an outcome but it fails to last and does little to change the long-term relations between the parties—and those in which acceptance is strong and enduring and results in changed relationships.

Mae Enga Peacemaking

Consider the following summary of Mae Enga peacemaking based on Meggitt's (1977) description of this society:

After a period of clan fighting there may come about a period of stalemate. Continuation of the war ensures the loss of more lives to no obvious advantage. Both owners of the quarrel (the clans which started the fighting) can negotiate from positions of equal strength. Allies of each create a pressure for peace and the Big Men of each clan begin negotiations, mainly involving homicide compensations, with both the enemy and then their own allies. Any agreement between groups, then, is subject to ratification within each group, so that while many people may still be disgruntled, any settlement reached has to be widely accepted. Finally, any agreement is ratified through a public meal sharing, speech making, and partial payment of the agreed compensation. The two warring sides stop fighting, they exchange some compensation payments, and agree to live in peace. But sooner or later the peace breaks down as allies demand support in their own conflicts, as only some of the earlier compensation payments are, in fact, met, or as incidents start to occur in the border area between the clans. (Meggitt 1977:113–143)

The problem here, from a conflict management point of view, is that the mechanisms that commit the parties to the peace agreement are in the medium run far weaker than the incentives for breaking it. In highland New Guinea generally, strong third parties able to impose a solution on warring groups are rare (Koch 1974); another explanation is that the agreement itself is not sufficiently beneficial to encourage both sides to stick to it. Ceasing to fight is a strategic, short-run decision, not one rooted in a new relationship between the parties. Parties know that payment of compensation will depend on strategic interests not abstract notions of justice. In terms of the three criteria noted above, this style of conflict management meets only one—acceptance—for the solution is not enduring and any changes in the relationship are only short-term strategic ones. However, even a temporary peace provides sufficient relief from violence to be termed a partial success.

Black-White Relations in the Southern United States

Throughout the 1960s, race relations was a source of intense conflict in many southern communities in the United States. During this period a wide range of self-help, joint problem solving, and third-party decision making methods were used in this conflict. How successful were they? More than twenty-five years later, according to the three criteria I would suggest that the civil rights protests produced an outcome which was more successful in terms of the first two criteria, and only a partial success by the third one.

In most communities, acceptance of the changes arrived at through joint problem solving and third-party decision making (mainly in the form of court decisions and federal legislation) came faster from blacks than whites, but by the 1980s public opinion data show moderately high support among whites for integrated schools, black voting rights, and other civil rights. In terms of endurance, the judicial, legislative, and other changes have lasted since the 1960s and there are no signs of their being threatened. Race is still a dominant concern in southern politics, but it is played out in more complex ways than in the past. For example, there are many areas of the region where stable, functioning coalitions between blacks and whites have developed to win important political offices. Among the examples are such white southern politicians as Jimmy Carter and Bill Clinton, who went on to win the Presidency, and many figures who won state office or were elected to Congress. Finally, black-white social relations in the South are certainly better than in the pre-civil rights era. Yet there is still a great deal of discrimination, distrust, racial tension, and latent conflict in daily life; by this criterion, conflict management to date has been only partially successful.

Labor-Management Relations in Industrialized Societies

A century ago, labor-management relations were far more conflictual and destructive than they are today in virtually every industrial and incipient industrial nation. Long, bitter strikes and owner-inspired violence against union organizers, members, and sympathizers were common. Only in a few cases did owners readily accept trade union representation of workers. Gradually the situation changed, sometimes as worker solidarity forced employers to recognize the union, but most often only when a third party, government, entered the conflict, guaranteeing the right of workers to organize and bargain collectively.

By the 1950s, the right of unions to organize and negotiate for workers was widely accepted in the industrial world, and while there were attacks on the power of unions (such as right-to-work legislation in the United States), the main elements of earlier solutions proved to be quite enduring. Although labor-management relations in particular industries and factories were sometimes extremely bitter and even violent,[4] on the whole bitter labor conflict declined significantly. Not only is the new order accepted and enduring, but relations between management and labor have taken new forms. Labor leaders now regularly sit on management councils and boards of directors, and neither side questions the other's right to exist. Bitter and destructive conflicts still occur, but they are now the exception. Although labor and management have competing interests, they discovered common concerns as well. Likewise, their mutually antagonistic images have, for the most part, given way to far more nuanced and individualized images, which makes it far easier for each to listen and even empathize with (if not accept) the perspective of the other and engage in constructive joint problem solving. Where management and labor continue to attack each other (especially in public), it is these exceptions that prove the extent of overall change in the past century. This case, then, seems relatively successful according to all three criteria.

France, Germany, and Postwar Europe

Sometimes a change imposed on one (or even both) of the parties somewhat against its will turns out to be successful when later generations come to accept it; it endures and constructively alters relationships. For example, over hundreds of years, France and Germany regularly went to war, taking territory and resources from each other. The post-World War II political and economic arrangements have linked the two at the core of a European union with a higher level of interdependence than

---

4. Disputes in the U.S. airline industry in the 1980s are a good example. In contrast, the auto industry, which saw some of the most violent confrontations in the 1930s, has witnessed the most extensive and peaceful industrial restructuring in the 1980s.

was imaginable in 1945. Accompanying the changes in economic, political, and military arrangements in Europe are basic shifts in how the people of each country view each other in addition to a capacity to put many fears of the past to rest (Montville 1991b). Although there is still periodic tension between the two, as in early 1990 when the French and others felt that German unification was advancing with too little consultation with other nations, there has been no threat of a return to the old military approach to conflict. The postwar arrangements are now widely accepted in each nation (although the Germans had little say in them initially), and they have endured and become even more firmly implanted with each decade. Finally, the French-German relationship, fundamentally different, especially since 1960, seems able to survive major changes in the European and international order.

Absolute and Relative Success

Not all conflict management efforts have an equal chance of success; differences are a function of the intensity of the dispute, the history of relationships between the parties, and the specific conflict management steps taken. A dispute between two parties with a long history of cooperation and a readily available third party to assist them is far more likely to be successfully managed than one between long-term antagonists without assistance.

Conflict management success can be evaluated in both absolute and relative terms. Evaluations at the absolute level concern the extent to which a conflict is put to rest. Relative judgments are concerned with the degree of difficulty of a dispute at the outset. The relative difficulty is a function of such factors as differences in interests, the intensity of feelings about these differences, the images that the disputants have of each other, and the history of prior relations between the parties: in short, many of the structural and psychocultural factors as they are manifest at the dispute level.

Consequently, expectations for conflict management success will vary as a function of the degree of difficulty. A parent who stops a fight between two of his children but fails to restore a peaceful, harmonious order will most likely be seen as a failure, while a diplomat bringing about a cease-fire or a separation of forces between two warring ethnic groups will be hailed as a real success although the second situation remains far more precarious than the first. In discussing conflict management successes and failures, judgments comparing what we might expect with what actually happened are necessarily involved. The larger the gap, the greater the relative success.

In practice, making such judgments is complicated: on the technical level it is difficult to evaluate the probabilities associated with outcomes that did not occur and compare them with those that did. Because such judgments are generally made after an outcome is known, hindsight frequently affects evaluations. In this regard, assessing conflict management (like much social science research) is much easier from the point of view of apparently self-evident outcomes than from the perspective of the unfolding events. But not all outcomes were most likely ones when viewed from the outset, and it is necessary to construct explanations in order to discern the ways initial expectations as well as proximate actions, nonactions, and other factors shape the outcomes.

The point is simple but critical: cases of successful conflict management cannot all be explained away as not-very-difficult conflicts from the start, while the failures are viewed as so formidable that no better outcome could have been imagined.[5] Complex and seemingly intractable conflicts are sometimes managed successfully, whereas situations that seem susceptible for easy resolution do not always prove to be so. The ways in which the actions of the parties in a dispute shape interests and interpretations make outcomes more or less successful.

A Land Dispute Among the Arusha: An Absolute Success

Many dispute outcomes which are both successful and predictable are handled through existing formal and informal conflict manage-

---

5. One way to evaluate the nonobvious relationship between expectations and outcomes in many disputes is experimental: Ask subjects to make judgments of the prospects for successful or unsuccessful conflict management for several conflict scenarios and for the likely outcomes. Then give them the outcomes which actually occur and ask the subjects to explain what they did and did not consider in their scenario in comparison with what actually took place. I would hypothesize that except for the more extreme situations, even expert subjects will not do terribly well. The series of public disputes in Susskind and Cruikshank (1988) provide a flavor of what this might entail; the reader first senses that a constructive solution is not obvious and then slowly learns how one was reached.

ment institutions (Nader and Todd 1978). Just because a dispute is handled successfully, however, does not mean that such an outcome is somehow automatic or the only one that could have occurred.

The Arusha live in a densely settled area of Northern Tanzania. The land dispute between two unrelated neighbors, taken from Gulliver (1979:234–252), shows how a conflict involving what first seems like a single issue often has another layer which is far more complex. Gulliver's account of the case, which I paraphrase below, also illustrates the extent to which constructive conflict management addresses both the interests and interpretations of participants.

Lashiloi and Kinyani both asserted their claims to two and a half acres lying between their farms following the death of Ngatio, who had been using the land as a tenant but never claimed it for himself. Although the two men had previously been on good terms, their relationship deteriorated following a series of incidents including violence against Lashiloi's son and accusations of the invocation of supernatural powers. Efforts to resolve their differences only produced anger and intransigence, so the two agreed to have a patrilineal moot hear the case.

The agenda grew much larger than the land question and soon included claims of trespass, damage to an irrigation gate, payment of an outstanding debt, interruption of irrigation water, illegal supernatural acts that required ritual purification, violence, compensation for violence, and accusations of slander. In the moot, the initial exchanges were quite acrimonious as each party, with the aid of supporters, asserted its claims. Little effective exchange occurred between the parties and there were frequent displays of anger including threats of independent action.

Eventually, with the help of their counselors, each side began making specific proposals to the other, a number of which were accepted, including one to divide the land between the two men. Members of each team not the most closely related to the two principals then pushed for a series of reciprocal concessions on the remaining issues. It turned out that while the land was important to both disputants, other emotional issues came to the fore as the conflict escalated. Lashiloi became very concerned about regular access to water for irrigation because the gate directing the supply was on Kinyani's share of the land; he also wanted purification from what he saw as Kinyani's supernatural offense against him. Kinyani, for his part, wanted recognition for the irrigation gate he had built, and acknowledgment that, given his right to control it, he would do so fairly. Only when these more dispositional concerns were addressed could a final solution be arranged which included a public ceremony in which Kinyani slaughtered a goat Lashiloi supplied, each fed the other symbolic pieces of meat, and both swore future friendship.

In the course of the moot, the interests and interpretations of each party changed. Each man had to decide which demands were the most important and which could be dropped or traded away. For example, when Lashiloi admitted that Kinyani had done no real harm to his son, Kinyani could admit that he had acted wrongly. At some level both must have known at the outset that some division of the disputed land was likely and acceptable. Each felt vulnerable on certain issues and only when the process began to offer reassurance could they become more flexible. Lashiloi could acknowledge Kinyani's right to operate the irrigation gate, as long as his supply of water was publicly assured. Kinyani was unwilling to admit that he had invoked an illicit supernatural curse against Lashiloi, who demanded purification. Both were willing to participate in a public ritual that marked an end to their dispute and relieved their fears.

This conflict could be seen as an "easy" one to manage.[6] Although relations between the parties had been effectively cut off, nothing either party had done was considered so heinous that restoration of ties was rejected by the other. Furthermore, both recognized a common set of norms; differences concerned matters of fact. Finally, both fully accepted the legitimacy of the settlement procedure.

Such a view, however, is too teleological, assuming that because a successful outcome was reached it was automatic. This denies the reality of the participants' intense feelings, their broken relationship, and the real animosity that had built up over time. This perspective also ignores the fact that in many communities, like the one Gulliver describes, neighbors like Kinyani and Lashiloi get into conflicts that cannot be settled, relationships are broken, and feuds develop. Successful conflict

6. Gulliver makes it clear that both parties accepted the outcome. He provides no data concerning the duration or changed nature of relationships between the parties, although his tone clearly suggests that the settlement proved to be viable and that Lashiloi and Kinyani's relationship moved from antagonism to one of good neighborliness.

management is not simply applying certain procedures to disputes that were bound to be settled; rather, it is a process that alters the situation so that constructive solutions become possible. By addressing and thereby modifying the interests and interpretations of disputants, constructive outcomes are produced. They do not happen by themselves.

The Camp David Accords: A Relative Success

If absolute conflict management successes can sometimes appear routine, few relative successes do. Here, because there is often little sense that conflict management efforts will get very far, even modest advances may receive attention. In some cases, such as the Arab-Israeli dispute, relative successes, such as the Camp David Accords, are a sign to some that a larger conflict is moving toward full settlement, when, in fact, it is only one, albeit significant, step on the way with no guarantee that others will follow.

Relative successes are important as reminders that the actions of disputants can make a difference in outcomes. They occur in difficult cases where most people believe little positive change will happen and serve as symbols of the efficacy of constructive conflict management. The hardest cases may also teach us some critical lessons about conflict management.

For more than fifty years the Arab-Israeli conflict has been one of the most intractable and violent in the world, involving five major wars and countless violent incidents. With the exception of the disengagement agreements U.S. Secretary of State Henry Kissinger negotiated after the 1973 war and the 1979 peace treaty between Egypt and Israel following the Camp David accords, there has been little constructive management of this conflict, and a good deal that was ineffective or destructive.[7]

The Kissinger agreements succeeded in disengaging the opposing armies. The Camp David agreement returned the Sinai lands Israel had captured from Egypt in 1967 in return for a peace treaty and institutionalization of normal relations between the two nations. As Rubin (1989)

7. Cohen (1990) offers an intriguing analysis of Israeli-Egyptian relations that emphasizes how cultural differences produced significant miscommunication between the parties which thwarted peacemaking and resulted in several military confrontations that might have been avoided if communication had been more effective.

suggests, in bitter disputes such as this one, the underlying conflict is not fully resolved, but particular differences can be settled, which in itself is no mean achievement.[8]

The Camp David accords, which provided the basis for the Egypt-Israel peace treaty signed six months later, grew out of two years of intense diplomatic activity, Egyptian President Anwar Sadat's dramatic visit to Israel in November 1977, and Israel's willingness to discuss a land-for-peace exchange with its largest neighbor. Upon taking office in January 1977, President Jimmy Carter made the attainment of a viable Middle East peace one of his highest foreign policy priorities (Quandt 1986). The countries in the region remained somewhat skeptical, but none rejected it entirely. After ten months of meetings, diplomatic exchanges, and public pronouncements, the Carter Administration came to an impasse, unable to get the parties to agree to the basis for talks, with the issue of Palestinian representation constituting the major (but not unique) stumbling block (Quandt 1986). At this point, Sadat, whose emissaries had already held secret meetings with top Israeli officials, launched his own peace initiative, traveling to Israel and addressing the Knesset, in large part to regain control over the agenda.

From that point it became increasingly clear that any breakthroughs on an overall peace would come from an Egyptian-Israeli agreement that might then draw the Jordanians and Syrians to the negotiating table. Although Carter had not originally favored such a strategy, he came to see it as the only one open to him, also recognizing that Egypt and Israel were quite content to talk without Syria, Jordan, or a Palestinian delegation. Carter hoped to obtain an Israeli withdrawal from the Sinai and agreement on a formula for peace which could be applied to the other occupied territories. When progress toward an agreement floundered, however, Carter decided to invite Sadat, Israeli Prime Minister Begin, and their top advisors to Camp David, where he hoped that once the two leaders could establish a personal relationship, the barriers to peace would tumble.

It was not so simple. The detailed accounts from Camp David

8. Rothman (written personal communication 1992) suggests that a crucial question involves the role of third parties. Although they are needed—Cohen (1990) sees them as welcome by both cultures—there is great concern with losing control over the process and fear that outsiders will impose solutions on the parties of the region. Third-party arrogance is often spoken of in the Middle East.

show that the intense hostility and distrust between the parties only partially gave way to the empathy and mutual concern that some textbook accounts of negotiation see as a prerequisite to progress (Carter 1982; Quandt 1986). In fact, after the third day of the thirteen-day talks, Begin and Sadat never met face-to-face because of their intense dislike of each other.[9] Carter then moved to a common-script strategy in which he carried a single document, often on his bicycle, to Sadat and Begin and each party, in turn, made suggestions until both were in agreement (Raiffa 1982). However, the move toward agreement was not smooth. Rather, the alternation between antagonism and cooperation that Gulliver (1979) describes as taking place at all phases of negotiations was evident. Right up until the end of the sessions it remained unclear to Carter whether success or failure would be the final result. At a number of critical junctures, Quandt (1986) says that Carter pressured Begin for concessions but without success; he then wound up getting Sadat, who was under greater pressure to reach an agreement, to make key concessions.

Quandt's account (1986) suggests that three crucial differences in the prioritizing of interests made the agreement possible: Israeli willingness to trade the Sinai for peace with Egypt in order to gain military disengagement, which was consistent with Begin's vision of an Israel which included the West Bank (Quandt 1986); Egyptian willingness to make a peace with Israel that was not tied to a broader resolution of the Palestinian issue in order to secure the return of the Sinai, to establish a new relationship with the United States, and to focus resources on internal development; and American political realities, meaning Carter's need for a foreign policy success and his willingness to settle for a much less comprehensive peace than he first hoped to achieve.[10] These different interests brought each party to the point where agreement was more

9. While communication between Sadat and Begin was not cordial, many sources report that the rapport between the Egyptian president and Israel's defense minister, Ezer Weizman, was very cordial and their conversations were characterized by effective, open exchange.

10. Although it is not a central concern in my analysis, third-party interests often play an important role in dispute management. When the third party is as powerful as the United States in this case, the "incentives" it may offer the disputants can be significant. Princen (1992) suggests that the interests of third parties and the resources they control can also limit their effectiveness as mediators; in this case Sadat and Begin were more interested in appealing to Carter than in dealing with each other.

attractive than nonagreement and where there was sufficient belief that the other side was likely to adhere to the agreement (partially brokered by U.S. guarantees).

The final agreement involved both general and specific shifts in each party's interests. Egypt and Sadat first thought they could broker a general peace in the region but came to accept the return of the entire Sinai, including the removal of all Israeli bases and settlements, and the establishment of a new relationship with the United States as a significant gain. Israel and Begin moved cautiously to exchange land for peace with Egypt in order to gain Arab recognition and, in effect, a more secure hold over the other occupied territories. What is clear from Quandt's account is how strong the Israeli fears were that returning the Sinai would increase its vulnerability; as a consequence, Begin raised a large number of issues which were used to bargain strategically but were also requests for reassurance. The United States and Carter, according to Quandt, were least clear about what they wanted to happen and what their interests were. As a result Carter had some trouble in adopting and pursuing a clear strategy. In the end, Quandt (1986) says domestic political concerns and pressures, which Carter never wanted to be important, came to play a significant role in many short-term decisions.

Several changes in interpretations of the situation in the 1977–1979 period can be identified, although they are harder to spell out in detail given the available data. Egypt and Sadat initially held negative, hostile images of Israel, overvalued their own capacity for action, denigrated that of the Israelis, and saw little chance for cooperation (Stein 1985a, 1985b). Following the 1973 war, Sadat developed a vision of peace in the region that would both restore Egypt's leadership of the Arab world and release vital resources needed for development. Between the time of his trip to Jerusalem and the signing of the peace treaty, he had to abandon this grandiose scheme, but he still found much that was appealing in the notion of the return of all captured Egyptian land and a new relationship with the United States. How Sadat and those around him developed and progressed through these alternative images is not completely clear. If data were available, however, we should be able to trace the reorganization of dispositions into new interpretations of the situation and of the parties involved.[11]

11. These data could be obtained from in-depth interviews or from public statements by political leaders. The data might not tell us all we wanted to know

Israeli leaders for years had said they would always return land in exchange for peace with the Arabs, but unfortunately for Sadat and Carter's view of a comprehensive peace, the most vocal of these were Israeli Labor politicians who lost power for the first time in 1977. Israeli fears were significant. The legacy of the Holocaust and the intense Arab-Israeli conflict led to a strong sense of isolation, a siege mentality, and a view that only military strength could produce security—what some have called the Masada complex (Bar-Tal 1986, 1990). Any retreat from military positions raised deep anxieties. One of the charges Begin had to face in making peace with Egypt was that the peace treaty was some kind of trick and that Israel was giving up land and military bases for a worth-less piece of paper. Yet Sadat's trip to Israel and the prospect of peace with its largest neighbor was appealing in terms of Israel's desire for security and international acceptance. Quandt suggests that in the end the most powerful image for Begin was that of the larger, Biblically inspired Israel which was more not less likely once peace was made with Egypt. Changes in interpretations thus made it possible for the parties to address differences of interest. Without this change, sparked by Carter's initiatives and Sadat's journey to Jerusalem, it is hard to see how Egypt and Israel would have moved toward military disengagement and diplomatic recognition.

The Camp David accords, which satisfied none of the principals at the time, were widely criticized in the Arab world for ignoring the interests of the Palestinians. Carter had first hoped to negotiate a com-prehensive peace treaty involving Jordan and Syria, and even when that was not possible he tried to make sure that the Palestinian issue was addressed. Sadat, who had first hoped that his dramatic visit to Israel in 1977 would provide the basis for a broad-based peace, settled for the return of all Egyptian lands, removal of Israeli settlements, and military disengagement permitting vital resources to be devoted to economic needs. Begin exchanged land for peace on the Egyptian front but faced a certain amount of opposition within his own party and was somewhat uneasy about Egypt's long-term commitment to the agreement.[12]

---

about deeply held dispositions but could reveal the interpretations derived from them.

12. Quandt (1986) suggests that of the three parties, Israel was clearest

Yet considering the intensity of the Arab-Israeli conflict in terms of the three criteria for successful conflict management suggested above, the Camp David Accords and the peace treaty that grew out of it represent an important relative success. Israel and Egypt have stuck to it (with some acrimonious verbal exchanges), exchanging ambassadors, some tourists, and a modest amount of trade, even though governments have changed in each nation. The relationship between Egypt and Israel is often strained, but it is strikingly different than the armed confrontation that characterized the previous three decades. In addition, as a direct consequence of the agreements, Egypt's relationship to the United States is far friendlier than it had been.

Conclusion

During successful conflict management processes, the interests and interpretations of the parties to a dispute change in important ways. Interests are transformed from general grievances to specific demands which can be acted upon, and disputants become clearer about which of their interests are most vital. Similarly, although core psychocultural dispositions rarely undergo fundamental change, the conflict management process can work toward rearranging existing ones, modifying interpretations growing out of them, and substituting for metaphors associated with ongoing mistrust and hostility other culturally appropriate ones more conducive to integrative outcomes. Such changes in interpretations and interests clearly occurred in the successes examined here.

The mechanism that drives this process forward is not always obvious (Gulliver 1979:179). It is too easy to assign a key role to single acts, such as Sadat's November 1977 trip to Israel; this was certainly important in altering some basic perceptions, but it took another year and a half before Egypt and Israel signed a peace treaty. More recently there has been rapid progress toward change in South Africa following President F. W. De Klerk's decision to free African National Congress

---

about its goals and achieved them most clearly in the agreement. While there were Israeli concessions on key points, especially involving settlements in the Sinai, Quandt says that Israel was quite content to sign a disengagement on the Egyptian front and make no concessions on the Palestinian issue.

leader Nelson Mandela and end the ban of the ANC. In this case there was clearly a long period of preparation for change and a shorter one of intense contact between members of the different communities which made rapid movement for change possible once the dramatic public step was taken. Central here are disputants' views of their alternatives, their perceptions of the situation, and political pressures to which they are responding. Exactly how these combine, however, still needs to be investigated.[13] One way to explore this question is by examining several cases of conflict management failure, the task I take up in the next chapter.

13. At this writing, the June 1992 elections in Israel led to a change in government and a shift in its intentions on how to proceed with the U.S.-initiated peace process. In its first few weeks a number of steps signaled a shift in intentions. Whether these will lead to a successful termination of the undeclared state of war with all its neighbors except Egypt remains to be seen. What is clear, however, is that the widespread, often informal, contacts between Israelis and Arabs over the past ten to fifteen years should improve dealings among all the parties.

7

Failed Conflict Management

Conflict management failures occur for a variety of reasons. Sometimes one party employs contentious self-help tactics against an opponent, producing retaliation. In other cases, the disputants talk to each other or to third parties, but progress toward a settlement stalls before an agreement is reached, either for lack of an arena, absence of agreement on an agenda, inability to find a zone of agreement on one or more issues, or failure to put together a package acceptable to all parties. Failures also grow out of what first seem to be at least partial successes. The parties go through all of the phases of conflict management Gulliver (1979) identifies and an agreement is implemented, but the solution fails to last because it does not address critical sources of the conflict. Like the Treaty of Versailles following World War I, poor agreements contain the seeds of their own downfall.

Underlying the many forms that conflict management failures take is a common pattern: the neglect of important interests and interpretations of the disputants. The three cases of failures discussed in this chapter share this element, although they come from different settings, have different histories, and are different kinds of conflict. The conflict between MOVE and the city of Philadelphia is one where an overdependence on self-help and third-party coercion with almost no joint problem solving proved to be disastrous. The return to warfare in highland New Guinea following twenty or more years of colonial peace shows some of the limitations to imposed solutions which fail to address important roots of conflict. In Northern Ireland, the site of a protracted ethnic conflict, a number of conflict management steps have been taken but none so far has proved successful. The goal of this chapter is to

136

explore these three cases in order to draw some lessons about conflict management failure.

The most important hypothesis to be examined is that in intense conflicts such as those examined here, interests can rarely be addressed effectively because the adversaries' interpretations of the situation are so antagonistic. For constructive conflict management to occur, disputants' hostile interpretations of each other must be altered, for only at that point can the real differences in interests be explored. In the conflict management failures examined here, serious efforts to address the opponents' deep-seated fears are all too infrequent, in great part because the parties see them as part of the "reality" of the situation, not as something which can be changed. The next chapter explores ways in which mutually antagonistic interpretations can be explicitly addressed, even in bitter, long-standing conflicts.

MOVE versus the City of Philadelphia

The conflict between MOVE, a mainly black back-to-nature group, and the city of Philadelphia is a dramatic example of the failure of all three dispute resolution strategies.[1] Self-help, joint problem solving, and third-party decision making all were used, for the most part unsuccessfully, in the course of the decade-long dispute that involved two armed confrontations resulting in deaths of twelve people (including five children), a fire that destroyed 61 homes and damaged many others, and severe psychological wounds not easy to calculate. It is a story of how a bitter but localized conflict over values and lifestyle ends with a city government headed by a liberal black mayor deciding to drop a bomb in a densely populated black middle-class neighborhood, starting a fire that the authorities let burn for over an hour.

---

1. The most important sources for information on MOVE's conflict with Philadelphia are the hearings of the Philadelphia Special Investigating Commission. The full transcripts are available at the Urban Archives Center at Temple University. Also see Anderson and Hevenor (1987), Assefa and Wahrhaftig (1990), Nagel (1991), and Wagner-Pacifici (1993).

Brief History

MOVE formed in Powelton Village, an integrated section of west Philadelphia, in the early to mid-1970s around the figure of John Africa (all members of the group took Africa as their last name). Its core philosophy stressed living naturally and respecting all living creatures. MOVE opposed using any machinery, consuming any processed foods, heating homes, or using soap; garbage was disposed of in the backyard to be recycled "naturally," where it attracted mice, rats, and other vermin. MOVE members used outhouses, had large numbers of dogs and cats, and refused to send their children to school.

During MOVE's early years, Frank Rizzo, the former police commissioner—best known for his vituperative denunciation of the rights of gays, hippies, women, and others who dared advocate cultural difference—was mayor. Soon after MOVE established its headquarters in a house in Powelton Village, lifestyle conflicts arose with neighbors and there were several confrontations with the police. MOVE used these confrontations and resulting court appearances to show disdain for the system, to spread the teachings of John Africa, and to demand the release of jailed members (Assefa and Wahrhaftig 1990). Incidents with the city escalated, and in July 1976 MOVE built an eight-foot wall to keep out the city and its inspectors. This was followed by a ten-month siege, an agreement between the city and MOVE in May 1978 (which then broke down), and an August 1978 shoot-out that left one police officer dead and several police officers and firefighters wounded. Police brutality against MOVE members occurred during the confrontation and nine MOVE members were arrested and later convicted of third-degree murder; three police officers, however, were acquitted on the charges of beating Delbert Africa.

In the early 1980s, a core of MOVE members not in prison relocated to a row house on Osage Avenue in a black middle-class area in west Philadelphia. Over the next few years tensions with the neighbors escalated for many of the same reasons they had in Powelton. In addition, MOVE members set up loudspeakers through which they harangued residents day and night; they believed that only through confrontation would they achieve their diverse goals, particularly the release of their jailed members. There were verbal exchanges with neighbors, threats to city and federal officials, and high tension resulting from the cult's lifestyle and disruption of normal life in the area. The other Osage residents sought help, but little more than sympathy was forthcoming from the city after Wilson Goode's election as the first black mayor in 1983.[2] City departments viewed MOVE as a police matter, and indeed, the city had no interest in getting a water or gas meter reader shot. The mayor's office did not want to provoke a violent confrontation over a sanitation violation nor to appear "soft" on MOVE (Nagel 1991). It did nothing at all: it took no unilateral action, did not seek third-party help in problem solving, nor did it turn to the courts for a judgment.

By late 1984 MOVE began to fortify its house and construct a "bunker" on its roof. Although the Department of Licenses and Inspections noted these changes, like the other civilian departments it took no action on what it considered a "police matter." By winter the neighbors, increasingly upset, formed a group, "The United Residents of Osage Avenue." Having gotten little action from the city, they appealed to the Republican governor of Pennsylvania, Richard Thornburgh, for aid, held a press conference giving lurid details about the stresses of living on the same block with MOVE, and demanded action.

Early in May 1985 there were reports that MOVE was hoisting gasoline stockpiles onto its roof. The mayor, finally feeling the neighborhood pressure, concluded, as did the police department, that an armed conflict involving MOVE was increasingly probable. Goode asked the district attorney, Ed Rendell, to reexamine the legal justification for the city taking action against the residents of the house, and on May 7 told Police Commissioner Gregory Sambor to prepare a tactical plan. By May 11 a court approved search and arrest warrants. The next day (Mother's Day) the police evacuated the neighborhood but never picked up the MOVE children, as had been ordered, despite the fact that the children left the house for part of the day for their daily exercise. Early the following morning the armed conflict began. When the MOVE members failed to surrender in fifteen minutes, the fire department trained high-power fire hoses on the bunker in an effort to dislodge it, and the police fired tear gas and smoke projectiles to provide cover for police teams trying to enter the houses on either side to teargas the MOVE house.

In the next few hours the police fired over ten thousand rounds of

2. The city offered counseling for the children of Osage Avenue who were encountering severe stress. Otherwise, the mayor and other city officials simply told the residents that nothing could be done at present and that they should be patient.

ammunition and had to order more. Their powerful arsenal included 50mm guns, Uzi submachine guns, and antitank weapons. At some point during the late morning or early afternoon, most of the front of the first floor was blown off the MOVE house, but none of the top police commanders was apparently ever informed. The police had no backup plan, for they never considered the possibility that their assault would be unsuccessful. In the midafternoon the police commissioner, in the presence of the city managing director, retired general Leo Brooks, instructed the head of the bomb disposal unit to put together an explosive device to be dropped from a state police helicopter onto the roof in the hope of dislodging the bunker. At about the same time a press helicopter took pictures of the MOVE house's roof which showed at least two cans clearly marked gasoline.

The bomb was to be made of an explosive used in mining which is considered "nonincendiary," but it also included a significant amount of the military explosive C-4. Experts later testifying before the Special Investigating Commission pointed out that the bomb failed to land where it was intended, that it never should have combined the two explosives used, and never should have been dropped from the air. Instead of damaging the bunker, the bomb started a small fire among the debris on the roof and ignited one of the gasoline cans. Just before 6 p.m., a half hour after the bomb was dropped, the mayor and then the city managing director ordered the fire, which was still quite small, put out. The police commissioner in charge of the operation did nothing, saying later that he assumed that the fire commissioner who had been in the room with him also heard the order. However, a few minutes later the police and fire commissioners decided together to let the fire burn the bunker before trying to put it out. In a short time the bunker, in flames, collapsed, starting a fire that was now out of control, especially given the unfeasibility of conventional firefighting methods due to fear that fire fighters would be shot. At about 7:30 p.m. two MOVE members, a child and a woman, escaped and were taken to safety. The commission the mayor appointed to investigate the conflict concluded (despite denials by the police) that at least one other member tried to flee but was driven back to the burning house by police gunfire. During the televised hearings, Father Paul Washington, a black minister, asked one of the police officers on the scene how he could explain why a person would return to a burning house unless he was being shot at. The officer replied, "Father, I wish I could tell you. But those weren't people. They were MOVE members."

Flawed Conflict Management

Both MOVE and the city of Philadelphia relied primarily on self-help tactics in the conflict.[3] MOVE used deliberate noncompliance with a number of city regulations and widely accepted social norms. They engaged unilateral actions in harassing local residents and city workers, creating scenes during their court appearances, and demanding the release of their imprisoned members. Finally, they threatened the use of force (far more than they used it) variously to draw attention to their concerns and to pressure the neighbors and city. The city used unilateral force, first in the siege and confrontation in Powelton, and later in the attack on the Osage house.

The almost exclusive reliance on and failure of self-help strategies can be explained in several ways. The inequality between the two sides and the early confrontations with the city convinced MOVE that the system was thoroughly corrupt and intent on destroying them, leaving self-help as the only path. The city increasingly used force because it came to believe that MOVE members were incapable of reason and because of the city's anger at them first for their blatant rejection of social conventions and then for the death and injuries from the August 1978 shoot-out. Finally, the reliance on self-help arose from each side's limited conception of its own interests and those (often inaccurately perceived) of the other side. Given each party's goals, self-help proved to be unsuccessful, even in the case of the far more powerful city, which was constrained politically and in other ways.

Joint problem solving failed to resolve the conflict in great part because it was not used in a significant manner. Although there was no doubt that MOVE was difficult to negotiate with, Assefa and Wahrhaftig (1990) argue that viable agreements with MOVE were possible and that in both the 1978 and 1985 crises the potential for negotiated agreements

3. In addition to the conflict between MOVE and the city, there was the dispute between the Osage neighbors (and earlier with the Powelton neighbors) and both MOVE and the city, differences between the mayor and police, and the backdrop of racial tension in the city. In a more complete recounting of the MOVE crisis, each of these elements would receive attention (see Assefa and Wahrhaftig 1990). Katherine Conner (personal communication, 1990) points out that the fact that the city became a major actor in the conflict, rather than a third party assisting other disputants, is itself an important indicator of conflict management failure.

was not fully exploited. They note that MOVE reached an agreement with the Powelton neighbors over the disposal of garbage, and that with the help of several dedicated third parties MOVE resolved a dispute with the city over the evacuation of the house in 1978. The agreement broke down, Assefa and Wahrhaftig argue, not because MOVE members were irrational but because no one took responsibility for monitoring the agreement and clarifying key ambiguous points in it. By the time of the 1985 crisis, joint problem solving was all but abandoned as the city assumed that MOVE was "too crazy" and defined the problem as a "police matter." Differences in power, mutually hostile images, and an absence of trust all worked against development of a climate where joint problem solving would have been possible. The city never took seriously MOVE's claims concerning their right to their alternative lifestyle or that its imprisoned members were political prisoners, whereas MOVE never tried to understand the city or neighbors' point that its lifestyle was highly problematic in a city of two million people. As a result, as the crisis progressed the two sides communicated less and less. Neither believed that fruitful exchange was possible, so that opportunities were never pursued and were sometimes discouraged.[4]

The city used third-party decision making—the use of court rulings against MOVE members—to punish MOVE members and contribute to the further escalation of tensions. MOVE rejected the legitimacy of the legal process and continued to view the incarceration of its members entirely in political terms. Each new arrest and conviction led to increased demands for the release of MOVE members.

Lessons

The climate of distrust between the city and MOVE was so strong that serious conflict management efforts never got off the ground in the 1983–84 period. Nagel's (1991) compelling hypothesis is that given the mayor's extreme degree of defensive avoidance, the search for alternatives was half-hearted and no effort was expended on understanding the deep fears and concerns of MOVE or considering how they could have been addressed. Avoidance meant that joint problem solving, even with

4. Wagner-Pacifici (1993) argues that the city's construction of MOVE as a violent terrorist group then provided a rationale for its own use of uncontrolled violence.

third-party assistance, never progressed because each side assumed that the other would respond only to power-oriented moves. This became a self-fulfilling prophecy as each side continued to see the previous unilateral move of the other as confirming its own assumptions that joint decision making would not work. The MOVE hearings provide evidence that these same assumptions and fears of action were widespread among other top decision makers as well.

Both the police (and the city officials in general) and MOVE continually saw the other side as highly threatening. Like many stereotypes, of course, these images had a kernel of truth to them. Untempered by any other information or by personal contacts, each party's view of the other was confirmed and even reinforced by a number of incidents. The one-dimensional images provoked equally simplistic actions as both the police and MOVE accepted the inevitability of an armed confrontation which neither side took steps to avoid. Measures one side saw as defensive were viewed as offensive threats by the other. Fear dominated the mutually escalatory events and there was no effort to conceptualize other action strategies, for there was no sense that the other side would use anything except force.

The key to understanding the reluctance to use joint problem solving lies in the interpretations of the situation which dominated each party's thinking. MOVE assumed that the city was out to destroy it and that the officials would only consider the release of MOVE prisoners if sufficiently credible threats were made. Of course intimidation only reinforced the already strong view on the part of the city that MOVE members were irrational and that therefore the only effective way to deal with them was through the use of force. In addition, the anger that city officials, especially the police and fire departments, had toward MOVE after 1978 further colored their perceptions and affected their decision-making ability. The expectations on the part of the police commissioner and others that a violent confrontation was inevitable meant that nonviolent alternatives were never seriously considered.[5] Not only did the police view the confrontation in military terms, which is understandable though not excusable, but they also overestimated their own capacity to act efficiently and effectively. Police planners consistently

5. During the MOVE Special Investigating Commission hearings, Police Commissioner Gregory Sambor said he prayed an armed confrontation would not happen, but he never took any concrete steps to see that it did not.

misjudged what could be accomplished, how the other side would respond, and what subsequent steps to take.[6]

The interests of MOVE members, their neighbors, elected city officials, and the police were certainly highly diverse. But Assefa and Wahrhaftig's charge that there were insufficient efforts to bridge those differences is important. Because neither side could think of an outcome aside from the use of force, no other conflict management strategies were taken seriously. Assefa and Wahrhaftig (1990) are persuaded that skilled third parties could have helped both sides develop solutions that would have been better than what happened. Given the outcome, it is hard not to agree.[7]

The Return to Warfare in Highland New Guinea
Brief History

Warfare was a central feature of highland New Guinea societies in the precolonial period—until the 1950s (Berndt 1964; Brown 1982; Koch 1974; Meggitt 1977). Berndt observes, "In nearly all recorded cases, warfare was an accepted feature of ordinary social living; and the time spent in actual fighting and in direct preparation for it, alone, must have been considerable" (1964:183). Neighboring clans and tribes regularly fought one another, but also engaged in trade, ceremonial exchange, and intermarriage (Brown 1982).

Australian colonization of the region started in the 1930s and by the late 1950s and early 1960s, pacification of much of the highland

6. The pressure the conflict placed on Mayor Goode may have led him to avoid dealing with it for as long as possible. Nagel (1991) argues persuasively that the stress resulted in defensive avoidance and severely impaired his decision-making ability. For example, this supposedly hands-on leader heard only the barest outlines of the police department's plans and he asked no questions about it whatsoever. In addition, Goode, generally known for his attention to detail, never asked for a second opinion or a critique of the plan from anyone, including his managing director, Leo Brooks, a former Army general.

7. In June 1992 Ramona Africa, the only adult survivor of the fire, was released from prison. She would not discuss details of the confrontation publicly and continued to demand the release of MOVE members still in prison. She held a publicized meeting with newly elected Mayor Ed Rendell (who had been district attorney in 1985), after which it was suggested that the new city administration wanted a new, less confrontational relationship with MOVE.

region was complete. Observers remarked at the speedy and effective replacement of violent self-help tactics with a system of law and order and the widespread changes this produced in daily life. Fighting seemed to be a thing of the past.

In effect the situation of the Central Enga by 1960 appeared to express a colonial success story—a portrait of a people whose ready acceptance of Western values, attitudes, and technology was somehow solving a social problem, while at the same time they were being prepared for a modest future as pacific peasants secure under the aegis of British justice (Meggitt 1977:155).

But this did not turn out to be the case, for within the next decade, as the Australians prepared to grant self-rule to Papua New Guinea, intergroup violence returned to the highlands. There was a rise in tension everywhere, administrators were no longer able to resolve disputes peacefully, and large group battles, not unlike the precolonial fighting, took place throughout the region.[8] Finally, the newly independent government declared a state of emergency in the region.

Why the colonial peace of the region did not hold is a conflict management failure many have sought to explain (Brown 1982; Gordon 1983; Gordon and Meggitt 1984; Meggitt 1977; Sillitoe 1977, 1978; Strathern 1974, 1977). Most of the explanations are structural in nature, emphasizing resource scarcity and government ineffectiveness, conditions which surely exist. Only in a few cases are there hints concerning psychocultural factors which may explain why the use of dispute management strategies other than violent self-help are problematic in this situation.

Yet psychocultural factors are crucial to understand the strong support for self-help and discouragement of other forms of conflict management in highland New Guinea. Three key dispositional elements— competitiveness, fearfulness, and uncertainty—explain how the people of the highlands interpret their daily worlds. Each of these dispositions increases dependence on the local group as the source of psychological and social identity. The fusion of group and individual identities in the system of homicide compensation described below encourages collec-

8. The parallel with the former USSR and the states of eastern Europe in the post-1989 period is too tempting not to mention, but it is not my focus here.

tive group action and discourages any actions that limit group autonomy. Defending the group, from this perspective, is a collective defensive maneuver in a world with little security, and one which increases in intensity as external resource pressures rise.

Two core principles are central to understanding social and political life in most highland New Guinea societies. The first is the primacy of the patriclan, a group of related males generally living on clan lands and ready to take collective action in its name (Berndt 1964). Although clans can come together as phratries or tribes, the patriclan is effectively the highest unit of political organization. Second, accumulation and distribution of wealth through complex interpersonal networks beyond the clan provide a vehicle for important ceremonial exchanges and ways for individuals to obtain leadership and status. In both political and economic relations, the social order is subject to manipulation and rapid change. These layered systems come together in such a way that Brown (1982) says it is important to see clans and tribes as local units in a larger regional system of interdependence, not as fully autonomous units. Groups that fight each other also intermarry and engage in competitive exchanges.

Conflict Management Strategies

Highland New Guinea societies are easily classified as "self-help" societies (Gordon 1983:206) because of the frequent unilateral use of force particularly in the pursuit of land and pigs, and the absence of third parties to help end disputes (Koch 1974). The use of the term "self-help" with reference to New Guinea needs clarification, however. Individuals do not act alone but rather as clan members or with the clan in collective action against other clans. In fact, individuals cannot act alone even if they want to because of the cultural notions of collective liability and homicide compensation.

When a man of one clan is killed by a member of another, the first clan will be approached for compensation. It makes no difference whether the death was accidental or intentional, willed or unwilled. The notion of compensation extends to deaths of allies in battle. If in a conflict between two clans, they recruit other clans as allies, any deaths to members of the allied clans are the responsibility of the clan that recruited them, as "owners of the battle." The concept of collective liability means that it is not the responsibility of the individual(s) who caused the deaths to make the compensation payment, but that of their clan; retaliation for nonpayment, likewise, can be exacted against any member of a clan, not just the individual who was involved in the original act.

Rapid expansion of conflicts often occurs as a result. An event involving two people (such as an auto accident or a drunken fight, both of which have been common precipitating incidents in recent years), quickly turns into a conflict involving two clans. Not only do the number of people involved rise rapidly, but a redefinition of issues from the specific to the general occurs at the same time. Individuals who in other contexts may be hesitant to take unilateral action and are encouraged to engage in joint problem solving find themselves in just the opposite situation here, where groups vigorously pursue claims against each other and where social support is easy to obtain.

In New Guinea, clans use joint problem solving in terminating fighting and in organizing the important *moka* or *Te* ceremonial economic exchanges; without mutual agreements between individuals and groups these exchanges cannot occur. The elaborate negotiation between the "Big Men" (informal leaders who achieve prominence due to their wealth and personal influence) of enemy and allied clans concerning peacemaking and homicide compensations which precedes the end to overt fighting, as described in chapter 6 (Meggitt 1977:113–143) does not always effectively limit future escalation. In peacemaking efforts, negotiating compensation is often much easier than obtaining the payment, however. For both economic and strategic reasons, groups often wait years to fulfill agreements negotiated earlier. The absence of any binding third party means that self-help remains the surest method for defending interests (Koch 1974), and negotiated agreements last only as long as they continue to meet the interests of the parties.

Conflict Management and Colonial Rule

Only a few years after the imposition of colonial rule, the violent clan self-help system gave way to a more peaceful system of conflict management. Interestingly, the most obvious explanation for this rapid change, the use of superior force, does not figure prominently in most efforts to account for the rapid installation of the *pax australiana* in the region.[9] For one thing there were never a large number of colonial officers in the area, although their constant presence did seem to make a difference (Meggitt 1977:153). Local leaders seemed to accept the new arrangements. Meggitt says what mattered most were the newly established, readily available administrative courts

which [the Mae Enga] viewed as a mode of intergroup fighting that could be pursued without weapons . . . litigation appeared to be a speedy and effective way of achieving their individual and clan aims, one that was economical of time, energy, and blood, and that would permit them to get on with their gardening and exchanges without the annoying and painful interruptions posed by military mobilization, the evacuation of noncombatants and pigs, the rebuilding of burned houses and the replanting of ruined gardens. (1977:153)

Gordon (1983) describes the features of the colonial conflict management process to explain its effectiveness. After first trying to stamp out the Te exchange system, the *kiap* (colonial field administrators) used it to identify Big Men who were appointed to the lowest positions in the colonial administration, *bosbois* and *tultuls*, responsible for reporting attitudes and developments to the kiaps and giving administrative orders to the people.

Peace was achieved by organizing matters in such a way that these petty officials would watch one another, and be afraid of taking the lead in acting against the kiap and other citizens . . . Often all the kiap had to do was collect the names of warring groups or the wrongdoers from these officials and then issue summonses, an arrangement which suited both parties. (Gordon 1983:210)

Gordon also points out that the kiaps' chief concern was land disputes, which he says they attended to rather than settled, often by referring the matter to the local dignitaries who would hold an unofficial court or moot on the matter (1983:210–211), sometimes after a hearing

9. Brown's discussion of pacification among the Simbu is perhaps an exception. She describes the use of force by the colonial administration and Simbu fears of death and jailing and concludes that "pacification was a temporary effect in which fighting was suppressed by the colonial administration" (1982:540). I have no way of knowing whether the variations reflect differences in the experiences across the region, group reactions to the same behaviors, or interpretations among the authors.

in the government court. Although the fear of retribution if groups tried to settle matters with violence was present, Gordon argues that the open-ended nature of the informal hearings made them popular, effective, and especially consistent with a worldview that emphasizes the manipulability of the social order. Cases which could not be resolved could be referred to the administrative courts, but the unofficial courts were effective because of the strong cooperation between the kiap and local magistrates. Peace during the colonial period was the result of employing a structural strategy that fit neatly with the preexisting beliefs about action of groups in the region.[10]

There were also economic incentives for abandoning regular warfare. Gordon (1983:209) says that the importance of the provision of valued trade goods should not be underestimated. Many of these goods then entered into expanded elaborate ceremonial economic exchanges (Berndt 1964:185; Brown 1982:535; Strathern 1974), which served as an alternative to competitive aggression expressed through warfare. Strathern (1974) argues that the colonial peace redirected this competition in nonviolent directions.

The Return to Violence

Since the late 1960s and early 1970s there has been a clear rise in tension in the highlands and a return to intergroup violence, caused mainly by disputes over land.[11] Once again self-help is considered the only sure way for a clan to protect its interests, joint problem solving is viewed as ineffective, and third-party decision making seems either uncertain or subject to political manipulation (Gordon and Meggitt 1984).

Meggitt (1977) provides data on intergroup fighting in the postcolonial period that reveals a pattern very much like the precolonial one. Clans organize and direct large-scale fighting with land an even

10. Good data on dispositions and perceptions throughout this period are still needed to evaluate this psychocultural hypothesis effectively.

11. Although land is identified by Meggitt (1977) as the most basic cause of warfare in both the pre- and post-colonial periods, Brown warns against single causal explanations as "not always exclusive, necessary, or sufficient" (1982:528), which is similar to the argument I make in my study of cross-cultural conflict (Ross 1986b, 1993). Sillitoe (1977) also argues that land shortage is not an adequate explanation for warfare everywhere in New Guinea.

more important motive for fighting than in the past (1977:177). Strathern (1974) suggests that the expanded scale of postcolonial New Guinea warfare makes disputes more difficult to settle today. He describes two intergroup disputes (both of which began with traffic accidents) that resist settlement because there is no easy way to arrange dispute management between large-scale groups once tensions have hardened. Direct negotiations between leaders or people linked in other ways become impossible and the danger of physical conflict, rather than ritualized conflict through economic exchanges, becomes greater. Strathern sees creating and maintaining group boundaries as a prominent feature of contemporary fighting. Outside mediators have not been able to arrange mutually satisfactory solutions.

There is little disagreement that there has been renewed use of violent self-help; exactly why this has come about, however, is subject to widely different explanations. Meggitt (1977) argues that severe population pressure and the failures of new administrative procedures for management of land disputes are most responsible for the return to violent self-help.[12] Gordon (1983), while agreeing that land is the source of the problem, emphasizes the decline of joint problem solving associated with the colonial administrative officials as mediators and its replacement by a far more formal and ineffective form of third-party decision making. Podolefsky (1984) proposes a cultural materialist explanation, stressing a decline in intergroup trade and intergroup marriage which removed inhibitions on intertribal fighting. Strathern (1974) emphasizes the increasing scale of New Guinea society, where the new political arrangements no longer allow the face-to-face ceremonial exchanges to limit polarization and hostility. Sillitoe (1978) points to the political ambitions of Big Men seeking followers and control. All more or less agree that neither the government nor any other third party is very effective.

These elements seem plausible, yet it also is true that these same conditions of land scarcity, changing size, political ambitions, and al-

12. For example, he describes the unsuccessful efforts of demarcation committees which succeeded neither as informal arbiters nor as adjudicators in effectively deciding upon clan boundaries (Meggitt 1977:165–167). Of course the Enga view that boundaries should be regularly subject to change as a function of group power and needs did not encourage honesty or compromise in front of a group seeking to set the borders once and for all.

tered trade and marriage patterns are found elsewhere in the world without necessarily producing the same high level of violence.[13] The analysis of conflict to this point encourages us to consider psychocultural forces in order to complement these explanations and to wonder why they receive so little attention in the accounts of recent violence in New Guinea.[14]

An explanation for the return to violence including psychocultural factors would describe the interpretations of the world and the dispositions underlying them which make violent self-help actions frequent and diminish the likelihood of joint problem solving or third-party decision making. Socialization among the Mae Enga and other groups in the region produces psychocultural dispositions which encourage the use of violence (Ross 1993: chapter 6). Male gender-identity insecurity is high while the affection and warmth needed to develop social trust are lacking, and aggressive role models are plentiful. Object attachments are uncertain; boys develop ties to their mothers, but these must be severed for the boy to reach culturally defined manhood, a process filled with fear as well as ritualized and real aggression.[15]

Both Brown (1982) and Gordon (1983) discuss psychocultural dispositions likely to grow out of such a pattern affecting worldviews and shaping collective action. Brown emphasizes that competition and rivalry are dominant cultural themes found in both warfare and economic activity.[16] Pacification did not change this pattern: "The Simbu still hold a coercive theory of society. Intergroup rivalry and hostility do

13. Podolefsky's (1984) argument seems to me the least satisfactory. For one thing it does not account for colonial peace, nor are the data he presents anywhere near adequate to support his argument. He offers the simple correlation between a decline in intergroup trade (which he presents only as a qualitative finding) and intertribal marriage in the region. Interclan marriage, in contrast, is more relevant to weakening inhibitions on interclan fighting.

14. Although psychocultural explanations for the return to warfare are not as prominent as structural ones, both Koch (1974) and Herdt (1987) see psychocultural factors as central in explaining high levels of conflict and the persistence of warfare in the region.

15. Herdt's (1987) description of socialization among the Sambia contains a number of features which seem appropriate for other societies in the region with respect to gender and identity issues.

16. Brown notes, "I see the ethos of the Simbu as focused upon competition rather than political authority" (1982:532).

not yield to third-party intervention. Competition is the relationship between groups" (Brown 1982:541).

Gordon characterizes the regional cultural pattern as one of suspicion and distrust, citing Schwartz's description of Melanesia as dominated by a paranoid ethos (1983:207). The key to understanding such societies, Gordon argues, is that the basis of social order is not so much rules and obedience as the exchange relationships which constantly redefine the social universe. Such a worldview "is not conducive to predictability and trust but rather the opposite" (Gordon 1983:207). He argues that fear and insecurity are manifest in many ways and he cites Meggitt's observations concerning changes in settlement patterns. "Fear," Gordon writes, "is a far more potent force in shaping human and social destiny than bravery or entrepreneurial skill" (1983:208).

In a world of shifting and constantly renegotiated alliances, clan identity and territory are among the few constant elements. Is there any wonder that such attachments are so emotionally charged, that men organize their lives around its defense, that the actions of others are easily seen as highly threatening? It seems plausible to suggest that a clan's land, an inanimate object, can easily become a psychocultural expression of the longed-for security and nurturance only partially known in infancy which suddenly ends in childhood.[17] Threats to territory, from this perspective, rekindle the pain of the lost bond with one's mother. The memories, undoubtedly distressing, provoke a turn toward one's fellow clan members—the symbol of security and the only available means for its defense (Gordon and Meggitt 1984:155).

Intergroup fights over compensation payments take on an intensity for many of the same reasons. Obtaining compensation is a vehicle for affirming self and group worth and, in an insecure world, it attains an importance far exceeding what an outsider might see. The merger of individual and group identity, seen in the calculation of compensation payments, guarantees social support for claims. Given the manipulative, competitive worldview of most people in the highlands, group interests are not only synonymous with one's own interests but also mutually

17. This hypothesis could be extended to a view of clan lands as a transitional object, as Winnicott (1953) uses the term, that links early relationships and the adult world. Because of unresolved elements in the early relationship, the object becomes highly charged emotionally, and later psychological functioning fixates on this issue.

exclusive of those of other groups. Any effort at conflict management that diminishes group autonomy is likely to be rejected, for it increases the chances that another group will profit from the situation.[18]

Although the structural factors associated with conflict in highland New Guinea are real, they take on a particularly ominous meaning in this psychocultural context. Competition, insecurity, and fear grow out of a process by which individuals and group identities are merged psychologically, politically, and socially.[19] As a consequence, unilateral group action becomes the dominant strategy of conflict management, and the use of other methods is considered a defeat for the group and a further diminution of the already problematic sense of individual self-worth. Defending the group, I argue, is a collective defensive maneuver in a world with few points of security that increases in intensity as resources become scarce.

Lessons

The success and then failure of the colonial peace in highland New Guinea can be linked to both the structural features and the psychocultural context of the region. The colonial peace was less a function of a change in cultural values than an opportunity to pursue long-standing values in other ways, as Meggitt and others suggest. At no point was self-help (with limited joint problem solving) rejected as the most appropriate way to manage conflicts. The informal dispute management system worked best when it was most similar to the precolonial one, as Gordon points out. Efforts to institutionalize binding third-party procedures, as with land demarcation committees, were widely rejected. Land and control over it was important not only as a crucial economic re-

18. Interestingly, Nader (1990) describes another route to autonomy in the development and implementation of "harmony ideology," which provides outsiders with no pretext to intervene in the local affairs of a community.

19. The theme of the merger of individual and group identities and the consequences for group conflict is well developed in Freud's classic work *Group Psychology and the Analysis of the Ego* (1922) and his essay "Mourning and Melancholia" (1917). More recent discussion of these topics building on these ideas are found in Fornari (1975) and Volkan (1988), who is especially concerned about the consequences of the relationship between individual and group identity on intergroup behavior. Social identity theory raises the same issues from a nonpsychoanalytic perspective (Tajfel and Turner 1986; Turner 1988).

source, but also because it represented a central psychocultural attachment. When structural conditions grew more acute, the psychocultural factors worked as a kind of multiplier, setting off a renewed round of violence.

Northern Ireland[20]
Brief History

In 1920 both the British and the Irish governments agreed to accept the division of the island into the two entities that we now know as the Republic of Ireland and Northern Ireland (Ulster), setting off a bitter civil war in the south over unification. From its inception, Northern Ireland has been bitterly divided between the dominant unionists (Protestant) and the minority nationalists (Catholic). The majority Protestant population has insisted, in a variety of ways, on maintaining its "union" with Great Britain in the United Kingdom. The Catholic minority has professed, with varying degrees of enthusiasm, a desire to reunite the island. Despite intercommunal tension, overt violence in Northern Ireland was low from the mid-1920s until the 1960s.

From the outset the new regime in the north received little support from most of the nationalist community. Instead of trying to win over the Catholic minority, the Belfast regime did all it could to keep political and economic power in Protestant hands. For example, local government district boundaries were redrawn to make sure that as few nationalists as possible were elected and that Catholics did not control councils in cities and towns even when they were in the majority (Boyle and Hadden 1985; R. White 1989). Economic policies were also manipulated in order to locate as much industry as possible in Protestant areas; better and more plentiful public services were available for Protestants. Catholics were openly discriminated against in public and private sector employment and by 1970 had an unemployment rate twice that of Protestants. Even symbolically the regime sought to assert Protestant dominance—for example, making it illegal to name any streets in Gaelic or display the Irish flag (Boyle and Hadden 1985:59−61).

Continued discrimination against the Catholic community caused

20. Many of the ideas developed here out of collaboration with Robert Mulvihill (see Mulvihill and Ross 1989).

most of them to regard Northern Ireland as an illegitimate state (Rose 1971) and respond to it with resigned compliance. Britain and the Republic in the south were, at the same time, parties to the conflict and potential third parties who could help alter the situation (O'Malley 1983).[21] Many analyses of the conflict give both a central role (Whyte 1990). The traditional nationalist view sees Britain as the source of the problem in the region, whereas traditional unionists blame the Dublin government for its refusal to recognize the region as separate from the Republic (Whyte 1990). Only recently has there been an emphasis on the internal aspects of the conflict that places the burden on the Catholics and Protestants in the north to work with each other (Whyte 1990; Wright 1992). For many in both communities, until recently joint problem solving seemed fruitless, in part due to power differences between the two groups and each side's image of itself as a vulnerable minority. The majority Protestants felt they could only lose in negotiations and that Catholic pressure was not strong enough to make the costs of the present policies untenably high. Catholics, in contrast, saw the Protestants (backed by the British) as too strong to yield on any significant matter. Self-help strategies were all that remained. Probably the most common response was avoidance, as the Catholic community created a full complement of communal institutions for its members, in addition to Catholic nonparticipation in Protestant institutions, including much of the public domain. Catholic use of exit, meaning emigration mainly to Britain or the United States, was far higher than that of the Protestants, as many saw little chance of improvement in the region's conditions. Noncompliance was certainly found in Catholic rejection of the political and social systems' demands. Finally, unilateral action occurred in the continued criticism of the constitutional arrangements, but active protest steadily dropped off. By 1962, even the Irish Republican Army (IRA) and its political arm Sinn Fein were relatively inactive (R. White 1989).

Northern Ireland was self-governing, meaning that the Protestants completely dominated its political and economic life. In the late 1960s,

21. The active role of the British is obvious in that Northern Ireland is part of the United Kingdom, and although Ulster was treated as an autonomous region from the 1920s until 1973, it has been ruled directly from London since 1973. The role of the Republic in the conflict is both emotional and political; it is the symbolic focus of identity for many Catholics and its constitution, for example, claims the six counties which make up Ulster as part of the Republic.

internal tensions erupted in the form of a civil rights movement demand-ing an across-the-board end to discrimination against the Catholic popu-lation. The movement achieved startling gains in some areas despite violent resistance by unionist factions claiming that it was a cover for militant nationalists. Intergroup violence spread as the Protestant Ulster Defense Force (UDF), which included many supporters of the Reverend Ian Paisley, and the IRA battled each other in the names of their religious communities (Lebow 1978; R. White 1989). The British sent in troops which the Catholic community first welcomed but later opposed when the Catholics became the object of regular harassment and internment. Deaths from violence peaked in 1972 but have continued over the past twenty years. The region is still ruled from London and there has been only modest change in the situation.

The standard explanation for the persistence of the conflict in Northern Ireland is more structural than psychocultural, emphasizing the division of the region into two religious camps with mutually exclu-sive interests and few overlapping ties (Whyte 1990; McFarlane 1986).[22] Structural theories of conflict identify incompatible, or at least different interests in a community. In a region like Ulster, it is easy to see how the differences in each community's access to resources have created privi-leges the Protestants want to maintain and the Catholics seek to alter. Structurally, the intensity of each side's position is best understood in terms of the absence of cross-cutting ties. Northern Ireland is a classic divided society in which one social cleavage takes precedence over all others (Boyle and Hadden 1985). Not only do members of each commu-nity attend different churches, but they also live in separate areas, often work in different places, enjoy different leisure activities, and attend separate primary and secondary schools.[23] The separate social worlds are reinforced through powerful stereotypes which are rarely countered by evidence to the contrary and are reinforced through strong social norms and prohibitions on communications challenging the social order of daily life (Fitzduff 1992; Harris 1972). In this situation, a critically important social unit, especially in Belfast and other cities, is the strong,

22. Lipjhardt (1975) presents ten images of Northern Ireland, all of which are primarily structural and none of which could be called psychocultural.

23. Only about 4 percent of the children in Northern Ireland attend what are called integrated schools, i.e., those with a significant number of Protestant and Catholic students.

localized male groups which form within each community and perpetrate many of the region's violent incidents (Lebow 1978).

A psychocultural account of this conflict also yields important insights, turning our attention to an important source of the *intensity* of feelings underlying each community's demands. Deep-seated fears and projective aggression, in this formulation, provide a motivation for one's own action as a function of aggressive motives attributed to the other side (Fornari 1975; White 1984; Volkan 1988). The frustrations, projections, fears of extinction, and sense of low self-esteem, as well as the development of positive in-group and negative out-group images identified as basic causes of ethnocentric conflict, are all present and determine how people in the region view their divided world. The psychocultural environment, the evidence suggests, does little to encourage the compromise, openness, and sharing needed for effective joint problem solving (Fitzduff 1992); rather, it promotes a sense of a polarized world in which aggressive self-help is often the only possible appropriate action.[24]

The differences in Protestant and Catholic interpretations of the

24. Although the evidence is less direct, many of the psychocultural dispositions the cross-cultural study identifies in high-conflict cultures are found in Ireland, but I must note that rural Irish communities in the Republic are not openly conflictual. More prevalent is the severe psychological repression and the absence of institutional mechanisms for the expression of grievances. Even in the North, many rural communities (fewer in the border areas) have little overt conflict. McFarlane (1986) describes how local community ideologies emphasize harmony even in the face of religious divisions, in part by blaming outsiders, hotheads, and special factors for violence when it occurs, rather than seeing it as an ongoing feature of community life. Even when psychocultural dispositions increase the chances of violence, community structure and social support are also needed before such acts regularly occur. Only in larger, polarized urban communities of the north has this taken place. Severe male gender-identity conflict and low levels of affection and warmth are central themes in Irish culture, although early socialization does not seem especially harsh. Messenger (1971) and Scheper-Hughes (1979) describe a strong Irish fear of intimacy, extremely low levels of social trust and sociability, great emotional distance between fathers and children —none of the predispositions needed to deal with political differences in a democratic context. Some male bonding occurs in the context of drinking relationships in local pubs (where females are almost never present). There are also powerful sexual fears on the part of both men and women. McGoldrick (1982) describes powerful feelings of aggression and a preoccupation with sin and death, which are dealt with through social withdrawal and isolation, for their expression within the family context is simply unacceptable. A plausible hypothesis is

conflict are seen most clearly around the issue of the hunger strikers in 1980–81 (O'Malley 1990; Wright 1992). The dramatic strikes developed after the British decided to abolish the special status of IRA prisoners who insisted they were political rather than criminal prisoners. Unionists saw the IRA as murderers of their friends and relatives, while many Catholics who did not support the IRA still identified with army harassment in their neighborhoods, extralegal internment, and Diplock courts, in which convictions occurred without a jury or direct confrontation of witnesses. When first Bobby Sands, then other hunger strikers stood for election for the British Parliament, "to many Protestants it looked like a vote for murder. To many Catholics it seemed the only way to deny the British government's claim that the prison issue was a conflict between civil society and terrorism" (Wright 1992:245).

Elsewhere I have described the Northern Ireland conflict in greater detail (Mulvihill and Ross 1989; Ross 1993); here my concern is explaining the failure, to date, of peacemaking efforts. Most peace proposals for the region emphasize structural features of the conflict, which are indeed important, but virtually neglect its psychocultural aspects. There has been insufficient effort to develop an understanding of each side's real fears and concerns as well as their objective interests as part of conflict management. An examination of four different efforts to resolve the conflict since 1920 suggests how such partial efforts are ineffective when conflicts are deeply rooted in the fears of the parties.

Failed Conflict Management Efforts

A review of four past attempts at conflict management—the creation of Northern Ireland, a power-sharing executive, the women's peace movement, and the Anglo–Irish Agreement—shows three crucial reasons why they failed. First, they did not involve all the key parties and therefore ignored crucial interests; second, they made virtually no effort to build on any feelings of understanding or good will, however meager,

---

that the aggression is either turned inward (evidenced in high rates of schizophrenia and alcoholism) or outward toward acceptable targets when they are available, as in the divided social worlds in the cities in north. For more discussion of the psychocultural situation in Northern Ireland see Mulvihill and Ross (1989) and Ross (1993).

between the communities; third, they addressed either structural or psychocultural aspects of the conflict and failed to combine the two.

Creation of Northern Ireland. In 1912 on the eve of World War I, home rule to Ireland was passed in the British House of Commons, but it was suspended with the outbreak of the war and led to a major constitutional crisis, pitting unionist leaders and their Tory allies against the British government. At the war's end, under great pressure from the Unionists, the Home Rule Bill was discarded in favor of the Government of Ireland Act which partitioned the island of Ireland. The failure to enact home rule ultimately led to the nationalist war with Britain and subsequently to the civil war in Ireland over the question of accepting the Government of Ireland Act. The imposition of a British decision on Ireland aroused the anger of Protestants and Catholics at times, and both availed themselves of self-help through the use of force. At the time, few people in either sectarian community or in Britain encouraged joint problem solving. Behind this was the apparent assumption that the interests of the parties were so incompatible that no mutually acceptable solution could be developed. As a result, a third party, the British political process, fearing unilateral Protestant action (if there were no partition), produced a binding decision that was then imposed through force.

Power-sharing executive. Following partition, the British granted home rule to Northern Ireland and had little to do with its affairs until the Catholic-led nonviolent civil rights movement in the late 1960s demanded changes in the system of religious patronage in jobs and housing and in economic discrimination. The British stepped in to remedy some of the more egregious social policy grievances. Moderate Protestant leaders recognized the need for change in the political area as well, but when they tried to respond to the demands for change, unionist militia groups launched a terrorist campaign, and under the Reverend Ian Paisley's leadership all Catholic civil rights marches were met with Protestant countermarches (Wichert 1991). Soon thereafter daily life became increasingly violent, British troops were stationed in Ulster, the Northern Ireland parliament was dissolved, and direct rule from Britain was imposed. A major attempt at resolution occurred in 1974 with the agreements at Sunningdale on the creation of the so-called "power-sharing" executive, which formally included representatives of the nationalist community and established a parliament based on proportional representation. It met with approval largely from moderate unionists whose main aspiration was maintaining the link with Great Britain, but it did not have popular Protestant support (Wright 1992). Its short life ended when the British government refused to try to end the general strike called by a coalition of unionist groups, the Ulster Worker's Council, in opposition to the plan.

The power-sharing executive arose from a combination of joint problem solving and third-party decision making, and failed for several reasons. First, it was certainly too narrow in scope: it tried to address the structure of political arrangements, but it failed also to pay attention to the underlying fears of people in both communities. Second, the process leading up to the power-sharing arrangement did not include all the parties to the conflict (See 1986:127). To the extent that the arrangement was imposed by a third party (the British) rather than developed by various groups in Northern Ireland, it was easy to reject. Unable to view the solution as their own, different parties in the north easily found fault with it. Finally, it turned out that third-party commitment to the solution was weak, for the British dropped the plan when serious opposition from the unionist community resulted in a general strike.

Women's peace movement. The women's peace movement rose to prominence in the mid-1970s, brought the Nobel Peace Prize to its founders, and then rapidly disappeared. In contrast to the three other efforts considered here, which were governmental-based and structural in nature, the peace movement was neither. Formed mainly by Catholic and Protestant women fed up with the ongoing violence, the movement had regular marches (with thousands of participants for a time) and other events calling for an end to the violence. It raised the hopes of moderates in both communities that the climate of fear and violence could be altered. It foundered, however, because of its inability to make structural changes in daily life and to convert its moral commitment and perceptions of the conflict into behavioral change in the region. The leaders of the movement were outsiders to the political processes of both communities, which was a real strength for a while but ultimately its greatest weakness. Some of the early leaders have since emigrated, and its activities no longer attract the large following they once did.[25]

25. The dilemma that all outsider-oriented change groups face is particularly poignant here. Major political figures, for the most part, adopt a wait-and-see attitude toward such movements before committing themselves. In the process they may deny them the short-term successes needed in order to gain credibility.

The outrage and commitment of the founders and supporters of the movement were insufficient to alter powerful fears and dispositions which continued to fuel the conflict from both sides. Nor did they address the differences in interests of the major parties. As representatives of Egypt and Israel found, even when there is a commitment to peace, actually working out the details can be exasperating and painful (Quandt 1986). Here the moral rejection of the ongoing violence was never converted into a specific set of proposals for changes in behavior, in great part because the deep mutual suspicions were never altered. As McLachlan (1987), a participant in the peace movement, has described, the psychocultural gap between the two communities has meant that the kind of communication required to change images has not developed.

Anglo-Irish Agreement. A fourth major attempt to manage the conflict was the Anglo-Irish Agreement adopted by the British and Irish governments in the autumn of 1985. This ingenious agreement was, in many ways, far less sweeping than partition or the power-sharing executive since it called for no major structural changes in the governance of Northern Ireland and because it maintained the status quo ante with regard to the constitutional status of Northern Ireland. On the other hand, the agreement's endorsement of the Irish dimension, in the establishment of a process for joint British-Irish decision making and cooperation in matters of concern to the north, clearly raised the prospect of unification, and hence the objections of Protestants. While it provides for British–Irish joint action, the agreement also provides an incentive to groups in the north for cooperation, as a way to limit the actions of the British and Irish governments. As of this writing, the agreement's fate is still to be decided, but its longevity, if not its impact, is impressive when compared to previous efforts.

The agreement is a curious one in that representatives of neither the Protestant nor Catholic communities in the north are a party to it, although it is generally approved by Catholics and rejected by Protestants. It calls for increased consultation and cooperation between the Republic and Great Britain on a wide range of matters concerning the north. While moderate Catholics welcome this move, more extreme nationalists categorically reject this as they have always rejected any British role in the north. On the Protestant side, unionists are wary of any arrangement that gives the Republic even the smallest toehold in Ulster.

The real problem with the agreement is that its exclusive focus on the structure of political interests (like the original home rule bill and the 1974 power-sharing proposal) poses a direct and formidable challenge to the dominant, majority Unionist population—with little reassurance that change will bring them concomitant benefits. By imposing an agreement upon them without their participation, it raises Protestant fears and distrust, which only stiffens their opposition (O'Brien 1986). Seen from the Unionist perspective, each of these efforts has constituted a major threat to the survival of Unionist identity, either in its Protestant or British forms. Because the Anglo-Irish Agreement failed to involve key parties to the conflict in the north, once again, it did nothing to lower the distrust between the communities, to increase their understanding of what the other sees as its vital interests, or even to exchange information. If the core of constructive conflict management lies in the development of creative solutions among the disputants, this agreement made little progress.

Yet this judgment needs to be tempered, for in the years following the agreement there is some indication that it has moved the parties closer to constructive joint problem solving. Using the perspective of family systems theory, Mulvihill (1992) has argued that the agreement has altered the relationship among the major parties in ways that bring them closer to breaking the current deadlock. While initial Protestant reaction to the agreement was hostile, resistance in 1985–87 was far less than it was to the power-sharing executive in 1973–74. In addition, the agreement clearly weakened some of the strong emotional ties between the Protestants and the British. On the Catholic side, there has been less blaming the British for the situation and greater thought given to what cooperation with the Protestants would require. One consequence has been a resumption of informal talks as well as the first formal discussions between the parties since the early 1970s (Fitzduff 1992). Although there are still significant unresolved issues (such as the role of Sinn Fein in the talks), there has been discussion involving the Protestants, the Catholics, and the British, as well as movement toward the inclusion of the Irish government.[26]

26. Although Sinn Fein leaders say they will talk with all parties, the British government and the Protestant parties refuse to talk with them until they renounce the use of violence. They refuse to do so and remain outside any discussions, at the same time threatening the legitimacy of any agreement to which they are not a party.

Lessons

Successful conflict resolution in Northern Ireland must consider both the structural and psychocultural roots of the conflict. The interests that members of each community define as real must be addressed. For Catholics, this means an end to discrimination in housing and other public services, more economic opportunities, and, most important, political involvement in decisions that affect their daily lives.[27] For Protestants, crucial interest concerns include fears of being subject to laws in a state tied to a church which is not their own, losing linkage to England, losing political voice, and enduring threats to their persons and property.

Both Catholic and Protestant interpretations of the conflict emphasize deeply held fears about threats to group self-esteem and legitimacy (Horowitz 1985). Both sectarian communities have real (and often legitimate) fears about what members of the other community might do given the opportunity. To address these fears, any conflict management process must differ from that which accompanied the 1974 power-sharing agreement or the 1985 Anglo-Irish accords. In addition to finding structural protections for each community, a concerted effort must aim at altering some of the deeply ingrained images and beliefs each holds about the other. The dominant analogies and metaphors which connect deep-seated fears and actions of the other side will have to be replaced, at least in part, with alternative metaphors and an understanding of the world that is based more on cooperation and trust. One of the key characteristics of highly polarized disputes such as this one is that members of each community have very simplistic, undifferentiated images of their adversaries (Fitzduff 1992). Protestants, then, see all Catholics as potential Republicans and potential IRA supporters, and Catholics view all Protestants as potential Paisleyites.[28]

In the late 1980s and early 1990s, perhaps as a consequence of the

27. Simple one-person, one-vote solutions are not relevant here, or in other ethnically divided societies where voting is, as Horowitz (1985, 1991) notes, really a form of census taking which confirms existing majority-minority status but is not political choice making.

28. It may be that a more differentiated view of the other side will develop only when the moderate elements in each community feel sufficiently secure that they can challenge the extremists in their own community directly. For this to occur, some confidence-building measures among moderates in each community are needed.

Anglo-Irish Agreement, there was an increased effort to arrange all-party talks that would include all the key participants. On several occasions, there were extended sessions, serious efforts to engage in joint problem solving, with only Sinn Fein not involved because of its refusal to renounce violence. Underlying these new peace efforts is an apparent realization of shared interests and some recognition of the vital interests of the other disputants. Whether this will eventually produce a viable "peace" agreement is hard to say. On the basis of the analysis offered here, however, it would seem that this will result only if each side's worst fears of the other are mollified.

Conflict management in Northern Ireland has not yet reached this point. Joint problem solving involving the major parties in the region (and probably some from outside) is necessary. A sense that success is possible and the availability of models of success and a language to describe them is also important. It is hard to see how any success can occur without third-party assistance, although identifying a potentially effective third party and assigning it a role is not for outsiders. An enduring peace cannot be imposed; it must consider the interests of all the parties to the dispute and address the deep-seated fears of all.

Conclusion: Commonalities Among Failures

The three cases here show different ways conflict management can fail. In all three cases imposition of a solution was tried at one point or another, and in all three it proved to be of little value. Imposed solutions may last for a time when they reflect important power inequalities. Without other efforts to address real fears and concerns, however, they did not produce viable changes. The passage of time did not improve bad situations; if anything, there is reason to believe that they got worse.

Because imposed solutions without subsequent steps often fail, the remaining options are continued intense conflict, exit, submission, or development of a solution that involves the disputants. Exit is a viable strategy only under certain conditions (see chapter 5). When population pressure is high and attachments are geographically focused, as in highland New Guinea, leaving the area is not useful. In other situations, a strong power may foreclose exit, as slave owners or dictatorial regimes have done throughout history, and as many democratic governments do when confronted by secessionist movements. Finally, exit is perhaps an answer for those people who leave, but it does nothing for those group members who remain. Submission (with selective noncompliance) is the response of many minority groups facing a far more powerful opponent. It is a strategy of survival, but does not solve any long-term problems, as the New Guinea and Northern Ireland examples show.

From a conflict management perspective, the most attractive option is one that involves all the parties in a dispute in developing an alternative to ongoing conflict and violence. This means addressing the interests and interpretations that separate disputants. In none of the three cases did the adversaries ever address each other's central interests effectively; they addressed mutual fears even less. Given the psychocultural context of each conflict this is not surprising. None of the adversaries was prepared to hear much about the other side's needs without feeling intensely threatened and fearful, just as Israelis and Egyptians did prior to the Camp David agreement.

What is completely absent from conflict management failures such as the ones explored here is the recognition of any set of common interests or any notion of linked fate which could provide the basis for a settlement of differences. Mutual images are so negative that acceding to any of the demands of the other side is seen as the worst possible outcome as well as a denial of the value of one's own group (Horowitz 1985).

The structure and intensity of dispositions associated with some intense conflicts clearly prevents the adversaries from ever getting to the point where they are able to explore common interests and integrative solutions. This hypothesis suggests that there are certain dispositional prerequisites for constructive conflict management that need to be in place before interests can be addressed adequately. Prenegotiation is one way to think about a place where these steps can be taken so that negotiation serves as consolidation (Rothman 1991). In situations where opponents' interpretations of each other are so hostile or suspicious that conflict management breaks down (or never gets started), attention to dispositions may be the first order of business.

If the fears and threats each side feels are significant barriers to dealing with interests, conflict management strategies need to address them directly by helping parties develop more complex views of adversaries, rearranging dispositional elements, finding common elements that emphasize what is shared, and finding alternative salient metaphors and analogies to replace those which evoke the strongest fears. Psychocultural complexity means that there are alternative ways in which a group's central dispositions can be arranged. Constructive conflict management needs to build on this. Changing fundamental worldviews (at least in the short run) will fail, whereas reorganizing and selectively emphasizing existing elements offers a much greater prospect for success.

8

Psychocultural Prerequisites for Constructive Conflict Management

The argument that effective conflict management needs to address both interests and disputants' interpretations says little about the order in which the two are considered. The discussion in the last two chapters, however, strongly supports the contention that, at least in the case of severe disputes, some modification of hostile psychocultural interpretations must precede efforts to negotiate conflicts of interest. Only when there is sufficient working trust among the parties, the hypothesis suggests, is there the possibility of addressing substantive issues through joint problem solving, often with third-party facilitation. This suggestion differs from traditional approaches to conflict management which emphasize altering incentives for cooperation through legal or constitutional change or international diplomacy in which psychocultural considerations typically have a small role. Horowitz (1985, 1991), for example, in discussing ethnic change in general and South Africa in particular, emphasizes that adoption of particular electoral reforms which offer incentives for cross-ethnic cooperation as the most likely path toward stable democracy.

The hypothesis that attention to psychological and/or psychocultural dispositions is required for effective problem solving to occur applies to conflict at several levels. It is at the core of psychoanalytic assumptions, which consider perceptions of the world to be barriers to intrapsychic and interpersonal relations. By learning about and then altering core dispositions, a person can modify the character of his or her relationships with others. I do not intend to evaluate this central tenet of psychoanalytic theory and practice, but I will focus on an extension of this hypothesis as it applies to the intergroup and even international levels: that intensely held psychocultural interpretations form the basis of mutual, hostile perceptions which thwart the development of constructive conflict management in intergroup conflicts. Where psychoanalysis tries to address the critical dispositions directly, the proposals considered here are more indirect, focusing on widely shared intergroup interpretations, not the core dispositions of intrapsychic worlds of members of opposing groups.[1] Strategies to alter psychocultural interpretations aim to influence the beliefs of important actors in a society and to alter public opinion more generally.

After discussing this hypothesis, I turn to strategies for modifying disputants' interpretations and discuss problem-solving workshops, Track Two diplomacy, and personal and cultural exchanges, all of which are aimed at modifying mutual hostile interpretations, particularly in international disputes. Finally, I argue that we have few institutions and practices that facilitate psychocultural change, in part because so much attention in conflict management is devoted to bridging interests defined in zero-sum terms. If, however, more effort is directed at finding ways to address hostile interpretations, the likelihood that disputants will be able to develop effective integrative solutions will increase. My argument is not, however, that changes in psychocultural interpretations, by themselves, are sufficient to produce constructive management of most conflicts. Quite the contrary: simply getting disputants to better understand each other is only one step; they still need to address the substantive issues which divide them. The two processes reinforce each other. As disputants alter interpretations, bridging interests can become easier, and as they experience success in addressing interest differences, new interpretations take hold.

Modifying Psychocultural Interpretations

The recent literature on peacemaking offers ideas about fruitful ways to manage conflicts. The notion that joint decision making (with or without the help of third parties) produces the best possible decisions is commonly argued (Fisher and Ury 1981; Pruitt and Rubin

1. Kelman (1991) offers a good discussion of the links between psychoanalytic theory and problem-solving workshops he has developed to address intense intergroup disputes. He also points out important differences in emphasis such as the one noted here. See also Montville and Davidson (1981–82).

1986; Susskind and Cruikshank 1988; Ury, Brett, and Goldberg 1988). However, joint decision making requires a mutual willingness to work toward a solution. In situations of high distrust, or where each party questions the fundamental legitimacy of the other side (as is the case in many bitter ethnic conflicts), there is often a formidable barrier to even engaging in discussions (as in Northern Ireland or the Middle East), let alone arriving at a solution.[2] In such severe conflicts, the need to modify perceptions of an adversary and his motives (and sometimes one's own as well)—what I have been calling psychocultural interpretations—is a prerequisite to joint problem solving (White 1984; Kelman 1978, 1987).

This hypothesis lies at the core of Kelman's analysis of the prospects for Israeli-Palestinian peacemaking. A fundamental obstacle to peace, he says, is that each side's acceptance and recognition of the other in this conflict raises the deepest fears about its own basic identity and continued existence (1978, 1987).[3] Successful peacemaking between the communities, he argues, must take these fears seriously in order to create a climate in which a consideration of substantive interests becomes possible. Kelman then proposes a series of psychological prerequisites for peacemaking, which, if met, would alter the intense, hostile interpretations on both sides and permit substantive negotiations to begin. Constructive interpretations must allow each side to: (1) acquire some insight into the perspective of the other; (2) believe that there is someone to talk to on the other side and something to talk about; (3) distinguish between the dreams and the operational programs of the other side; (4)

2. In highly polarized disputes, such as intense ethnic conflicts, the act of openly talking with the other side (and sometimes even suggesting the reasonableness of communication with an adversary) can be sufficient to delegitimize a person or group in the eyes of the wider community. In such a setting the task of beginning any direct discussions involving the major disputants is difficult. Evidence of this are the length of time needed for arranging any public discussions between the Israeli government and the PLO, between the South African government and the ANC, and between Protestants and Catholics in Northern Ireland.

3. The parallel to Northern Ireland is clear. Whether one focuses on Republican-British or Nationalist-Unionist cleavage, the question of identity is striking, as is the asymmetry that results from the way both sides approach it. Many Catholic nationalists define their identity in terms of their opposition to the British while Protestant loyalists define themselves in contrast to the Catholic population of the entire island of Ireland. The two extremist factions, in effect, bypass each other. For a more detailed discussion applying Kelman's prerequisites to Northern Ireland see Mulvihill and Ross (1989).

be persuaded that mutual concessions will create a new situation, setting into motion a process of change; (5) be persuaded that structural changes conducive to a stable peace have taken place or will take place in the leadership of the other side; and (6) feel a sense of responsiveness to its human concerns and psychological needs on the part of the adversary.

The hypothesis that opponents' mutual fears must be addressed as a first step in constructive conflict management is also at the heart of White's (1984) discussion of the U.S.-Soviet conflict written just prior to Gorbachev's assumption of power and the thaw in U.S.-Soviet relations.[4] He suggests that explicit consideration of motives and perceptions can help develop interpretations that are more accurate and make the peaceful resolution of disputes more likely. Realistic empathy, says White, is needed before longtime enemies can make peace. By this term, he means understanding but not necessarily sympathizing with an opponent's position. Non-empathy creates barriers to conflict management because an adversary's actions are consistently misinterpreted in three basic ways: failing to see their fear of being attacked, their desire for peace, and their understandable anger. Empathy, White says, is critical for developing interpretations which can help constructively manage what he calls defensively motivated (as opposed to power-motivated) aggression, which arises from inner needs and is an outward projection of inner concerns. Empathy can modify "exaggerated fear" rooted in unacknowledged aggressive impulses in ones' own mind. One way it does this is by building support for the attribution of hostile acts to situational forces as opposed to the innate dispositions of opponents (Pruitt and Rubin 1986; Rothman, personal communication 1992). Drastic tension reduction, without necessarily altering underlying motives and perceptions, is a crucial first step from White's viewpoint. Arms reduction alone will not work, he contends, because fears produce arms build-ups, not the reverse.

Listing prerequisite conditions to conflict management which are clearly absent in many bitter conflicts directs us to consider the order in which specific actions should be taken and alerts us to possibilities for new initiatives or for reinforcement of existing approaches. Moreover, identifying specific prerequisites reminds us about the interactive nature

4. The book indicated a number of important changes needed in the relationship between the two nations which, in fact, did occur over the next five years or so.

of conflict management processes. As progress is made on some conditions, the achievement of others may become easier as the disputants' interpretations of the conflict are modified.

Psychocultural Conflict Theory Considerations

According to psychocultural conflict theory, deeply rooted dispositions combine with particular, recent events and collective memories of historical occurrences to form psychocultural interpretations relevant to a specific conflict.[5] By taking psychocultural dispositions into account, conflict management efforts can attempt to modify hostile interpretations that help perpetuate destructive conflicts. Underlying dispositions cannot be magically removed or reshaped. However, given an understanding of the complexity of these dispositions, effective action strategies can address the interpretations associated with them. They may alter the connection between the dispositions and current events either by suggesting the relevance of a disposition not previously emphasized, by proposing that the link to certain events is less appropriate than it was believed to be, or by offering new or different connections (analogies, metaphors, or images) among existing dispositions and current events. As a result, parties that were too fearful or too angry to negotiate with each other may develop a more nuanced and more complex view of an adversary, as well as of themselves, enhancing the prospect that joint problem solving will produce beneficial results. Certainly this can be seen in the conflict management successes, such as the maintenance of Franco-German peace since 1945[6] or the Camp David accords, discussed in chapter 6.

5. Although there is no room to elaborate on the point here, it is important to recognize how particular historical events continue to have intense emotional significance decades or even centuries after everyone who participated in them has died. Psychoculturally, these events symbolize group identity in important ways. Volkan (1988) and Montville (1991a) encourage us to consider ways in which these events represent significant group losses which were never properly mourned.

6. Montville (1991a) recounts the story of Irene Laure, a participant in the French resistance and leader of the national organization of French socialist women. Laure reluctantly participated in a Moral Rearmament meeting in Switzerland in 1947 although previously she had refused to even remain in the room when Germans spoke. At this meeting she encountered the widow of Adam von Trott whom the Nazis killed after the failed assassination attempt on Hitler in July 1940. Laure felt a sense of common humanity and announced to the plenary

A central psychocultural dynamic in many conflict scenarios involves the development of a bipolar, black-and-white, image of the world in which each side in a dispute sees itself as the embodiment of all that is good and views the enemy as not just evil but even inhuman. Consider how a strategy aimed at altering such psychocultural interpretations might proceed. It must recognize the importance of the psychoanalytic process of splitting, in which the good parts of the self are internalized, and the bad ones are projected onto an external object, as a primary, universal dynamic whose intensity increases with the level of tension (Fornari 1975; Volkan 1988). Warning disputants that this basic psychodynamic mechanism is potentially destructive and dysfunctional does little to help them overcome its effects. More likely to be effective is an intervention that recognizes the process of splitting and the dispositions underlying it and tries to invoke additional ones, so that this one dynamic is put in the context of others in order to limit its impact. When each party's dominant fears and images are articulated, there is a greater possibility that they can be successfully addressed.

Similarly, threats to identity are central in many protracted conflicts (Northrup 1989; Volkan 1988). For a third party or an opponent simply to tell a group that such fears are irrational rarely alters the cognitive, let alone the affective interpretations of a conflict. It is much more useful for disputants to engage in interactions which first evoke mutual threats to identity and then to offer mutual assurances which communicate an acceptance of each other's core identity and right to exist. Finally, because so much intense feeling around the issue of identity in intergroup conflict involves unresolved past suffering, it is important to encourage the mutual expression of sorrow for losses which allows each party to fully mourn them, a necessary step for establishing new relationships (Montville 1991b; Volkan 1988).

Alteration of either the intensity or the content of these interpretations can occur in several ways. One is to structure intergroup interactions in order to emphasize the common human needs of all parties to

---

session that her hatred was wrong. Later she travelled extensively in Germany telling the story of her own losses and suffering, asking for an end to hatred, and holding out the vision of a cooperative future Europe. Montville argues that her effort was powerful because it allowed each side to acknowledge and mourn its losses as a first step toward building a new relationship.

the conflict,[7] and in so doing weaken the belief that those on the other side are less than human. Another step is to encourage the parties to see how their own actions, whatever the intentions, are partially responsible for the threats an opponent perceives.

The key strategy in modifying disputants' mutually hostile interpretations requires providing strong proximate evidence countering an existing interpretation, weakening the link between this interpretation and particular dispositions, and providing new evidence, both affective and cognitive, which links new interpretations to other basic dispositions. For example, whereas the view of an opponent as inhuman is linked to a bipolar image of the world, sharing experiences of loss and hurt can create empathy while invoking core dispositions about security and nurturance. Sometimes apparently small actions having great symbolic significance accomplish these changes. In this sense, small agreements sometimes have wider meaning. From the conflict management point of view, affectively rooted changes in interpretations can have significant impact on intergroup relations when they are shared and supported in a community.[8]

Targets of Efforts to Modify Interpretations

If the goal is altering strongly held psychocultural interpretations which prevent effective joint problem solving, it is important to consider who should be the target of these efforts. Although there may be a desire to concentrate on leaders most responsible for the day-to-day course of a conflict, this approach poses two problems. One is that access to critical elites is often highly limited; few leaders, particularly at the national level, have the time or inclination to engage in such a process in the heat of a conflict. Just as important is the fact that leaders who develop new interpretations of adversaries which are not shared beyond their inner circles are likely to be politically vulnerable and reluctant to act on their new views without wider support for them.

7. This differs from the notion of superordinate goals (Sherif et al. 1988) in that rather than being focused on specific tasks and primarily cognitive in nature, the idea of shared needs has a large affective component and is clearly more diffuse.

8. In many ways it is easier to create such changes in interpretation than to diffuse them effectively and the person who trumpets a changed view too loudly may become suspect to other members of the group.

Therefore, efforts are more likely to target near-elites, those people in a society who have access to leaders or might be future leaders, as well as influence public opinion more broadly. Certainly this has been the case with various attempts to alter U.S. images of the Soviet Union since the mid-1950s. While tension between the superpowers went up and down throughout the post-Stalin period, by the time Mikhail Gorbachev came to power in 1985 there was a significant shift in American interpretations of the Soviets so that when Gorbachev took the first steps toward a fundamental restructuring of the relationship between the superpowers and began radical reform in his own society and in Eastern Europe, these actions were greeted warmly and understood in terms of prior shifts in interpretations of the Soviets. In South Africa it is clear that the extensive contact between many white and black leaders in the five years prior to the government's release of Nelson Mandela from prison in 1990 and the subsequent legalization of the African National Congress prepared the way to the rapid movement toward preparations for establishing a post-apartheid regime. In the Middle East and Northern Ireland as well there have been many occasions for exchange and dialogue involving a wide range of members from the different communities.

While the main focus in this discussion is on shifts in interpretations that result from face-to-face experiences, the media can also play a vital role in this process. At the simplest level, the transmission of powerful, emotional images—Sadat arriving in Israel and being greeted by his former enemies, or Mandela and de Klerk meeting each other for the first time in public—communicates significant changes. As the media tell a story they generally humanize and contextualize the key actors in ways that do not support intensely hostile images. A striking example is the way American and European media portrayed Gorbachev and his wife, Raisa. With each international summit, more and more human details were presented, making it virtually impossible for Americans to see Gorbachev or the USSR as an implacable foe or, interestingly, to understand his serious domestic political problems and limitations.[9]

Although the pressure of particular conflicts promotes a wish to affect political leaders as quickly as possible, the importance of multiple influence strategies for long-term peacemaking efforts should not be ig-

9. In the late 1980s the following joke circulated in Moscow: What is the difference between the United States and the USSR? Gorbachev could be elected president of the United States.

nored. Efforts to affect the views of near or future elites as well as concern with public opinion more broadly are also important.

Strategies for Modifying Disputants' Interpretations

Although there are many books and self-help manuals purporting to explain how the divergent interests of opponents can be resolved, much less is available on ways to alter hostile interpretations. In this section my goal is to indicate a particular direction rather than to offer concrete suggestions.

Most of the strategies reach individuals typically in face-to-face small groups and are based on the need for disputants to address fears and mutually hostile interpretations before they can deal with substantive differences in interests. Psychoanalysis is a specific strategy for altering disputants' interpretations and dispositions, yet its methodology is hardly appropriate in toto to large-scale social disputes. What psychoanalysis does provide, however, is a theoretical justification for specific methods aimed at modifying mutually hostile interpretations.

Interactive problem solving involves "workshops . . . designed to encourage an analytic approach to joint problem solving of a conflict that will be conducive to the emergence of creative 'win-win' solutions satisfying the basic needs of both parties" (Kelman 1991:145). Track Two diplomacy "is an unofficial, information interaction between members of adversary groups or nations that aims to develop strategies, influence public opinion, and organize human and material resources in ways that might help resolve conflict" (Montville 1991a:162). Other broad-based personal and cultural exchanges also have the aim of altering stereotyped, negative, and rigid images and thereby paving the way for constructive joint problem solving.[10] All are forms of prenegotiations which establish the prerequisite conditions for serious discussions in long-term disputes by deepening parties' understanding of each other's positions and increasing the sense of mutual empathy. Such strategies also aim at providing people with skills that help them to understand the conflict in which they are engaged and meet their basic needs (Rothman 1992).

10. While these labels are relatively new, the underlying ideas are not and we can find many historical examples of the same processes.

Problem-solving Workshops

Problem-solving workshops bring together members, but typically not official representatives, of opposing communities in a variety of formats. Those that have received the greatest attention have focused on significant international disputes, but the method has also been utilized to address conflicts within organizations and disputes in local communities. The workshop is designed to bring together individuals from the different groups in a "safe" setting to address questions which are otherwise difficult, if not impossible, to discuss. While the participants have no official positions, it is hoped that they might influence decision makers or policy decisions in a variety of ways, at minimum through the example that dialogue between the two communities can be productive. As workshop models have developed, there are important differences in what their organizers have tried to achieve.

For example, in the late 1960s three Yale University faculty members with experience in Africa brought six Somalis, six Ethiopians, and six Kenyans to a secluded location in South Tyrol for two weeks to discuss the border dispute between Somalia and its two neighbors, which involved a good deal of armed fighting (Doob 1970). The researchers employed a modified form of sensitivity training (T-groups) to try to build a more complex understanding of the issues among the participants and to produce specific proposals for ending the conflict. Although there was a good deal of time allocated to general training, involving building personal links among the participants, before the specific border disputes were discussed, in comparison with more recent designs there was very little attention devoted to participants' developing any empathy for each others' core beliefs. When the Somalis continued to emphasize the importance of self-determination and the Kenyans and Ethiopians stressed the sanctity of international borders in Africa, the trainers apparently did not push the participants to identify the needs beneath these positions. In addition, the naïve and ambitious goal of having the participants' design a settlement for the two disputes contrasts with more modest goals such as having the participants develop the skills to identify their own underlying needs and fears, develop a sense of the deep-seated fears and needs of members of the opposing group, or design first steps the disputants might take to resolve the dispute. The failure of this attempt, like the women's peace movement in

Northern Ireland, illustrates the fact that generalized efforts to alter psychocultural orientations are not sufficient. Rather what is needed is sophisticated changes in interpretations which then allow for specific redefinition of interests.

Interactive problem-solving workshops, which Kelman (1978, 1991; Kelman and Cohen 1986) has designed, emphasize building a more nuanced understanding of the conflict among participants, meaning the development of a mutual appreciation of the fears and threats the other side feels. These workshops are seen as a form of mediation, for Kelman and the other organizers hope that the participants will share their insights with others in their own community, including those in decision-making roles. Important goals in this kind of workshop are strengthening the perception that further dialogue among the parties is likely to be fruitful due to a responsiveness to each other's human concerns and psychological needs, increased insights into each other's perspectives, and the sense that there are people on the other side worth talking to (Kelman 1978). There is relatively little effort to have the parties develop specific solutions to the conflict and little interest in the development of interpersonal bonds among the workshop participants.[11]

Other workshop designs focus more exclusively on participants' psychocultural interpretations. In one form there is an emphasis on participants articulating their central human needs, such as security, identity, recognition, and development, and recognizing both the shared and nonnegotiable character of these needs and how they are central to the dispute (Burton 1969, 1990). Once such a step is taken, disputants consider ways in which the basic human needs of all can be met as part of a solution to a conflict. Problem solving, for Burton, situates a conflict in a local context, and emphasizing what is common to the disputants increases the likelihood of developing a long-term solution.

Another model emphasizes the identification of basic needs, as the Burton and Kelman approaches do, and then encourages participants to use these insights to develop the skills to focus on a concrete problem which divides the communities (Rothman 1992). For example, Rothman has run workshops in which Jews and Palestinians develop

11. Kelman stresses that the focus of concern is at the intergroup, rather than the interpersonal level (1991:146). In fact, if participants get too close personally to those on the other side, their credibility in their own community may be weakened.

proposals to address intercommunity tensions, which rose when there was a heavy influx of Jewish immigrants into a predominantly Arab town in Israel, and others to offer recommendations to meet the needs of both Jews and Arabs living in Jerusalem. By emphasizing the differences among basic needs, interests, and bargaining positions, these workshops attempt to both produce shifts in how each side views the other, and help participants develop problem-solving skills so that even when bargaining positions seem incompatible, common needs can be identified, and proposals that meet the basic needs and many common interests of all parties may be developed.

Track Two Diplomacy

"Track Two diplomacy" is a catchall term that refers to a wide range of contacts and exchanges between opposing groups (particularly in the international arena) which supplement, rather than replace, traditional (Track One) diplomacy. It developed out of the recognition that official government-to-government or leader-to-leader relationships can be highly constraining. In contrast, Track Two efforts can be more open ended and exploratory and can build bridges that can later influence Track One efforts (Montville 1991a). The Track Two effort relies on the hypothesis that altering hostile interpretations of the other side is a critical prerequisite to reaching agreements. Only when psychological barriers involving the accumulated historical grievances of all parties are lowered, mutual acceptance of responsibility for hurts afflicted is established, and mourning of losses is carried out, can Track One and other conventional conflict management efforts succeed. Three distinct processes are part of Track Two efforts to date (Montville 1991a; Montville and Davidson 1981–82): small, facilitated problem-solving workshops or seminars (much like those just discussed); efforts to influence public opinion through the media and in other ways; and the development of cooperative economic (and other) activities which provide incentives and institutional support for continued cooperation among the parties.

Workshops and seminars obviously involve only small numbers of people. Track Two efforts to modify public opinion involve educating people on each side about the legitimate concerns of the other side, shared interests and fears, and peacemaking successes when they occur. Crucial to this effort is not only building a more sophisticated view of the hopes and fears of each side, but building support for political leaders who can use Track One channels to reach binding agreements.

Recently a good deal of attention has been paid to prenegotiation, pointing out the need for disputants to have an opportunity to exchange ideas, understandings, and perspectives before formal talks begin (Rothman ed. 1991; Saunders 1985; Stein 1989). Although most of the attention has focused on international disputes, this work is relevant to intransigent conflict at all levels.

Finally, cooperation in economic and other activities is vital to the Track Two effort for several reasons. Unlike the other two steps, it addresses the interests of the conflicting parties directly and offers concrete examples of ways in which working together to solve a common problem can make people on all sides better off and can serve as a model for the future.[12]

Personal and Cultural Exchanges

Diffuse and wide-ranging efforts to build personal, intellectual, and even political ties among groups and nations in conflict are often justified on the grounds that such contacts will alter hostile stereotypes, increase understanding of the other side's fears and help pave the way for formal intergroup peacemaking efforts (Saunders 1991). Contact between representatives of hostile groups is expected to alter prior mutually hostile images. For example, the Dartmouth Conference has since 1960 brought together Soviet and American citizens, who have engaged in policy-related nonofficial dialogue (Saunders 1991).[13]

In polarized situations, a critical first step may be for people from

12. The emphasis on the achievement of superordinate goals includes the assumption that when such goals are met, they will be accompanied by a shift in interpretations. It is important to recognize the limitations to this argument. Even in postwar Europe, one of the best cases of the growth of cooperative institutions among previous enemies, it is uncertain whether this was due to the demonstration of effects of European institutions or to other political factors. In any case it came far more slowly than institutional changes.

13. The focus on such contacts varies widely. The Dartmouth Conference tries to focus on substantive issues. In some cultural exchanges there is greater concern with developing interpersonal contacts of a more diffuse sort. In contrast, groups like Moral Rearmament are interested in addressing the core psychocultural assumptions of members of different communities.

different communities to learn about the hopes and fears of the other side, to perceive that common ground may exist, and to select problems to consider together. Educational, cultural, and sports-related exchanges may be very diffuse in their goals. At the most basic level, it is hoped that interpersonal and group exchanges may offer a more nuanced and human view of an adversary. It is also hoped that such exchanges can be part of a broader attempt to shift public opinion to be receptive to political leaders' bold peacemaking efforts (Kriesberg 1992).

Lessons

Problem-solving workshops, Track Two diplomacy, and personal and cultural exchanges are all strategies for modifying psychocultural interpretations, a crucial step before effective joint problem solving can occur in many polarized conflicts. Unlike psychoanalysis, some of whose core assumptions are reflected in each of these methods, the emphasis in the context of conflict management is on modifying psychocultural interpretations disputants hold, not in changing the underlying dispositions. In the approaches discussed here, the emphasis is on facilitating participation in situations that challenge previous interpretations of an adversary and offering the possibility of linking the new information to a disposition not emphasized before. It is hoped that new metaphors will develop, allowing adversaries to view each other differently, and that disputants may acquire skills that will allow them to solidify and build on this change in interpretations.

By itself, contact between members of hostile groups does not necessarily lead to improved mutual images, however. In many conditions contact exacerbates intergroup tension rather than lowering it. Differentiation and personalization, Brewer and Miller (1984) argue, require the weakening of categorization of group members. In situations of high stress, unequal status, competition, and different group social norms, contact without facilitation may often reinforce negative images and fears of the other side. Simply bringing warring factions together can be a formula for failure as much as for success.

Interests Must Also Be Addressed

Modifying psychocultural interpretations can pave the way to effective joint problem solving but does not in and of itself address interest differences among disputants, even when goodwill is present. The Camp David Accords between the United States, Egypt, and Israel offer a dramatic example of major shifts in the central actors' and the public's interpretations of the situation and each other following Sadat's trip to Israel. Yet another two and a half years of intense, often very tense, negotiations were needed to arrive at a peace treaty all parties could accept. Goodwill and changed images are not enough; adversaries must also deal with the substantive differences which divide them. When they do so successfully, disputants reinforce the newly developed interpretations, furthering the possibility of a long-term change in relationships.

Addressing interests effectively often requires a combination of patience and exceptional negotiating skill (Raiffa 1982). In intergroup conflicts, interests are frequently stated as explicit positions which more often than not seem completely incompatible with each other (Fisher and Ury 1982; Rothman 1991). Reaching an agreement requires separating interests and positions, but this in no way guarantees success. In the Egyptian-Israeli case, for example, it took a long time for the two parties to move from recognizing that each party had an interest in lowering tension and avoiding another war to accepting the specifics of a land-for-peace formula consistent with the common interests.

Agreements that resolve conflicts of interests are important in and of themselves but may also modify psychocultural interpretations and in so doing affect future problem-solving efforts. Substantive agreements do this when they address underlying needs and give parties a real sense that their deepest concerns are being met. In addition, when needs are met, each party develops a stake in maintaining and even expanding an agreement. For example, during periods of bitter tension (such as around the 1982 Israeli invasion of Lebanon and in the period following the onset of the *intifada* on the West Bank and Gaza), Egypt recalled its ambassador from Israel for a period but never broke off relations or threatened to cancel the treaty.

Interests can be addressed, and protected, through constitutional arrangements that provide incentives for parties to cooperate. Horowitz argues that if the electoral arrangements found in most democratic nations are applied to severely divided societies, majority domination with little prospect for minority representation will result. What is needed in nations like South Africa or in Northern Ireland, he says, are electoral systems that reward cross-ethnic cooperation (Horowitz 1991). Where plurality systems such as first-past-the-post (where the person with the highest total wins) encourage self-sufficiency within majority groups, approval voting with vote pooling and a fifty percent requirement for victory offers incentives for political leaders and followers to build coalitions across ethnic divisions which address the interests of more than one group. The argument in this chapter does not challenge such proposals, but is based on the hypothesis that cooperative constitutional engineering of this sort will not occur as long as opposing parties hold intensely hostile images of each other.

Conclusion

Conflict management efforts must consider institutions and practices that address both hostile interpretations and disputants' interests. Far more attention is currently devoted to addressing the interests involved in social disputes. The argument here is that equal effort should be devoted to establishing and maintaining effective institutions and practices that allow disputants to get beyond intense mutual distrust.

Many recent discussions of conflict management emphasize ways in which disputants can make best use of joint problem solving, implicitly assuming a desire for a common solution but a lack of know-how regarding its development (Fisher and Ury 1981; Pruitt and Rubin 1986; Susskind and Cruikshank 1988; Raiffa 1982; Ury, Brett, and Goldberg 1988). Yet in situations where the parties have not yet committed themselves to searching for a common solution because they perceive the conflict in mutually exclusive, zero-sum terms, the more specific proposals for addressing interest differences can be employed only when these hostile interpretations are altered.

Problem-solving workshops, such as those Kelman has designed, and the range of Track Two diplomacy methods Montville has described are certainly steps in the right direction. At the same time there remains a need for more extensive institutionalization of procedures to facilitate psychocultural changes. In the same way that police and courts can be thought of as necessary institutional mechanisms for maintaining law and order, modern societies need to develop institutional mechanisms to facilitate constructive conflict management that addresses disputants' deepest fears and needs.

In most situations where conflict is intense and perceived threats to identity are great, it is naïve to think that such changes are easy to achieve. In many cases, disputants will be skeptical of any process that limits their freedom of action. As a result it may be hard to utilize a third party who may, in fact, be able to facilitate conflict management if given the chance.[14] Similarly, polarized groups involved in bitter disputes will probably not be able to be very introspective.

Facilitated efforts to achieve psychocultural change will typically involve relatively few people, making it important to consider how to provide support and reinforcement for those who do change. One step is to combine intense efforts to modify psychocultural interpretations, as in workshops, with a more general campaign to influence public norms and opinion to the same end, through the media or educational system. Another useful step is to dramatize ways in which changes in interpreta-tions are accompanied by meaningful behavior change in an adversary. Emphasizing small reciprocal successes can sometimes overcome the belief that no constructive changes are possible.[15]

It is important to understand that facilitated psychocultural change will not lead to one-shot resolution of complex conflicts (as the naïve organizers of the workshop on the border conflict between Somalia and its neighbors hoped it might). More realistically, participants on all sides should identify a series of small but meaningful steps that they would be prepared to take and that people on the other side could interpret as a sign of a sincere desire to improve relations. Each side could also articu-late its fears in response to each step it takes and identify the fears likely to be aroused by the steps it asks of the other party. Such an exchange could produce a number of significant benefits. It would direct attention to future positive steps rather than dwelling on past negative actions,

14. This dynamic was certainly involved during the Gulf crisis between early August 1990 and mid-January 1991 when neither Saddam Hussein nor George Bush seemed interested in supporting third-party efforts to negotiate an agreement between Iraq and the United States.

15. Osgood's (1962) Graduated Reciprocation in Tension Reduction (GRIT) is a concrete proposal about how such a pattern might be implemented. Larson (1988) provides a detailed application of the GRIT approach in a specific bargain-ing situation, the Austrian State Treaty.

and focus on conflict management as a process involving a series of reciprocal moves rather than a single dramatic action. Finally, it would invite responses in kind from the other side, providing a mechanism for maintaining a reciprocity that can dramatically alter public opinion and disputants' perceptions of a situation.

Two elements are central to such proposals. One is that significant change often has to originate from the parties in a conflict. Imposing solutions from outside only increases the disputants' feelings of vulnerability. The second is that altering the fundamental relationship among actors can produce meaningful changes in their behavior toward each other (Bowen 1978; Mulvihill 1992). Given the hypothesis that any long-term bitter conflict contains dysfunctional patterns, many of which the parties are unaware, then a process that alters the relationship between the parties is often a first step in producing meaningful change. Although external changes may affect the internal dynamics of a system, constructive conflict management is most likely when the central parties in a dispute assume new, more constructive roles vis-à-vis each other.

The specific proposals for changing interpretations may seem modest, given the overwhelming need. In part this is because the framework for a great deal of conflict management to date, as Ury, Brett, and Goldberg (1988) point out, has emphasized either the rights or power of each party rather than their needs and interests. Both rights- and power-based conflict management strategies emphasize incompatible interests. Rights-based approaches appeal to a third party who renders a decision declaring one side the winner and the other the loser, as in a court or bureaucratic decision. Power-based conflict management is pure self-help. Neither approach assumes that the needs of all parties are legitimate or that there may be solutions that are acceptable to all parties. No wonder, then, that we have few institutions and practices that address opponents' hostile interpretations and emphasize joint decision making as a strategy for bridging differences.

As long as public expectations about the possibility of constructive conflict management are low, successful solutions will be difficult to achieve. Recent efforts to develop, teach, and institutionalize procedures for managing interest differences are important steps in the right direction. In modern industrial settings this matter is often so neglected that even modest efforts to institute interest-based conflict management produce a striking effect on outcomes (Susskind and Cruikshank 1988; Ury,

Brett, and Goldberg 1988). My main argument in this chapter, however, presented as a working hypothesis, is that the implementation of such procedures often requires that mutually hostile psychocultural interpretations be addressed as a prerequisite to dealing with substantive differences to allow each party to "hear" what others are saying. Good data on if and when changes in interpretations affect the capacity of parties to address interest differences would tell us a great deal about the value of efforts in this direction.

9

Toward More Constructive Conflict Management

Too many participants in intense social disputes, and too many observers, accept the idea that there is little or nothing constructive that can be done to alter their course. I contend that conflict management can make a difference in many disputes. Believing that effective actions can be taken is, of course, not the same thing as knowing what specific steps to take in a particular situation, but in and of itself this attitude can contribute to a disputant's sense of efficacy and expectations and motivate a continuing search for constructive solutions.

Three ideas are central to my argument: conflict as a cultural process; the importance of psychocultural interpretations, along with structural interests, as sources of conflict; and the strong linkage between how we understand conflicts and how we try to manage them. In this concluding chapter I highlight the possibilities for increasing constructive conflict management by way of three points. First, we need well-developed models (and concrete examples) of the successful management of conflicts, especially those that are bitter and intense (also see Kriesberg 1992). Second, the psychocultural dimension of conflict, particularly the reorganization and refocusing of interpretations is a crucial and underdeveloped aspect of constructive conflict management. Third, managing more conflicts more constructively requires both the belief that this is possible and the development of supportive institutions and practices. Successful conflict management cannot depend on extraordinary efforts of especially gifted or far-sighted individuals; rather, the lesson from the constructive conflict societies examined in chapter 3 is that it must be institutionalized in such a way that ordinary people can engage in it and benefit from it in all aspects of their daily lives.

Models of Successful Conflict Management

Models of successful conflict management serve two purposes. First, they identify specific approaches that may be applied to a wide range of conflicts. In recent years a small cottage industry of scholars and practitioners teaching specific methods of conflict management with an emphasis on joint problem solving in a variety of settings has developed in opposition to the belief that conflicts need to be left alone or halted by third parties. This effort needs to be evaluated in a theoretically informed way in order to be relevant to conflicts in many cultural settings, and an important part of this task involves a better understanding of conflict management success.

A second purpose is more overtly political and aimed at changing the conventional wisdom that conflict, particularly large-scale intransigent conflict such as that between ethnic groups, is inevitable and irremediable. The success of the alternative dispute resolution movement and new methods of mediation and negotiation has been greatest in universities and large-scale organizations in industrial societies. In these settings, where conflicts are often low to moderate in intensity, both the interpersonal and economic rewards of innovation are often quickly apparent.[1] It is harder for many to sustain the belief that more bitter conflicts may be similarly manageable.[2]

Successful conflict management needs to be studied in its own right (Kriesberg 1992). Study of failures can teach us many things about what not to do or what went wrong in particular cases but it neither contributes to a belief that constructive conflict management is possible nor tells us how to do it. The practices and institutions in constructive conflict societies have distinctive features that cannot be deduced from societies in which conflict is destructive and bitter, and the lessons of successfully managed conflict are not simply the inverses of cases that were failures.

I was first struck by the need for examples of successful conflict

1. There may be a kind of Hawthorne effect here; in many large organizations, perhaps the fact that change is introduced is more important than the specific innovations.

2. Some (e.g., Rifkin 1991) argue that the emphasis on mediation and problem solving promoted by alternative dispute resolution advocates focuses on the resolution of interpersonal disputes, at the expense of structural inequalities and group-based conflicts.

management of intense conflict a few years ago when I discussed the Israeli-Palestinian dispute with Herbert Kelman. He made it clear that peacemakers like himself needed to focus on the idea that conflict could be managed constructively as a way of empowering those disputants who were interested in this goal. We talked about parallel conflicts —Northern Ireland, South Africa, Sri Lanka, and Cyprus—and I remember asking him for examples of similar bitter disputes that did not end in one-sided domination but in some kind of success that could be used as an example of the possibility of an alternative to continued confrontation and violence. Neither of us found it easy to respond, and the examples we eventually discussed (Switzerland, Belgium, and Holland of earlier centuries) were not contemporary.

It may indeed be the case that there are very few examples of ethnic conflict management with peace and justice. Alternatively it may be that the way we think about such situations limits our ability to identify appropriate cases. The greatest conceptual danger comes, I think, from the post hoc nature of many analyses. Cases where some kind of accommodation is achieved are dismissed as not relevant to the situation at hand, because an improvement in the situation is used as evidence that the conflict must not have been severe in the first place. Maybe—but good data on ethnic relations over time would probably show that this is often not the case.

If we had such data, I believe that we would see that there is rarely, if ever, dramatic change in group relations overnight (Kriesberg 1992:235). Most change is incremental and modest. Second, the evidence would show that few situations shift from high to low levels of conflict in the short run without the intervention of significant external factors. We need a language for the management of the most intransigent disputes that is much more nuanced than the current terms found in the conflict resolution field. A book like Fisher and Ury's *Getting to Yes* (1981) is important in showing that joint problem solving can be effective, but its usefulness is limited by the fact that the authors do not indicate the kind of conflicts in which their method is less likely to be successful. They also implicitly label anything short of complete agreement as failure.

Too often, imperfect intergroup relations are considered to be "bad." Instead, the incremental improvements interventions can make need to be more appreciated. The answer to the question "What would have happened without any intervention?" is often that the situation would have been far worse. As long as people continue to see only "fully resolved" conflicts as successes, there will be a tendency to ignore many worthwhile partially successful interventions and lose the opportunity to learn from them. In part this comes from difficulties we have in accepting the idea that no effectively functioning society is without conflict, but that when conflict occurs it is not inevitably destructive. It is ironic that our anxiety about the destructive possibilities in human conflict in some ways prevents us from developing institutions and practices which might, in fact, weaken its negative effects and constructively channel its potential for positive change.

Consider the case of Scandinavia, where Norwegians, Swedes, Danes, Finns, and Icelanders fought for domination over each other until early in this century. From the perspective of Northern Ireland or the Middle East, ethnic relations in Scandinavia look very calm today. Yet when I talk to people who know the area intimately, they tell me about such lingering suspicions as Norwegian and Danish resentment over Sweden's neutrality in World War II, mutually negative stereotypes, and ethnic jokes. While this is all true, what is missing is a sense of proportion, a recognition that the intensity of conflict among the different groups in the region is lower than it has ever been, that disputes there are regularly handled peacefully, and that many solutions involve mutual gain. Constructive conflict management does not require the end of group differences, and if the tensions associated with them are found in jokes rather than overt fighting, so much the better.

Another example (although not without ambiguities) is the change in black-white relations in Kenya, Zambia, and especially Zimbabwe between the colonial and independence periods. As colonies, each of these areas had sizeable white settler communities, which to different degrees fought to prevent African majority rule. Upon achieving independence, however, African leaders made a particular effort to assure whites that they were welcome and needed in the new nation, and that their rights and property would be protected. In each case, many whites chose to leave, but some stayed partly due to the fact that they could not take all their wealth with them. Because exit was a viable option, Africans often felt that most whites who remained were different from those who left. What is most significant is the sharp reduction in mutual tension and the sense of linked fate now found in black-white relations. Whites are now a small and wealthy ethnic enclave that is careful to respect majority rule. In some cases this is accompanied by a shift in beliefs as well (see Smith 1984).[3] Successful conflict management need not mean that tensions and differences between groups completely disappear; rather, as in this case, they may simply be less destructive than before.[4]

We need to be able to look at cases such as Scandinavia or East and Central Africa (and other areas where change has been significant if less dramatic) over time in order to build models of successful conflict management applicable to contemporary cases. Donald Horowitz (1985, 1991) offers several examples of success, most notably Malaysia, the Nigerian constitution of 1979, and even the current electoral system in Sri Lanka. I have already discussed French-German reconciliation since 1945 (Montville 1991a), changes in race relations in the United States (especially in the South) since 1950, and Israel and Egypt following Sadat's trip to Jerusalem in 1977. Other potentially more problematic cases include Canada—which avoided the worst-case scenarios many foresaw in the late 1960s—reconciliation in Nigeria since the failed Biafran succession, relations in selected states in India, Nicaragua under Chimora, and the generally peaceful management of social change in much of Spain since Franco.

Success and failure in conflict management is signaled in the changes in interests and interpretations. As suggested in chapter 6, indicators of success with regard to addressing disputants' interest-based demands would include: movement from general grievances to more specific demands; the emergence of clear ranking of each party's interests; the identification of inclusive interests benefiting all and making intergroup agreements attractive; and the degree to which each side perceives flexibility in the opponent with respect to important demands. Indicators of successful shifts in the state of disputants' interpretations of a conflict could include: the extent to which each side develops empathy but not necessarily sympathy for the other(s); the degree to which each side accepts the existence of an opponent rather than wanting to see it annihilated or removed from the territory; the ability of members of each community to conceptualize how they would be better off if

4. One must not forget that the economic inequalities and the assumptions of cultural superiority and inferiority that dominated black-white relations in the African nations just mentioned still exist. Nonetheless, relations between the groups have improved significantly.

there were intercommunity cooperation as opposed to continued conflict; and the extent to which each community believes that opponents understand and accept its core needs.

Specific changes in language can be particularly good indicators of these changes. How do leaders as well as ordinary people talk about their own group and the other side? Do the adjectives change, over time? Is there an alteration in the metaphors used to discuss the conflict and express grievances? Is fear or threat expressed differently? What in the disputants' language suggests shifts in the degree of empathy and acceptance of the other side's basic needs?

Considering the language of ethnic conflict management requires us to recognize the Whorfian position, that language shapes our perceptions of reality. To the extent that this is the case, the ways participants talk about conflict not only reflect their view of what conflict management can accomplish, but also affect how they behave. If language stresses inevitability, threat, polarization, and biologically driven conflict, then disputants are not likely to consider intergroup conflict management very promising. Constructive approaches are more likely to develop when disputants possess a language that expresses different ways disputes can be (and have been) successfully managed, including images of mutual gain, a sense of trust, and a modest degree of mutual empathy.

The Importance of Psychocultural Interpretations

In the conclusion of my cross-cultural analysis, I argued:

Conflicts aren't just about what people do to each other. They are also about what one group of people think or feel that another group of people are doing, or trying to do, or wanting to do. This, of course, is what makes them so difficult to contain and manage at times. In a context of suspicion not only actions, but also presumptions about the intentions and meanings behind the actions (or inactions), play a central role. In few conflict situations do events themselves provide clear explanations for the motives underlying them; individuals turn to internal frameworks as well. This interpretive element in conflict behavior shapes subsequent action. (Ross 1993:177–178)

This idea is central to my analysis of conflict management as well.

Making sense of key symbolic elements is often essential in understanding the role of psychocultural dynamics of a conflict. During the period when Turkish Cypriots were confined to enclaves surrounded by U.N. troops, for example, raising parakeets as a hobby flourished and then disappeared when some Turks returned to their villages after intercommunal talks permitted restricted travel on the island (Volkan 1988). Volkan argues that the caged birds came to symbolize the feeling of lack of freedom and served as an externalization of intense anxiety.

Shared, [the parakeets] were suitable reservoirs to hold and protect by externalization the imprisoned self-images of Cypriot Turks . . . This externalization helped [the Cypriot Turk] to repress his own feeling of want: As long as the little creatures sang, remained fertile, and were looked after, they embodied the hope that the human population might also thrive and receive care. Anxiety created by the sociopolitical stress was thus allayed by the actualization of the old concept of a bird's free nature, this externalization providing a safety value for mass anxiety. In their dilemma, the Turks of Cyprus had become what could be described as helpless helpers . . . Although they paradoxically clung to the abstract notion of a longed-for savior, they became themselves the saviors of the birds that represented their own imprisoned selves. This example of the Cypriot Turks indicates the use of some existent object to absorb the common unwanted characteristics so that the population in question could feel more cohesive as individuals and more closely bound to their group of allies. (1988:80)

Interpretation is central to conflict behavior because conflicts evoke deep-seated emotions in situations that are highly ambiguous and often unstructured. Emotion runs high when what are felt to be important interests are involved. Ambiguity is great when the meaning of actions or intentions is unclear. The combination of emotion and ambiguity readily produces psychic threat and regression with a return to intense, primitive feelings. The dispositions invoked in such situations are rooted in early experiences and shape how participants react to a conflict. Yet worldviews are cultural, not just personal, when they are nurtured and socially reinforced, linking individuals in a collective process.

Although participants in any dispute claim that they know exactly what the conflict is about, in most situations, different parties do not agree on what a conflict is about, when it started, or who is involved. As Schattschneider (1960), Coleman (1957), and many others have noted, the substance of conflicts, the parties, and their goals change over time. A conflict is less a one-time event than a fluid, changing phenomenon. Many disputes, whether they are between families in a community or nations in the world, involve parties with a long history, which, of course, includes lists of accumulated grievances that can be trotted out and appended to newer ones as conditions change.

The same factors that push actors to make sense of an ambiguous and unstructured situation also lead to cognitive and perceptual distortion because, in effect, the desire for certainty often is greater than the need for accuracy. Not only are individuals likely to make systematic errors in their perceptions of social action in which they are involved, but the homogeneous nature of most social settings will also reinforce their self-serving mistakes. Interpretations of a conflict offer a coherent account that links discrete events and actors. Central to such interpretations is the attribution of motives to parties. Once identified, the existence of such motives makes it easy to "predict" another's future actions, and through one's own behavior to turn such predictions into self-fulfilling prophesies. The infusion of events with emotion makes it especially likely that processes of externalization and projection involved in the construction of interpretations will evoke a group's inner needs as well as external events. In this sense, it is appropriate to suggest that rather than thinking about particular objective events that cause conflicts to escalate, we ought to be thinking about *interpretations* of events that are associated with escalation and those that are not.

Psychocultural insights are particularly useful in understanding the intensity of emotions found in so many conflicts which to outsiders often seem to be about trivial matters. Where outsiders can easily devise simple solutions, disputants often remain incomprehensibly unyielding. Why? The high emotional investment of the parties means the matter is no longer trivial, which third parties must recognize and not dismiss as irrational. Often the emotional intensity of bitter conflicts is rooted in perceived threats to group and individual identity, and any satisfactory outcome must take this into account. Only when these identity issues are addressed can any progress on the substance of the dispute be made, since powerful insecurities and fears feed projection, externalization, and displacement and become prime barriers to the consideration of interests, the ostensible focus of the dispute. Of course emotion-laden conflicts can be especially difficult to settle. Sometimes the fact that each side feels the same intense emotions makes it difficult to recognize what they may, in fact, share. For example, precisely because both Protestants and Catholics in Northern Ireland see themselves as a threatened minority, each has trouble understanding how the other can feel the same thing. One party's emotional concerns may be difficult for another to accept, especially when its own actions may be the cause.

Shared in-group images of the world and plans for action are predicated on a shared conception of the difference between one's own group and others. The interpretive processes involved in intense conflict situations emphasize the homogeneity of each party, often using minor objective differences to mark major social distinctions. Outsiders then can serve as objects for externalization, displacement, and projection of intense negative feelings, which are present but denied within the group.

Recognizing the role that interpretive factors play offers the possibility of modifying them, rather than accepting their consequences as somehow inevitable. The conflict management process, for example, can first recognize and then address the fears of adversaries in a variety of ways. Each party's articulation of the importance of what is at stake and recognition of the ambiguity associated with actions and statements on both sides can be a first step toward lowering fear and insecurity. When such fears are made self-conscious and their sources addressed, the prospects for constructive conflict management increase.

My emphasis on the central role that psychocultural interpretations play in conflict behavior is not an argument that all differences are reducible to psychocultural states. People do fight about real interests, be they material or symbolic, but the way this is done, the intensity of feelings, and the lengths to which disputants go to defend or acquire what they believe is their due are evidence that the pursuit of interests has an important psychocultural component which is not yet well understood.

We need better data and a richer understanding of the worldviews, metaphors, analogies, and images used to characterize actions, presumed intentions, and values of one's own group and of others to understand their role in conflict behavior more completely. In particular, the argument that changes in interpretations are central to the conflict management process needs systematic empirical elaboration.

Expanding Constructive Conflict Management

The idea of the constructive conflict society (or constructive conflict communities) draws attention to the fact that not only may individual conflicts be managed well, but communities may also have effective conflict management as their norm. As with societies in which ethnic relations are not intensely hostile, there is always a temptation to dismiss constructive conflict societies as situations where people have no reason to fight, as opposed to viewing them as places where they have as much reason to fight as anyone else but conflict is handled differently.

Implicit in my analysis is the idea of borrowing institutions and practices from constructive conflict societies, but this transplantation hypothesis needs more careful consideration. The alternative dispute resolution movement in the United States, sometimes without great self-consciousness, borrowed many ideas concerning conflict management from small-scale societies in which legal anthropologists have worked (e.g., Gibbs 1963; Nader and Todd 1978). Replacing self-help or adjudication with mediation, negotiation, moots, and other kinds of joint problem solving has proven very popular in some organizations and communities, although the overall success of these approaches is still uncertain. We need to understand more about the adaptation of such practices to new settings, the importance of psychocultural and structural features of target communities, and what is needed to make such new institutions legitimate or to increase the legitimacy of existing institutions in which new practices are developed.

This issue was brought home to me during the Gulf crisis of 1990–91. Along with several colleagues I participated in a teach-in and a series of weekly meetings to discuss the conflict and war that followed. A colleague who had devoted many years to studying the region attended several sessions and was clearly upset with both our expressions of discomfort about the course of the conflict and our discussion about ways to end it. Finally, he wrote an open letter to the college newspaper charging us with trying to inappropriately impose western social science concepts of conflict resolution on the region. What he failed to understand, from our point of view, was that all cultures grapple with the question of managing conflicts and that the notion of peacemaking is just as appropriate to the Middle East as anywhere else. Where he was probably right, however, was that our lack of familiarity with the specific cultures made it difficult to talk about psychocultural interpretations or structural interests with the degree of specificity he would have been able to accept.

Ultimately, improved conflict management depends upon the development of institutions and practices that address both the psychocultural interpretations and structural interests underlying disputes. Especially in severe social conflicts, such as intense ethnic conflicts, far more can, and should, be done. No longer should we accept self-help strategies based on power differences among the parties as adequate. Similarly, there is a real danger in relying on authoritative third-party interventions, whether by police and court systems or international peacekeeping forces. Although such tactics may be better than available short-run alternatives, they rarely address deep underlying causes or alter the basic relationships between the parties and thus do little to prevent the conflict from breaking out at the next opportune moment.

A viable approach to constructive conflict management must assign a primary role to the parties to the dispute. In addition, there is a pressing need for norms that make it clear to disputants that sooner or later they will be expected to engage in such a process; likewise institutions and practices that will support joint problem solving efforts must be created or strengthened. Good solutions are those the disputants ultimately accept and feel that they "own," which is most likely when they participate in the definition of alternatives and maintain control over outcomes. A process rooted in disputants' involvement must by its very nature address both hostile interpretations and substantive differences in interests.

A language that helps parties conceptualize constructive conflict management and identifies various successful models must be accompanied by specific skills. Joint problem solving, even when third-party assistance is available, is difficult, especially in emotionally charged situations. For example, there is little reason to believe that many ethnic political leaders possess the necessary skills; they have often been selected for their experience articulating grievances not their solutions. In most cases of protracted conflict, negotiations with long-time adversaries easily produce, I suspect, a great deal of moralistic position taking, overemphasis on one's own demands, reliance on the language of rights, and insufficient attention to the deeper needs and fears of the other side. None of these lead to successful conflict management.

In his work on Middle East conflict, Jay Rothman brings members of the Jewish and Arab communities in Israel together in interactive workshops. His goal is not to make participants like one another; in fact, he notes that the development of personal ties with those on the other side often creates problems for people returning to their own communities. Instead, he wants them to be able to deal with one another more constructively. Among the skills he identifies are a vocabulary they can use to talk to each other and the ability to frame the issues in a conflict cooperatively, to identify common needs, and to creatively define solutions for mutual gain (Rothman 1992).[5]

Another effort to extend constructive conflict management is found in training programs developed for educational settings ranging from primary school to university levels (National Institute for Dispute Resolution 1991).[6] These programs aim both to empower individuals to manage disputes constructively and to create a culture in the school that views constructive conflict management as appropriate and effective. The most common element of these programs is an emphasis on peer mediation, and Rifkin (1991) reports that assessments to date show high levels of teacher and student satisfaction, a decrease in fighting, lower suspension rates, and improvement in school climate (1991:2). Evaluation of the Resolving Conflict Creatively Program in Brooklyn, New York, shows an impact on teachers as well as students in more spontaneous use of conflict resolution skills, greater acceptance of differences, and increased skill in understanding other points of view (Mettis 1988, 1990).

Although Rifkin applauds these results, she notes with concern that the emphasis in many programs is on individual rather than structural conflict and that there is little effort to extend the skills to other conflicts, such as those between the community and schools, or to issues of cultural and racial bias (Rifkin 1991:3). She calls for a greater effort to develop programs that facilitate collaboration with courts, social service agencies, communities, and schools.

Finally, there is the important question of evaluating school-based and other types of dispute resolution programs. Although some programs have conducted self-evaluations, there is a need for longitudinal

5. Programs in many American elementary and secondary schools aimed at providing training in conflict and peacemaking make the same claim: that it is the particular skills which are lacking and that providing them can change the culture of conflict in a school in important ways.

6. An overview of dispute resolution programs in educational settings is found in a special issue of *Forum* (Spring 1991), published by the National Institute for Dispute Resolution, and a special issue of *Peace Reporter* (Fall-Winter 1991) published by the National Peace Foundation. Each describes a number of school-based initiatives in various regions of the United States and at different educational levels.

data (Rifkin 1991) and a clearer sense of the ways in which such programs do and do not succeed. In this regard, Campbell's notion of "the experimenting society" (1988) is particularly appropriate. His argument that explicit evaluation should accompany social policy innovation in order to identify when and how policies do and do not achieve their intended goals seems especially appropriate to conflict management innovation in any setting.

It is easy to obtain widespread support for the goal of peaceful management of conflict. Consensus on goals, should not, however, blur the fact that some steps toward achievement of common goals are more effective than others. In fact, twentieth-century history provides ample evidence that some of the most sincere and committed peacemakers, often relying on moral suasion alone, have been among the most unsuccessful.

Conclusion

The proactive approach advocated here will not always succeed in producing constructive resolution of disputes or conflicts. But this does not necessarily mean that dispute management efforts need to be more selective. Interventions that fail are one kind of error, although they may contain important lessons. However, I am even more concerned, at this point, with failures that result when conflict management efforts that might succeed are not tried. An example of this overly cautious approach is Haass' (1990) analysis of intense ethnic conflicts, which he argues can only be dealt with effectively when they are "ripe" for resolution. This somewhat tautological point may be correct, but Haass, in advising the makers of foreign policy to be cautious about intervening in these conflicts prematurely, offers little in the way of proposals for fostering this "ripeness," which is described in terms that are almost more biological than social or political. "No conflict shall be resolved before its time." Perhaps no peacemakers will look foolish for having failed for intervening in disputes not yet ripe for resolution, but how many disputes might have been resolved but were not because no one took any steps to try to bring the dispute closer to the point of being "picked"? If we do not have many conflict management failures, it may be because we are too cautious in our interventions.

Conflict management institutions and practices affect the course of specific disputes. They also affect norms and expectations that shape the disputes in broader ways. One effect is communicating to adversaries that differences can be managed without violence. Another result is creating moral, economic, and political pressures on parties who refuse or hesitate to engage in joint problem solving within established institutional frameworks. Finally, by setting high expectations for disputants, conflict management institutions and practices can shape community behavior, often increasing the number of incidents settled by the parties themselves.

I began this book by noting that while conflict in human societies is inevitable, what people do about disputes when they occur is highly variable. A major goal of my analysis has been to suggest ways in which peacemakers as well as those who are themselves involved in conflicts can manage them more constructively as they better understand the causes of disputes.

Unlike the human technology for fighting, which has improved significantly in recent centuries, our ability to manage conflict effectively has increased far less rapidly. This is in part due to long-standing beliefs not only that conflicts are inevitable, but that there is little that can be done about them once they are underway. My argument, contrary to this view, is that conflict is rooted in a set of social and psychocultural circumstances that needs to be understood, but which when recognized offers the possibility for actions that can significantly alter the dispute's path.

Not all disputes are equally good candidates for constructive conflict management, and constructive conflict management is not crisis management. At the same time, my analysis suggests that many more disputes could benefit from constructive management. Incremental improvement in conflict management is a realistic goal and one that can be realized given our present level of resources, skills, and motivation. My goal in examining conflict and conflict management in cross-cultural perspective has been to suggest reasons why this effort is worthwhile and ways it can be achieved.

Bibliography

Abel, Richard. 1973–74. "A Comparative Theory of Dispute Institutions in Society." *Law and Society Review* 8:217–347.

Altschuler, Milton. 1965. "The Cayapa: A Study in Legal Behavior." Ph.D. diss. University of Minnesota.

Anderson, John, and Hilary Hevenor. 1987. *Burning Down the House: MOVE and the Tragedy of Philadelphia*. New York: Norton.

Assefa, Hizkias, and Paul Wahrhaftig. 1990. *The MOVE Crisis in Philadelphia: Extremist Groups and Conflict Resolution*. Pittsburgh: University of Pittsburgh Press.

Aubert, Wilhelm. 1969. "Law as a Way of Resolving Conflicts: The Case of a Small Industrial Society," in Laura Nader, ed., *Law in Culture and Society*, pp. 282–303. Chicago: Aldine.

Avruch, Kevin. 1991. "Introduction" in Kevin Avruch, Peter W. Black, and Joseph A. Scimecca, eds., *Conflict Resolution: Cross-Cultural Perspectives*, pp. 1–17. New York: Greenwood Press.

Avruch, Kevin, and Peter W. Black. 1991. "The Cultural Question and Conflict Resolution." *Peace and Change* 16:22–45.

Axelrod, Robert. 1984. *The Evolution of Cooperation*. New York: Basic Books.

Badinter, Elisabeth, et al. 1989. "Profs, ne capitulons pas." *Le Nouvel Observateur*. (2–8 November 1989) 1304:58–59.

Balinkska, Maria. 1988. "SOS-Racisme." *Patterns of Prejudice* 22:46–48.

Bar-Tal, Daniel. 1986. "The Masada Syndrome: A Case of Central Belief," in N. Milgram, ed., *Stress and Coping in Time of War*, pp. 32–51. New York: Brunnor/Mazel.

———. 1990. "Israeli-Palestinian Conflict: A Cognitive Analysis," *International Journal of Intercultural Relations* 14:7–29.

Barth Fredrik. 1952. "Subsistence and Institutional System in a Norwegian Mountain Valley." *Rural Sociology* 17:28–38.

———. 1960. "Family Life in a Central Norwegian Mountain Community," in Thomas D. Eliot et al., eds., *Norway's Families: Trends, Problems, Programs.* Philadelphia: University of Pennsylvania Press, pp. 81–107.

Beriss, David. 1990. "Scarves, Schools, and Segregation: The Foulard Affair." *French Politics and Society* 8:1–13.

Berndt, Ronald M. 1964. "Warfare in the New Guinea Highlands." *American Anthropologist* 66:183–202.

Berobe, Maurice, and Marilyn Gittell. 1969. *Confrontation at Ocean Hill-Brownsville: The New York School Strikes of 1968.* New York: Praeger.

Bolton, Ralph. 1984. "Notes on Norwegian Non-Violence." Paper presented to the Annual Meeting of the Society for Cross-Cultural Research, Boulder, Colo.

Bowen, Murray. 1978. *Family Therapy in Clinical Practice.* New York: Jason Aronson.

Boyle, Kevin, and Tom Hadden. 1985. *Ireland: A Positive Proposal.* Harmondsworth: Penguin Books.

Brewer, Marilynn B., and Norman Miller. 1984. "Beyond the Contact Hypothesis: Theoretical Perspectives on Desegregation," in Norman Miller and Marilynn B. Brewer, eds., *Groups in Contact: The Psychology of Desegregation,* pp. 281–302. New York: Academic Press.

Briggs, Jean L. 1975. "The Origins of Nonviolence: Aggression in Two Canadian Eskimo Groups," in Warren Muensterberger and Aaron Esman, eds., *The Psychoanalytic Study of Society,* pp. 134–203. Vol. 6. New York: International Universities Press.

Brown, Paula. 1982. "Conflict in the New Guinea Highlands." *Journal of Conflict Resolution* 26:525–546.

Brown, Roger. 1986. "Ethnic Conflict," in *Social Psychology,* pp. 531–634. 2d. ed. New York: Free Press.

Burton, John. 1969. *Conflict and Communication: The Use of Controlled Communication in International Relations.* New York: Free Press.

———. 1990. *Conflict: Resolution and Provention.* New York: St. Martin's.

Campbell, D. T. 1983. "Two Distinct Routes Beyond Kin Selection to Ultra-sociality: Implications for the Humanities and Social Sciences," in D. L. Bridgeman, ed., *The Nature of Prosocial Development: Theories and Strategies,* pp. 11–41. New York: Academic Press.

———. 1988. "The Experimenting Society," in Samuel Overman, ed., *Methodology and Epistemology for Social Science: Selected Papers of Donald T. Campbell,* pp. 290–314. Chicago: University of Chicago Press.

Carter, Jimmy. 1982. *Keeping Faith: Memoirs of a President.* New York: Bantam.

Castberg, Frede. 1954. *The Norwegian Way of Life.* London: William Heinemann.

Chagnon, Napoleon. 1967. "Yanomamo Social Organization and Warfare," in Morton Fried, Marvin Harris, and Robert Murphy, eds., *War: The Anthropology of Armed Conflict and Aggression,* pp. 109–159. Garden City, N.Y.: Natural History Press.

————. 1983. *The Fierce People.* 3d ed. New York: Holt, Rinehart and Winston.

Cobb, Roger, and Charles Elder. 1983. *Participation in American Politics: The Dynamics of Agenda Building.* 2d ed. Baltimore: Johns Hopkins University Press.

Cohen, Raymond. 1990. *Culture and Conflict in Egyptian-Israeli Relations.* Bloomington: University of Indiana Press.

————. 1991. *Negotiating Across Cultures: Communication Obstacles in International Diplomacy.* Washington, D.C.: United States Institute for Peace.

Coleman, James S. 1957. *Community Conflict.* New York: Free Press.

Connary, Donald S. 1966. *The Scandinavians.* London: Eyre and Spottiswoode.

Coser, Lewis. 1956. *The Functions of Social Conflict.* New York: Free Press.

Crozier, Michel. 1964. *The Bureaucratic Phenomenon.* Chicago: University of Chicago Press.

Cuomo, Mario. 1974. *Forest Hills Diary: The Crisis of Low-Income Housing.* New York: Vintage.

Darby, John. 1983. *Ireland: Background to the Conflict.* Syracuse: Syracuse University Press.

Dentan, Robert Knox. 1968. *The Semai: A Non-Violent People of Malaya.* New York: Holt, Rinehart and Winston.

————. 1978. "Notes on Childhood in a Nonviolent Context: The Semai Case," in Ashley Montagu, ed., *Learning Non-Aggression: The Experience of Non-Literate Societies,* pp. 94–143. New York: Oxford University Press.

————. 1979. *The Semai: A Non-Violent People of Malaya.* Fieldwork edition. New York: Holt, Rinehart and Winston.

————. 1992. "The Rise, Maintenance, and Destruction of the Peaceable Polity: Preliminary Eassay in Political Ecology," in James Silverberg and J. Patrick Gray, eds., *Aggression and Peacefulness in Humans and Other Primates,* pp. 214–270. New York: Oxford University Press.

Deutsch, Morton. 1973. *The Resolution of Conflict: Constructive and Destructive Processes.* New Haven: Yale University Press.

Deutsch, Morton, and Shula Shichman. 1986. "Conflict: A Social Psychological Perspective," in Margaret Hermann, ed., *Political Psychology,* pp. 219–250. San Francisco: Jossey-Bass.

Devereux, George. 1967. *From Anxiety to Method in the Behavioral Sciences.* New York: Humanities Press.

De Waal, Franz. 1989. *Peacemaking Among Primates.* Cambridge: Harvard University Press.

Divale, William T. 1974. "Migration, External Warfare and Matrilocal Residence." *Behavior Science Research* 9:75–133.

Doob, Leonard W., ed. 1970. *Resolving Conflict in Africa: The Fermeda Workshop.* New Haven: Yale University Press.

Draper, Patricia. 1978. "The Learning Environment for Aggression and Anti-

Social Behavior among the !Kung," in Ashley Montagu, ed., *Learning Non-Aggression*, pp. 31–53. New York: Oxford University Press.

Eckstein, Harry. 1966. *Division and Cohesion in Democracy: A Study of Norway*. Princeton: Princeton University Press.

Edelman, Murray. 1964. *The Symbolic Uses of Politics*. Urbana: University of Illinois Press.

Eibl-Eibesfeldt, Iranëus. 1979. *The Biology of Peace and War: Men, Animals, and Aggression*. New York: Viking.

Eidheim, H. 1969. "When Ethnic Identity is a Social Stigma," in Fredrik Barth, ed., *Ethnic Groups and Boundaries*. 39–57. Boston: Little Brown.

Ember, Carol R., Melvin Ember, and Bruce Russett. 1992. "Political Participation and Peace: A Cross-Cultural Test of the 'Democracies Rarely Fight Each Other' Hypothesis." *World Politics*. 44:573–599.

Erikson, Erik H. 1950. *Childhood and Society*. New York: Norton.

Escoube, Pierre. 1971. *Les Grands Corps de l'Etat*. Paris: Presses Universitaires de France.

Etienne, Bruno. 1989. *La France et l'Islam*. Paris: Hachette.

Fabbro, David. 1978. "Peaceful Societies: An Introduction." *Journal of Peace Research* 15:67–83.

Fairbairn, W. R. D. 1954. *An Object-Relations Theory of Personality*. New York: Basic Books.

Felsteiner, William. 1974–75. "Influences of Social Organization on Dispute Processing." *Law and Society Review* 9:63–94.

Felsteiner, William, Richard Abel, and Austin Sarat. 1980–81. "The Emergence and Transformation of Disputes: Naming, Blaming, Claiming . . ." *Law and Society Review* 15:631–653.

Ferguson, R. Brian. 1984. "Introduction: Studying War," in R. Brian Ferguson, ed., *Warfare, Culture and Environment*, pp. 1–81. Orlando, Fla.: Academic Press.

———. 1992. "A Savage Encounter: Western Contact and the Yanomami War Complex," in R. Brian Ferguson and Neil L. Whitehead, eds., *War in the Tribal Zone: Expanding States and Indigenous Warfare*, pp. 199–227. Sante Fe, N.M.: School of American Research Press.

Firth, Raymond. 1949. "Authority and Public Opinion in Tikopia," in Meyer Fortes, ed., *Social Structure*, pp. 168–188. Oxford: Oxford University Press.

———. 1963 [1936]. *We the Tikopia: Kinship in Primitive Polynesia*. Abridged edition. Boston: Beacon Press.

Fisher, Roger. 1983. "Negotiating Power: Getting and Using Influence." *American Behavioral Scientist* 27:149–166.

Fisher, Roger, and William Ury. 1981. *Getting to Yes: Negotiating Agreement Without Giving In*. Boston: Houghton-Mifflin.

Fitzduff, Mari. 1992. "Move Sideways to Progress? Mediation Choices in Northern Ireland." Paper presented to the Ethnic Studies Network, Portrush, Northern Ireland.

Fornari, Franco. 1975. *The Psychoanalysis of War.* Bloomington: Indiana University Press.

Freud, Sigmund. 1917 [1963]. "Mourning and Melancholia." *General Psychological Theory,* 164–179. New York: Macmillan.

———. 1922 [1959]. *Group Psychology and the Analysis of the Ego.* New York: Norton.

Fried, Morton. 1967. *The Evolution of Political Society.* New York: Random House.

Gans, Herbert. 1969. "Negro-Jewish Conflict in New York City: A Sociological Analysis." *Midstream* 25:3–15.

Gibbs, James L., Jr. 1963. "The Kpelle Moot: A Therapeutic Model for the Informal Settlement of Disputes." *Africa* 33:1–11.

Gluckman, Max. 1955. *The Judicial Process Among the Barotse of Northern Rhodesia.* Manchester: Manchester University Press.

Gordon, Robert. 1983. "The Decline of the Kaipdom and the Resurgence of 'Tribal Fighting' in Enga." *Oceania* 53:205–223.

Gordon, Robert J., and Mervyn J. Meggitt. 1984. *Law and Order in the New Guinea Highlands: Encounters with Enga.* Hanover, N. H.: University Press of New England.

Gorer, Geoffrey. 1938. *Himalayan Village: An Account of the Lepchas of Sikkim.* London: M. Joseph.

Gowa, Joanne. 1986. "Anarchy, Egoism, and Third Images: Evolution of Cooperation and International Relations." *International Organization* 40:167–186.

Greenberg, Jay R., and Stephen A. Mitchell. 1983. *Object Relations in Psychoanalytic Theory.* Cambridge: Harvard University Press.

Gregor, Thomas. 1990. "Uneasy Peace: Intertribal Relations in Brazil's Upper Xingu," in Jonathan Haas, ed., *The Anthropology of Warfare,* pp. 105–124. New York: Cambridge University Press.

Grillo, R. D. 1985. *Ideologies and Institutions in Urban France: The Representation of Immigrants.* Cambridge: Cambridge University Press.

Gruter, Margaret, and Roger Masters. 1986. *Ostracism: A Social and Biological Phenomenon.* Special Issue of *Ethology and Sociobiology.* New York: Elsevier.

Gullestad, Marianne. 1984. *Kitchen-Table Society.* Oslo: Universitetsforlaget.

Gulliver, P. H. 1979. *Disputes and Negotiations: A Cross-Cultural Perspective.* New York: Academic Press.

Guntrip, Harry. 1968. *Schizoid Problems, Object-Relations, and the Self.* New York: International Universities Press.

Haas, Ernst. 1964. *Beyond the Nation-State.* Stanford: Stanford University Press.

Haass, Richard N. 1990. *Conflicts Unending: The United States and Regional Conflict.* New Haven: Yale University Press.

Harner, Michael. 1972. *The Jivaro: People of the Sacred Waterfalls.* Garden City, N.Y.: Natural History Press.

Harris, Marvin. 1979. *Cultural Materialism: The Struggle for a Science of Culture*. New York: Vintage Books.

Harris, Rosemary. 1972. *Prejudice and Tolerance in Ulster*. Manchester: Manchester University Press.

Herdt, Gilbert. 1987. *The Sambia: Ritual and Gender in New Guinea*. New York: Holt, Rinehart and Winston.

Hirschman, Albert O. 1970. *Exit, Voice and Loyalty: Response to Decline in Firms, Organizations and States*. Cambridge: Harvard University Press.

Hollos, Marida. 1974. *Growing Up in Flathill*. Oslo: Universitetsforlaget.

Horowitz, Donald. 1985. *Ethnic Groups in Conflict*. Berkeley and Los Angeles: University of California Press.

———. 1991. *A Democratic South Africa? Constitutional Engineering in a Divided Society*. Berkeley and Los Angeles: University of California Press.

Howell, Signe. 1989. " 'To Be Angry Is Not To Be Human, But To Be Fearful Is': Chewong Concepts of Human Nature," in Signe Howell and Roy Willis, eds., *Societies at Peace: Anthropological Perspectives*, pp. 45–59. London: Routledge.

Howell, Signe, and Roy Willis, eds. 1989a. *Societies at Peace: Anthropological Perspectives*. London: Routledge.

———. 1989b. Introduction, in Signe Howell and Roy Willis, eds., *Societies at Peace: Anthropological Perspectives*, pp. 1–28. London: Routledge.

Inkeles, Alex. 1972. "National Character and Modern Political Systems," in Francis L. K. Hsu, ed., *Psychological Anthropology*, pp. 201–240. 2d ed. Cambridge, Mass.: Schenkman.

Jervis, Robert. 1976. *Perception and Misperception in International Politics*. Princeton: Princeton University Press.

Jervis, Robert, Richard Ned Lebow, and Janice Stein, eds. 1985. *Psychology and Deterrence*. Baltimore: Johns Hopkins University Press.

Joseph, Alice, Rosamund B. Spicer and Jane Chesky. 1949. *The Desert People: A Study of the Papago Indians*. Chicago: University of Chicago Press.

Kelman, Herbert. 1978. "Israelis and Palestinians: Psychological Prerequisites for Mutual Acceptance." *International Security* 3:162–186.

———. 1987. "The Political Psychology of the Israeli-Palestinian Conflict: How to Overcome the Barriers to a Negotiated Solution?" *Political Psychology* 8:347–363.

———. 1991. "Interactive Problem Solving: The Uses and Limits of a Therapeutic Model for the Resolution of International Conflicts," in Vamik Volkan, Joseph V. Montville, and Demetrios A. Julius, eds., *The Psychodynamics of International Relationships*. Vol. 2. *Unofficial Diplomacy at Work*, pp. 145–160. Lexington, Mass.: Lexington Books.

Kelman, Herbert, and Stephen P. Cohen. 1986. "Resolution of International Conflict: An Interactional Approach," in S. Worchel and W. G. Austin, eds., *Psychology of Intergroup Relations*, pp. 323–342. 2d ed. Chicago: Nelson Hall.

Keohane, Robert O. 1986. "Reciprocity in International Politics." *International Organization* 40:1–27.

Klein, Melanie. 1957. *Envy and Gratitude*. London: Tavistock.

Knauft, Bruce M. 1987. "Reconsidering Violence in Simple Societies: Homicide Among the Gebusi of New Guinea." *Current Anthropology* 28:457–500.

Koch, Klaus-Friedrich. 1974. *War and Peace in Jalemo: The Management of Conflict in Highland New Guinea*. Cambridge: Harvard University Press.

Konner, Melvin. 1982. *The Tangled Wing: Biological Constraints on the Human Spirit*. New York: Harper Colophon.

Kriesberg, Louis. 1982. *Social Conflicts*. Englewood Cliffs, N.J.: Prentice-Hall.

———. 1992. *International Conflict Resolution: The U.S.-USSR and Middle East Cases*. New Haven: Yale University Press.

Larson, Deborah Welch. 1988. "The Psychology of Reciprocity in International Relations." *Negotiation Journal* 4:281–301.

Lebow, Richard Ned. 1978. "The Origins of Sectarian Assassination: The Case of Belfast." *Journal of International Affairs* 32:43–61.

Lebow, Richard Ned, and Janice Stein. 1987. "Beyond Deterrence." *Journal of Social Issues* 43:5–71.

Lee, Richard Borshay. 1979. *The !Kung San: Men, Women, and Work in a Foraging Society*. Cambridge: Cambridge University Press.

———. 1990. "Comment on Wilmsen and Denbow." *Current Anthropology* 31:510–512.

Levi-Strauss, Claude. 1944 [1967]. "The Social and Psychological Aspects of Chieftainship in a Primitive Tribe: The Nambikuara of Northwestern Mato Grosso," in Ronald Cohen and John Middleton, eds., *Comparative Political Systems: Studies in the Politics of Pre-industrial Societies*, pp. 45–62. Garden City, N.Y.: Natural History Press.

LeVine, Robert A. 1965. "Socialization, Social Structure, and Intersocietal Images," in Herbert Kelman, ed., *International Behavior: A Social Psychological Analysis*, pp. 43–69. New York: Holt, Rinehart and Winston.

———. 1973. *Culture, Behavior, and Personality*. Chicago: Aldine.

LeVine, Robert A., and Donald Campbell. 1972. *Ethnocentrism: Theories of Conflict, Ethnic Attitudes and Group Behavior*. New York: John Wiley.

Lichtenberg, Joseph D. 1983. *Psychoanalysis and Infant Research*. Hillsdale, N.J.: The Analytic Press.

Lindberg, Leon, and Stuart Scheingold. 1970. *Europe's Would-Be Polity*. Englewood Cliffs, N.J.: Prentice-Hall.

Lipjhardt, Arend. 1975. "The Northern Ireland Problem: Cases, Theories and Solutions." *British Journal of Political Science* 5:83–106.

Mahler, Margaret S., Fred Pine, and Anni Bergman. 1975. *The Psychological Birth of the Human Infant: Symbiosis and Individuation*. New York: Basic Books.

Mansbridge, Jane, ed. 1990. *Beyond Self-Interest*. Chicago: University of Chicago Press.

Marcus, George, and Michael M. J. Fischer. 1986. *Anthropology as Cultural Critique: An Experimental Moment in the Human Sciences*. Chicago: University of Chicago Press.

Marshall, Lorna. 1961. "Sharing, Talking and Giving: The Relief of Social Tension Among the !Kung Bushmen." *Africa* 31:231–249.

———. 1976. *The !Kung of Nyae Nyae*. Cambridge, Mass.: Harvard University Press.

Mather, Lynn, and Barbara Yngvesson. 1981. "Language, Audience, and the Transformation of Disputes." *Law and Society Review* 15:775–821.

McFarlane, Graham. 1986. "Violence in Rural Northern Ireland: Social Scientific Models, Folk Explanations and Local Variation (?)," in David Riches, ed., *The Anthropology of Violence*, pp. 184–203. Oxford: Basil Blackwell.

McGoldrick, Monica. 1982. "Irish Families," in Monica McGoldrick, John K. Pearce, and Joseph Giordano, eds., *Ethnicity and Family Therapy*, pp. 310–339. New York: Guilford Press.

McLachlan, Peter. 1987. "Northern Ireland: The Cultural Bases of the Conflict." *Conflict Resolution Notes* 4:21–23.

Meggitt, Mervyn. 1977. *Blood is Their Argument: Warfare among the Mae Enga Tribesmen of the New Guinea Highlands*. Palo Alto: Mayfield.

Melson, Robert, and Howard Wolpe. 1970. "Modernization and the Politics of Communalism: A Theoretical Perspective." *American Political Science Review* 65:161–171.

Messenger, John. 1971. "Sex and Repression in an Irish Folk Community," in Donald S. Marshall and Robert C. Suggs, eds., *Human Sexual Behavior*. 2–37. New York: Basic Books.

Mettis Associates. 1988. "The Resolving Conflict Creatively Program: A Summary of Significant Findings." Report submitted to William P. Casey, superintendent, Community School District 15, Brooklyn, New York.

———. 1990. "The Resolving Conflict Creatively Program: 1988–1989. Summary of Significant Findings." Report submitted to William P. Casey, superintendent, Community School District 15, Brooklyn, New York.

Midlarsky, Manus. 1975. *On War: Political Violence in the International System*. New York: Free Press.

Milgram, Stanley. 1974. *Obedience to Authority*. New York: Harper Colophon.

Mitrany, David. 1966. *A Working Peace System*. Chicago: Quadrangle Books.

Montagu, Ashley, ed. 1978. *Learning Non-Aggression: The Experience of Non-Literate Societies*. New York: Oxford University Press.

Montville, Joseph. 1991a. "The Arrow and the Olive Branch: A Case for Track Two Diplomacy," in Vamik Volkan, Joseph V. Montville, and Demetrios A. Julius, eds., *The Psychodynamics of International Relationships*. Vol. 2. *Unofficial Diplomacy at Work*, pp. 161–175. Lexington, Mass.: Lexington Books.

———. 1991b. "Psychoanalytic Enlightenment and the Greening of Diplomacy," in Vamik Volkan, Joseph V. Montville, and Demetrios A. Julius, eds., *The Psychodynamics of International Relationships.* Vol. 2. *Unofficial Diplomacy at Work,* pp. 177–192, Lexington, Mass.: Lexington Books.

Montville, Joseph V., and W. P. Davidson. 1981–82. "Foreign Policy According to Freud." *Foreign Policy* 45: 145–157.

Moore, Sally Falk. 1975. "Selection for Failure in a Small Social Field: Ritual Concord and Fraternal Strife among the Chagga, Kilimanharo, 1968–1969," in Sally Falk Moore and Barbara G. Meyerhoff, eds., *Symbol and Politics in Communal Ideology: Cases and Questions,* pp. 109–143. Ithaca: Cornell University Press.

Moses, Raphael. 1991. "Shame and Entitlement: Their Relation to the Political Process," in Vamik Volkan, Joseph V. Montville, and Demetrios A. Julius, eds., *The Psychodynamics of International Relationships.* Vol. 2. *Unofficial Diplomacy at Work,* pp. 131–141. Lexington, Mass.: Lexington Books.

Mulvihill, Robert. 1992. "Family Systems Theory and Ethnic Conflict Management." Paper presented to the First Ethnic Studies Network Conference. Portrush, Northern Ireland.

Mulvihill, Robert, and Marc Howard Ross. 1989. "Theories of Conflict, Conflict Management and Peacemaking in Northern Ireland." Paper presented to North American Conference on Conflict Resolution and Peacemaking, Montreal.

Murphy, Robert F. 1957. "Intergroup Hostility and Social Cohesion." *American Anthropologist* 59:1018–1035.

Nader, Laura. 1990. *Harmony Ideology: Justice and Control in a Zapotec Mountain Community.* Stanford: Stanford University Press.

Nader, Laura, and Harry F. Todd, eds. 1978. *The Disputing Process: Law in Ten Societies.* New York: Columbia University Press.

Nagel, Jack. 1991. "Psychological Obstacles to Administrative Responsibility: Lessons of the MOVE Disaster," *Journal of Policy Analysis and Management* 10:1–23.

Naroll, Raoul. 1983. *The Moral Order: An Introduction to the Human Situation.* Beverly Hills: Sage.

National Institute for Dispute Resolution. *Forum.* 1991. Special Issue on Dispute Resolution in Education. Washington, D.C.: National Institute for Dispute Resolution.

Newman, Katherine S. 1983. *Law and Economic Organization: A Comparative Study of Preindustrial Societies.* Cambridge: Cambridge University Press.

Nisbett, Richard, and Lee Ross. 1980. *Human Inference: Strategies and Shortcomings of Social Judgment.* Englewood Cliffs, N.J.: Prentice-Hall.

Noelle-Neumann, Elisabeth. 1984. *The Spiral of Silence: Public Opinion— Our Social Skin.* Chicago: University of Chicago Press.

Northrup, Terrell A. 1989. "The Dynamic of Identity in Personal and Social Conflict," in Louis Kriesberg, Terrell A. Northrup, and Stuart J. Thorson, eds., *Intractable Conflicts and Their Transformation*, pp. 55–82. Syracuse: Syracuse University Press.

O'Brien, Conor Cruise. 1986. "Ireland: The Mirage of Peace." *New York Review of Books*. April 24, 1986:40–46.

O'Malley, Padraig. 1983. *The Uncivil Wars: Ireland Today*. New York: Houghton-Mifflin.

———. 1990. *Biting at the Grave: The Irish Hunger Strikes and the Politics of Despair*. Boston: Beacon Press.

O'Nell, Carl W. 1989. "The Non-Violent Zapotec," in Signe Howell and Roy Willis, eds., *Societies at Peace: Anthropological Perspectives*, pp. 117–132. London: Routledge.

Osgood, Charles, 1962. *An Alternative to War or Surrender*. Urbana: University of Illinois Press.

Otterbein, Keith. 1970. *The Evolution of War*. New Haven: HRAF Press.

Paige, Karen Ericksen, and Jeffrey M. Paige. 1981. *The Politics of Reproductive Ritual*. Berkeley and Los Angeles: University of California Press.

Podolefsky, Aaron. 1984. "Contemporary Warfare in the New Guinea Highlands." *Ethnology* 23:73–87.

Princen, Thomas. 1992. *Intermediaries in International Conflict*. Princeton: Princeton University Press.

Pruitt, Dean G., and Jeffrey Z. Rubin. 1986. *Social Conflict: Escalation, Stalemate and Settlement*. New York: Random House.

Quandt, William. 1986. *Camp David: Peacemaking and Politics*. Washington, D.C.: Brookings.

Raiffa, Howard. 1982. *The Art and Science of Negotiation*. Cambridge: Belknap Press.

Ramsøy, Natalie Rogoff, ed. 1974. *Norwegian Society*. New York: Humanities Press.

Rifkin, Janet. 1991. "An Overview of Dispute Resolution in Educational Institutions." *Forum* 1–4.

Robarchek, Clayton A. 1979a. "Conflict, Emotion and Abreaction: Resolution of Conflict among the Semai Senoi." *Ethos* 7:104–123.

———. 1979b. "Learning to Fear: A Case Study of Emotional Conditioning." *American Ethnologist* 6:555–567.

———. 1986. "Helplessness, Fearfulness, and Peacefulness: The Emotional and Motivational Contexts of Semai Social Relationships." *Anthropological Quarterly* 59:177–183.

———. 1989a. "Primitive Warfare and the Ratomorphic Image of Mankind." *American Anthropologist* 91:903–920.

———. 1989b. "Hobbesian and Rousseauan Images of Man: Autonomy and Individualism in a Peaceful Society," in Signe Howell and Roy Willis, eds., *Societies at Peace*, pp. 31–44. London: Routledge.

———. 1990. "Motivations and Material Causes: On the Explanation of Conflict and Wars," in Jonathan Haas, ed., *The Anthropology of War*, pp. 56–76. Cambridge: Cambridge University Press.

―――. 1992. "Culture of War, Culture of Peace: A Comparative Study of the Waorani and the Semai," in James Silverberg and J. Patrick Gray, eds., *Aggression and Peacefulness in Humans and Other Primates*, pp. 189–213. New York: Oxford University Press.

Robarchek, Clayton A., and Robert Knox Dentan. 1987. "Blood Drunkenness and the Bloodthirsty Semai." *American Anthropologist* 89:356–365.

Rose, Richard. 1971. *Governing Without Consensus: An Irish Perspective.* Boston: Beacon Press.

Ross, Marc Howard. 1981. "Socioeconomic Complexity, Socialization, and Political Differentiation." *Ethos* 9:217–247.

―――. 1983. "Political Decision Making and Conflict: Additional Cross-Cultural Codes and Scales." *Ethnology* 22:169–192.

―――. 1985. "Internal and External Violence: Cross-Cultural Evidence and a New Analysis." *Journal of Conflict Resolution* 29:547–579.

―――. 1986a. "A Cross-Cultural Theory of Political Conflict and Violence." *Political Psychology* 7:427–469.

―――. 1986b. "The Limits to Social Structure: Social Structural and Psychocultural Explanations for Political Conflict and Violence." *Anthropological Quarterly* 59:171–176.

―――. 1986c. "Female Political Participation: A Cross-Cultural Explanation." *American Anthropologist* 88:843–858.

―――. 1988. "Why Complexity Doesn't Necessarily Enhance Participation: Exit, Voice and Loyalty in Pre-Industrial Societies." *Comparative Politics* 21:73–89.

―――. 1991a. "The Role of Evolution in Ethnocentric Conflict and Its Management." *Journal of Social Issues* 47:167–185.

―――. 1991b. "The Political Uses of Fission." Paper presented to the Annual Meeting of the Society for Cross-Culture Research. San Juan, Puerto Rico.

―――. 1992a. "The Language of Success and Failure in Ethnic Conflict Management." Paper presented to the Ethnic Studies Network, Portrush, Northern Ireland.

―――. 1992b. "Ethnic Conflict and Dispute Management," in Austin Sarat and Susan Silbey, eds., *Studies in Law, Politics and Society*, pp. 107–146. Vol. 12. Greenwich, Conn.: JAI Press.

―――. 1993. *The Culture of Conflict: Interpretations and Interests in Comparative Perspective.* New Haven: Yale University Press.

―――. Forthcoming. "Managing Ethnocentric Conflict: Competing Theories and Alternative Steps Towards Peace." *Journal of Conflict Resolution.*

Rothman, Jay. 1989. "Supplementing Tradition: A Theoretical and Practical Typology for International Conflict Management." *Negotiation Journal* 5:265–277.

―――. 1991. "Negotiation as Consolidation: Prenegotiations in the Israeli-Palestinian Conflict." *Jerusalem Journal of International Relations* 13:22–44.

―――. 1992. *From Confrontation to Cooperation: Resolving Ethnic and*

Regional Conflict in the Middle East and Beyond. Beverly Hills: Sage Publications.

Rothman, Jay, ed. 1991. Special Issue on Prenegotiations. *Jerusalem Journal of International Relations.*

Rubin, Jeffrey Z. 1989. "Some Wise and Mistaken Assumptions about Conflict and Negotiation." *Journal of Social Issues* 45:195–209.

Rule, James B. 1988. *Theories of Civil Violence.* Berkeley and Los Angeles: University of California Press.

Safran, William. 1985. "The Mitterrand Regime and Its Ethnocultural Accommodation." *Comparative Politics* 18:41–63.

Saunders, Harold. 1985. "We Need a Larger Theory of Negotiation: The Importance of Pre-Negotiating Phases." *Negotiation Journal* 1:249–262.

———. 1991. "Officials and Citizens in International Relationships," in Vamik Volkan, Joseph V. Montville, and Demetrios A. Julius, eds., *The Psychodynamics of International Relationships.* Vol. 2. *Unofficial Diplomacy at Work,* pp. 41–69. Lexington, Mass.: Lexington Books.

Schattschneider, E. E. 1960. *The Semi-Sovereign People.* New York: Holt, Rinehart and Winston.

Schemla, Elisabeth. 1989a. "Ecole: Le piège religieux." *Le Nouvel Observateur* (26 October–1 November 1989) 1303:72–75.

———. 1989b. "Jospin: Accueillez les foulards!" *Le Nouvel Observateur* (26 October–1 November 1989) 1303:78–79.

Scheper-Hughes, Nancy. 1979. *Saints, Scholars, and Schizophrenics: Mental Illness in Rural Ireland.* Berkeley and Los Angeles: University of California Press.

Schneider, Robert. 1989. "Immigres: L'Enquête qui dérange." *Le Nouvel Observateur* (23–29 November 1989) 1307:72–73.

Schwartz, Richard D., and James C. Miller. 1964. "Legal Evolution and Societal Complexity." *American Journal of Sociology* 20:159–169.

Sears, R. R., E. E. Maccoby, and H. Levin. 1958. "The Socialization of Aggression," in E. E. Maccoby, T. Newcomb, and E. L. Hartley, eds., *Readings in Social Psychology,* pp. 350–358. 2d ed. New York: Holt, Rinehart and Winston.

See, Katherine O'Sullivan. 1986. *First World Nationalisms: Class and Ethnic Politics in Northern Ireland and Quebec.* Chicago: University of Chicago Press.

Sharp, Gene. 1990. *Civilian-Based Defense: A Post-Military System.* Princeton: Princeton University Press.

Sherif, Muzafer, et al. 1988. *The Robbers Cave Experiment: Intergroup Conflict and Cooperation.* Middletown, Conn.: Wesleyan University Press.

Sillitoe, Paul. 1977. "Land Shortage and War in New Guinea." *Ethnology* 16:71–81.

———. 1978. "Big Men and War in New Guinea." *Man* 13:252–271.

Smith, Alec. 1984. *Now I Call Him Brother.* Basingstoke: Marshalls.

Snidal, Duncan. 1991. "Relative Gains and the Pattern of International

Cooperation." *American Political Science Review* 85:701–726.

Solway, Jacqueline, and Richard B. Lee. 1990. "Foragers, Genuine or Spurious? Situating the Kalahari San in History." *Current Anthropology* 31:109–146.

Stein, Janice G. 1985a. "Calculation, Miscalculation, and Conventional Deterrence I: The View from Cairo," in Robert Jervis, Richard Ned Lebow, and Janice G. Stein, eds., *Psychology and Deterrence*, pp. 34–59. Baltimore: Johns Hopkins University Press.

———. 1985b. "Calculation, Miscalculation, and Conventional Deterrence II: The View from Jerusalem," in Robert Jervis, Richard Ned Lebow, and Janice G. Stein, eds., *Psychology and Deterrence*, pp. 60–88. Baltimore: Johns Hopkins University Press.

Stein, Janice G., ed. 1989. *Getting to the Table: The Processes of International Prenegotiation*. Baltimore: Johns Hopkins University Press.

Stern, Daniel N. 1985. *The Interpersonal World of the Infant*. New York: Basic Books.

Strathern, Andrew. 1974. "When Dispute Procedures Fail," in A. L. Epstein, ed., *Contention and Dispute*, pp. 240–270. Canberra: National University Press.

———. 1977. "Contemporary Warfare in the New Guinea Highlands—Rival or Breakdown." *Yagl-Ambu* 4:135–146.

Susskind, Lawrence, and Jeffrey Cruikshank. 1988. *Breaking the Impasse: Consensual Approaches to Resolving Public Disputes*. New York: Basic Books.

Swartz, Marc J. 1968. Introduction, in Marc J. Swartz, ed., *Local-Level Politics*, pp. 1–46. Chicago: Aldine.

Swartz, Marc J., Victor Turner, and Arthur Tuden. 1966. Introduction, in Marc J. Swartz, Victor Turner, and Arthur Tuden, eds., *Political Anthropology*, pp. 1–41. Chicago: Aldine.

Tajfel, Henri. 1981. *Human Groups and Social Categories*. Cambridge: Cambridge University Press.

Tajfel, Henri, and John C. Turner. 1986. "The Social Identity Theory of Intergroup Behavior," in Stephen Worchel and William G. Austin, eds., *Psychology of Intergroup Relations*, pp. 7–24. 2d ed. Chicago: Nelson-Hall.

Thoden Van Velzen, H. U. E., and W. van Wetering. 1960. "Residence, Power Groups and Intra-Societal Aggression." *International Archives of Ethnography* 49:169–200.

Todd, Harry F., Jr. 1978. "Litigious Marginals: Character and Disputing in a Bavarian Village," in Laura Nader and Harry F. Todd, Jr., eds., *The Disputing Process—Law in Ten Societies*, pp. 86–121. New York: Columbia University Press.

Trevarthen, Colwyn, and Katerina Logotheti. 1989. "Child in Society and Society in Children: The Nature of Basic Trust," in Signe Howell and Roy Willis, eds., *Societies at Peace: Anthropological Perspectives*, pp. 165–186. London: Routledge.

Turnbull, Colin. 1961. *The Forest People*. New York: Doubleday Anchor.

———. 1978. "The Politics of Non-Aggression," in Ashley Montagu, ed., *Learning Non-Aggression: The Experience of Non-Literate Societies*, pp. 161–221. New York: Oxford.

Turner, John C. 1988. *Rediscovering the Social Group: A Self-Categorization Theory*. Oxford: Basil Blackwell.

Turner, Victor. 1957. *Schism and Continuity in an African Society*. Manchester: Manchester University Press.

Turney-High, Hugh H. 1949. *Primitive War*. Columbia: University of South Carolina Press.

Tversky, A. and D. Kahneman. 1980. "Causal Schemas in Judgments Under Uncertainty," in Martin Fishbein, ed., *Progress in Social Psychology*, pp. 49–72. Vol. 1. Hillsdale, N.J.: Erlbaum.

Underhill, Ruth M. 1939. *Social Organization of the Papago Indians*. Columbia University Contributions to Anthropology, 30:1–280.

———. 1946. *Papago Indian Religion*. New York: Columbia University Press.

Ury, William L., Jeanne M. Brett, and Stephen B. Goldberg. 1988. *Getting Disputes Resolved: Designing Systems to Cut the Costs of Conflict*. San Francisco: Jossey-Bass.

Volkan, Vamik D. 1988. *The Need to Have Enemies and Allies: From Clinical Practice to International Relationships*. New York: Jason Aronson.

Wagner-Pacifici, Robin. Forthcoming. *Discourse and Destruction: The City of Philadelphia vs. MOVE*. Chicago: University of Chicago Press.

Wallace, Anthony. 1962. *Culture and Personality*. New York: Random House.

Waltz, Kenneth. 1959. *Man, The State, and War*. New York: Columbia University Press.

White, Douglas. 1989. "World System Explanations of War Viewed from the Community Level." Typescript.

White, Ralph K. 1984. *Fearful Warriors: A Psychological Profile of U.S.-Soviet Relations*. New York: Free Press.

White, Robert. 1989. "From Peaceful Protest to Guerrilla War: Micromobilization of the Provisional Republican Army." *American Journal of Sociology* 94:1277–1302.

Whiting, Beatrice B. 1980. "Culture and Social Behavior: A Model for the Development of Social Behavior." *Ethos* 8:95–116.

Whiting, Beatrice B., and John W. M. Whiting. 1975. *Children of Six Cultures: A Psycho-Cultural Analysis*. Cambridge: Harvard University Press.

Whyte, John. 1990. *Interpreting Northern Ireland*. Oxford: Oxford University Press.

Wichert, Sabine. 1991. *Northern Ireland Since 1945*. New York: Longman.

Wildavsky, Aaron. 1987. "Choosing Preferences by Constructing Institutions: A Cultural Theory of Preference Formation." *American Political Science Review* 81:3–21.

———. 1989. "Frames of Reference Come from Cultures: A Predictive

Theory," in Morris Freilich, ed., *The Relevance of Culture*, pp. 58–74. New York: Bergan and Garvey.

———. 1991. "Why Self-Interest is an Empty Concept Outside of a Social Context: Cultural Constraints on the Construction of 'Self' and 'Interest'." Typescript.

Wilmsen, Edwin N. 1989. *Land Filled With Flies: A Political Economy of the Kalahari*. Chicago: University of Chicago Press.

Wilmsen, Edwin N., and James R. Denbow. 1990. "Paradigmatic History of San-speaking Peoples and Current Attempts at Revision." *Current Anthropology* 31:489–507.

Wilson, William Julius. 1980. *The Declining Significance of Race*. 2d. ed. Chicago: University of Chicago Press.

Winnicott, Donald W. 1953. "Transitional Objects and Transitional Phenomena." *International Journal of Psycho-Analysis* 34:89–97.

Wright, Frank. 1992. *Northern Ireland: A Comparative Analysis*. Dublin: Gill and Macmillan.

Yngvesson, Barbara. 1978. "The Atlantic Fisherman," in Laura Nader and Harry F. Todd, eds., *The Disputing Process—Law in Ten Societies*, pp. 59–85. New York: Columbia University Press.

Yngvesson, Barbara, and Lynn Mather. 1983. "Court, Moots, and the Disputing Process," in Keith O. Boyum and Lynn Mather, eds., *Empirical Theories About Courts*, pp. 51–83. New York: Longman.

Zinnes, Dina A. 1980. "Why War? Evidence on the Outbreak of International Conflict," in Ted Robert Gurr, ed., *Handbook of Political Conflict*. New York: Free Press.

Index

217